BBC

# DOCTOR WHO
# TIME LORD VICTORIOUS

"As the Doctor would say, brilliant!"
BIG COMIC PAGE

"I can't say enough good things about this. It's everything that *Doctor Who* does best."
BUT WHY THO?

"This is one book newcomers and old fans alike are sure to enjoy. 9/10!"
EXPLORE THE MULTIVERSE

"All of the creative team work together to produce a solid adventure which is sure to win the hearts of the fans."
MONKEYS FIGHTING ROBOTS

"Houser nails it."
NEWSARAMA

"Perfectly captures the look and voices of the characters!"
ADVENTURES IN P

"This is a great place to get an extra dose of *Doctor Who.*"
COMICBOOK.COM

"Houser is just on fire at the moment."
NERDLY

"Highly recommended... Bold, sassy, intelligent, and accessible to new fans. 5 out of 5!"
GEEK SYNDICATE

"5 out of 5!"
KABOOOOOM

"A radical romp through time and space!"
NERDIST

"The art team continues to excel!"
FI PULSE

# Doctor Who Backlist

Editor
**Jake Devine**

Senior Designer
**Andrew Leung**

## Titan Comics

Managing Editor
**Martin Eden**

Senior Creative Editor
**David Leach**

Production Controller
**Caterina Falqui**

Senior Production Controller
**Jackie Flook**

Art Director
**Oz Browne**

Sales & Circulation Manager
**Steve Tothill**

Publicist
**Imogen Harris**

Direct Marketing Assistant
**George Wickenden**

Marketing Manager
**Ricky Claydon**

Head Of Rights
**Jenny Boyce**

Editorial Director
**Duncan Baizley**

Operations Director
**Leigh Baulch**

Executive Director
**Vivian Cheung**

Publisher
**Nick Landau**

For rights information contact Jenny Boyce
jenny.boyce@titanemail.com

Special thanks to James Goss, Chris Chibnall, Matt Strevens, Mandy Thwaites, Suzy L. Raia, Gabby De
Matteis, Ross McGlinchey, David Wilson-Nunn, Kirsty Mullan and Kate Bush for their invaluable assistance.

## BBC Studios

Chair, Editorial Review Boards **Nicholas Brett** | Managing Director, Consumer Products and Licensing **Stephen Davies**
Head of Publishing **Mandy Thwaites** | Compliance Manager **Cameron McEwan** | UK Publishing Co-Ordinator **Eva Abramik**

**DOCTOR WHO: TIME LORD VICTORIOUS: DEFENDER OF THE DALEKS**
ISBN: 9781787733114

Published by Titan Comics, a division of Titan Publishing Group, Ltd. 144 Southwark Street, London, SE1 0UP.
Titan Comics is a registered trademark. All rights reserved.

A CIP catalogue record for this title is available from the British Library.
First edition: November 2020.

10 9 8 7 6 5 4 3 2 1

Printed in Spain

Titan Comics does not read or accept unsolicited DOCTOR WHO submissions of ideas, stories or artwork.

BBC
# DOCTOR WHO
# TIME LORD VICTORIOUS

STORY
## JAMES GOSS

WRITER
## JODY HOUSER

ARTIST
## ROBERTA INGRANATA

COLORIST
## ENRICA EREN ANGIOLINI

FLATTERS
## SHARI CHANKHAMMA
## & SABRINA DEL GROSS

LETTERER
## RICHARD STARKINGS OF
## COMICRAFT

TITAN
COMICS

BBC

BBC

DOCTOR WHO

# TIME LORD VICTORIOUS

## PREVIOUSLY...

In a twist of fate, the Tenth Doctor and the Thirteenth Doctor were brought together to face off against their deadly enemies. Unfortunately, the universe doesn't quite like the idea of a Time Lord meeting up with their past or future self - the consequences of such a paradox could cause a reality-altering shift that destroys the entire universe! Lucky for them it all worked out, until the Tenth Doctor was pulled into an impossible Time Vortex...

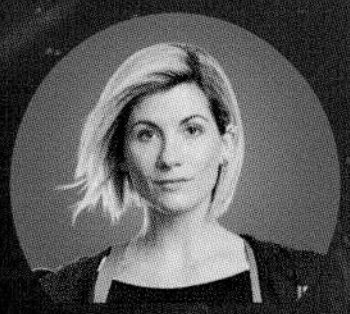

### Thirteenth **Doctor**

The Thirteenth Doctor is a live wire, full of energy and fizzing with excitement and wit! She is a charismatic and confident explorer, dedicated to seeing all the wonders of the universe, championing fairness and kindness wherever she can.

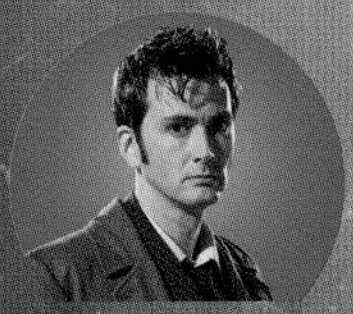

### Tenth **Doctor**

The Tenth Doctor still hides his post-Time War guilt beneath a happy-go-lucky guise. While oftentimes plucky and adventurous, he feels a deep loss for those he has loved. Never cruel or cowardly, he champions the oppressed across time and space.

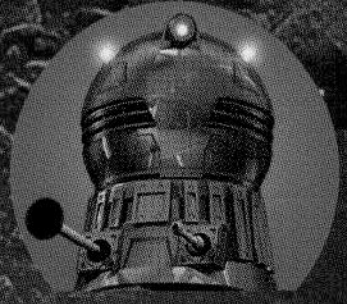

### The Emperor

The almighty leader of the Daleks - the Doctor's greatest enemy - his golden battle armor portrays his royal superiority. Merciless, the Emperor strives for universal domination.

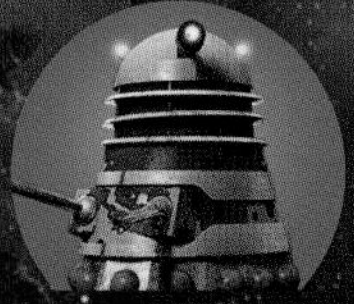

### The Strategist

Seemingly obsolete, this Dalek is the Prime Strategist for the Empire, so don't be deceived by his battered and broken looks. A law unto itself, this is one cunning Dalek.

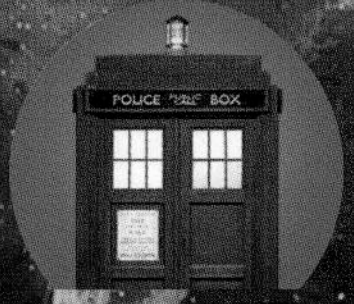

### The TARDIS

'Time and Relative Dimension in Space'. Bigger on the inside, this unassuming blue police box is your ticket to amazing adventures across time and space!

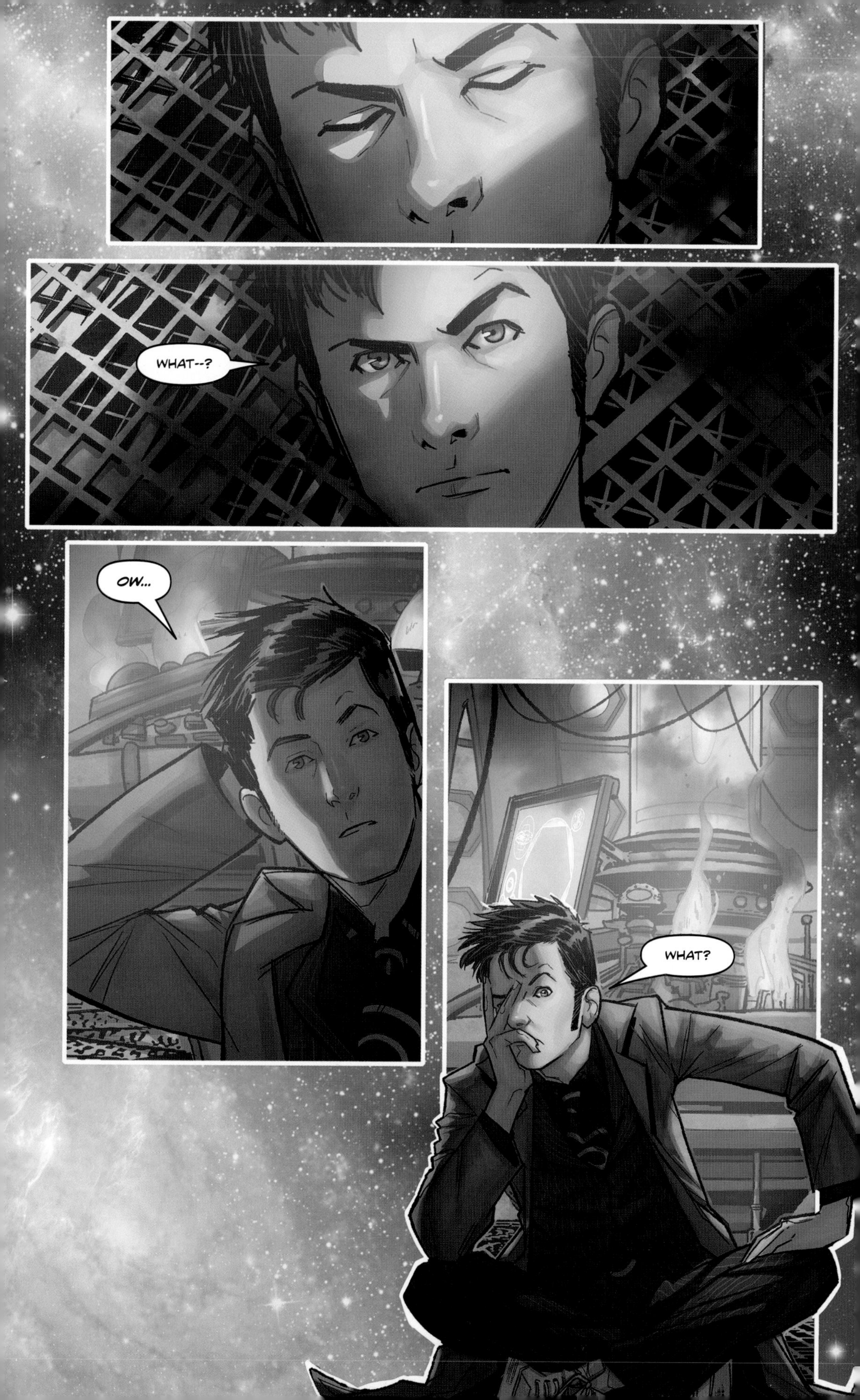
WHAT--?
OW...
WHAT?

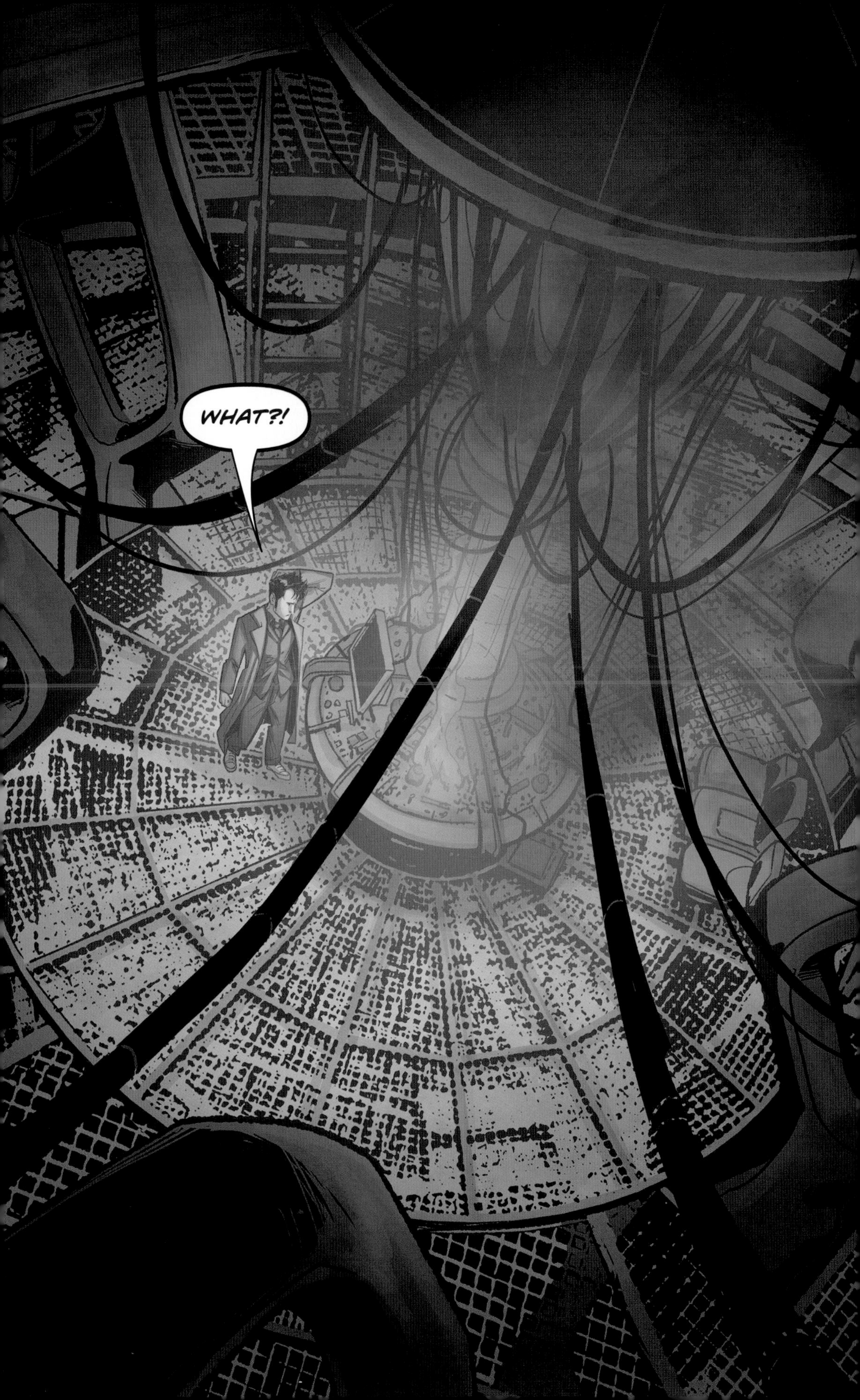
WHAT?!

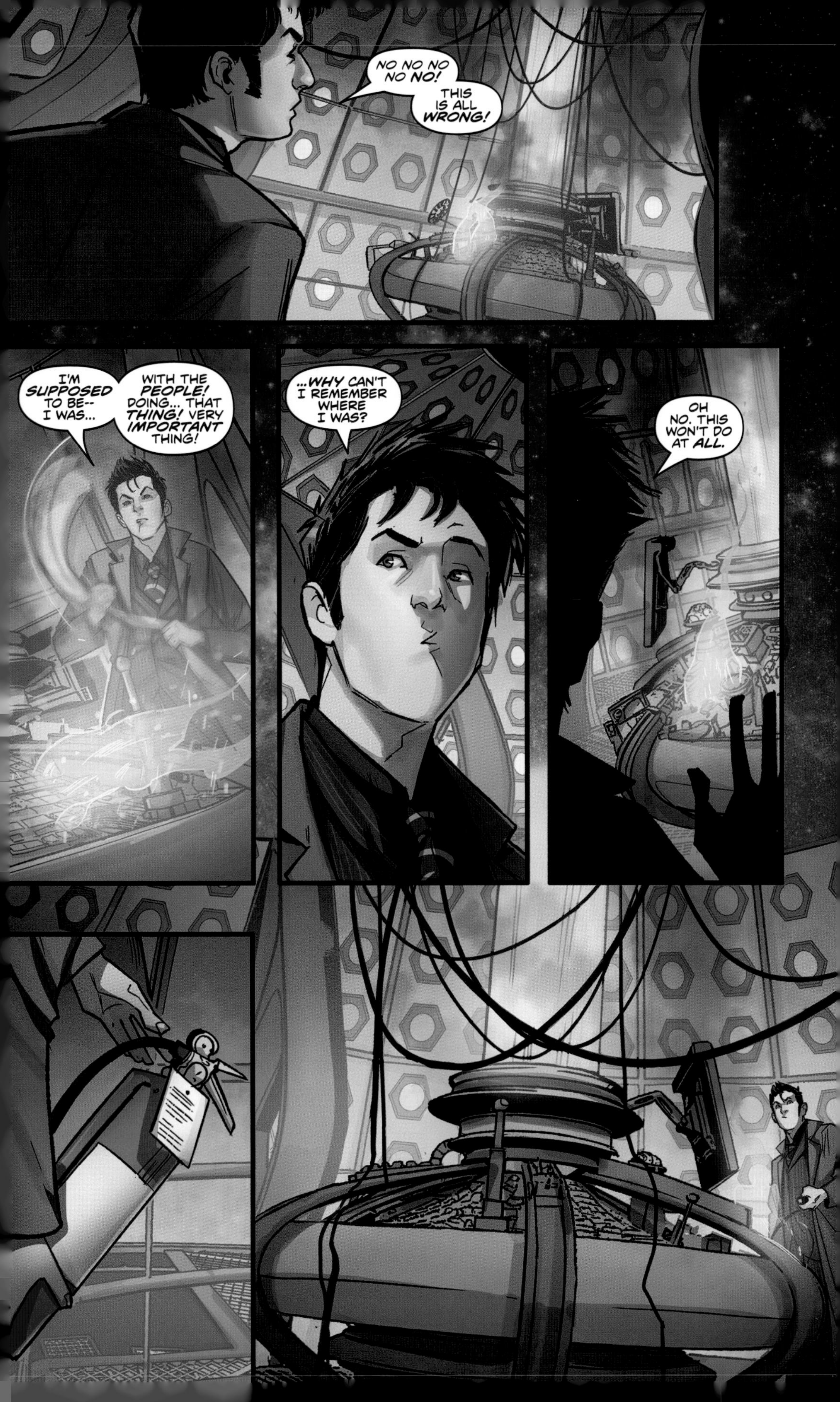
NO NO NO NO NO!
THIS IS ALL WRONG!
I'M SUPPOSED TO BE-- I WAS...
WITH THE PEOPLE! DOING... THAT THING! VERY IMPORTANT THING!
...WHY CAN'T I REMEMBER WHERE I WAS?
OH NO. THIS WON'T DO AT ALL.

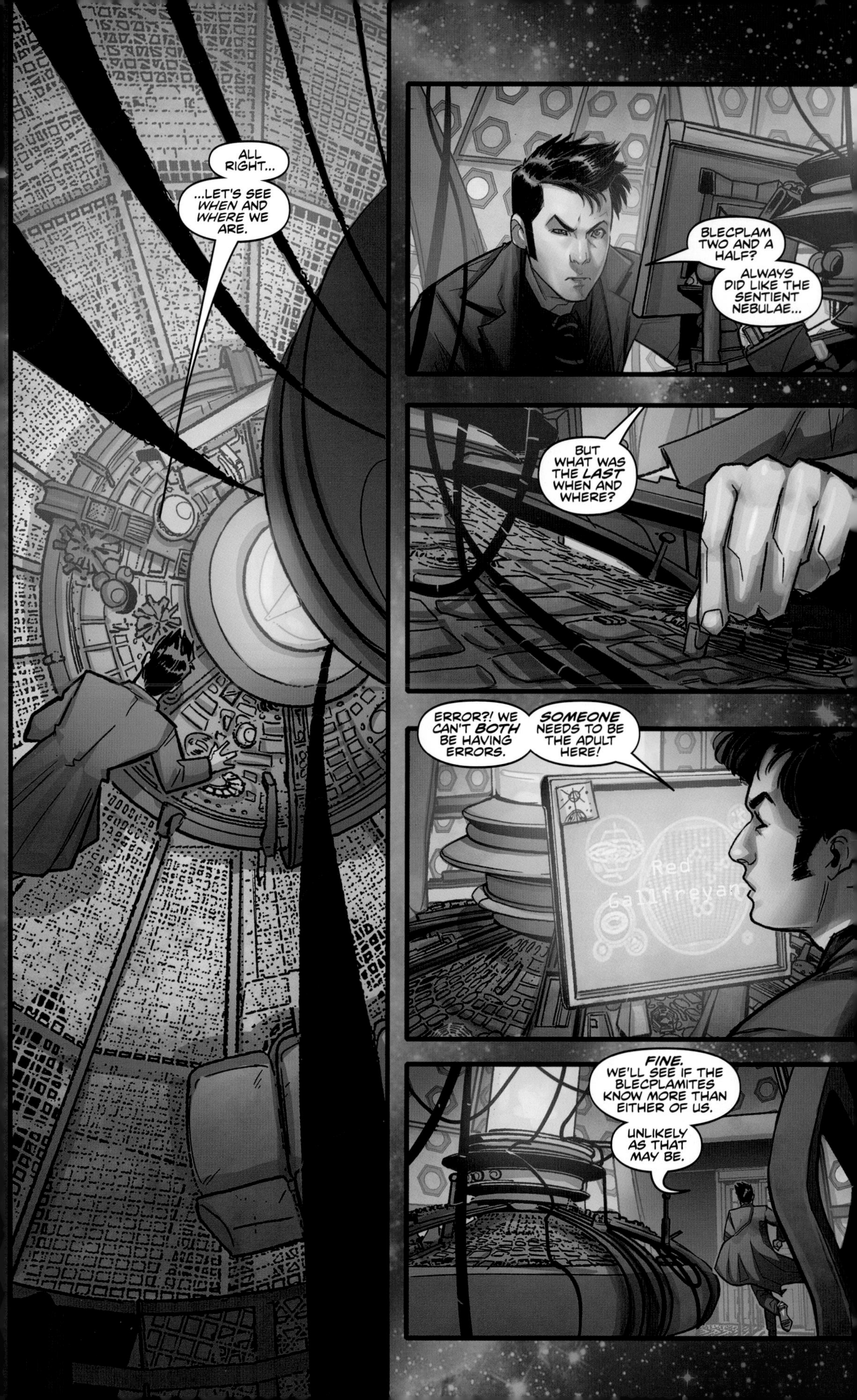
ALL RIGHT...
...LET'S SEE WHEN AND WHERE WE ARE.
BLECPLAM TWO AND A HALF?
ALWAYS DID LIKE THE SENTIENT NEBULAE...
BUT WHAT WAS THE LAST WHEN AND WHERE?
ERROR?! WE CAN'T BOTH BE HAVING ERRORS.
SOMEONE NEEDS TO BE THE ADULT HERE!
FINE. WE'LL SEE IF THE BLECPLAMITES KNOW MORE THAN EITHER OF US.
UNLIKELY AS THAT MAY BE.

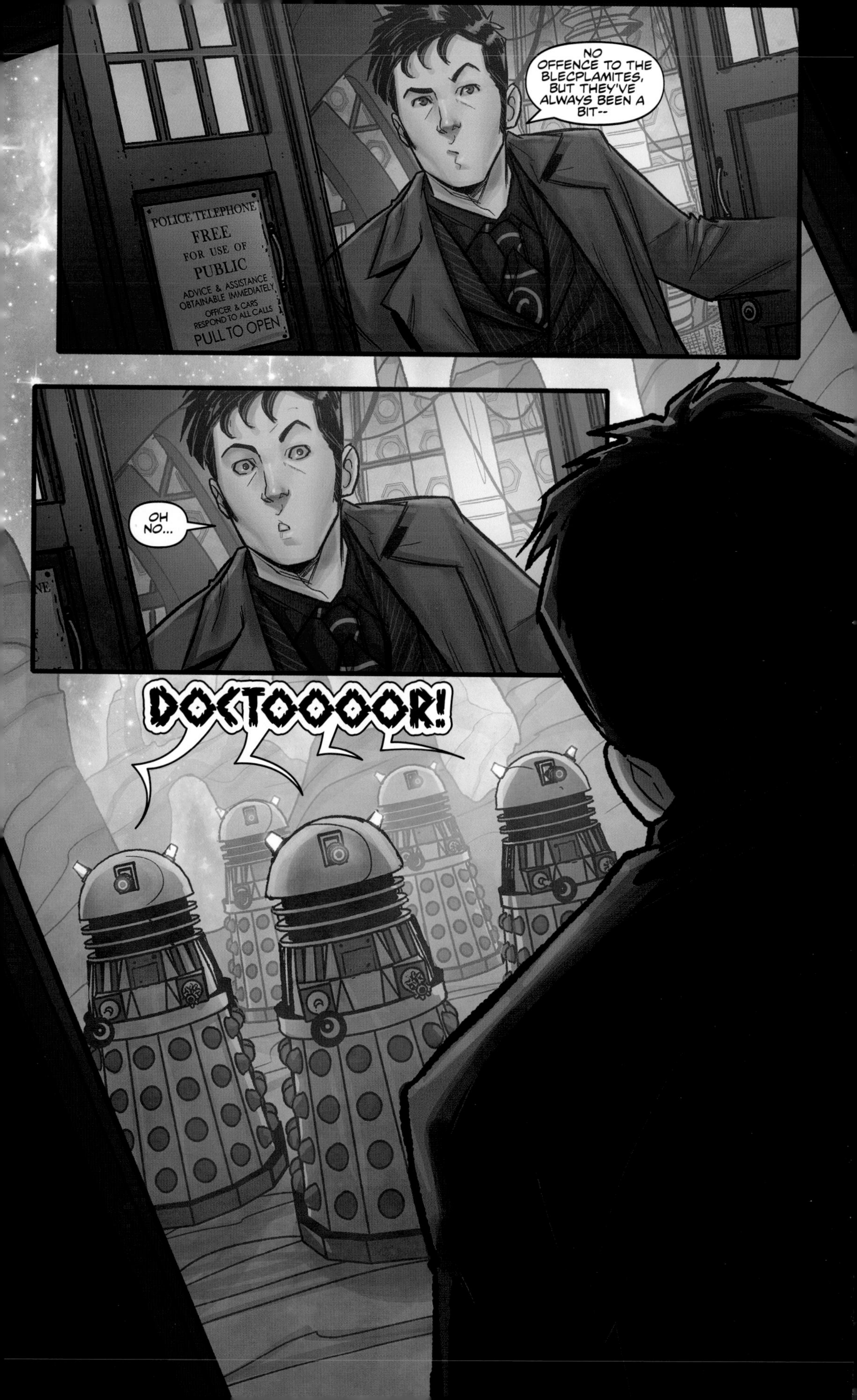
NO OFFENCE TO THE BLECPLAMITES, BUT THEY'VE ALWAYS BEEN A BIT--
POLICE TELEPHONE
FREE
FOR USE OF
PUBLIC
ADVICE & ASSISTANCE OBTAINABLE IMMEDIATELY
OFFICER & CARS RESPOND TO ALL CALLS
PULL TO OPEN
OH NO...
DOCTOOOOR!

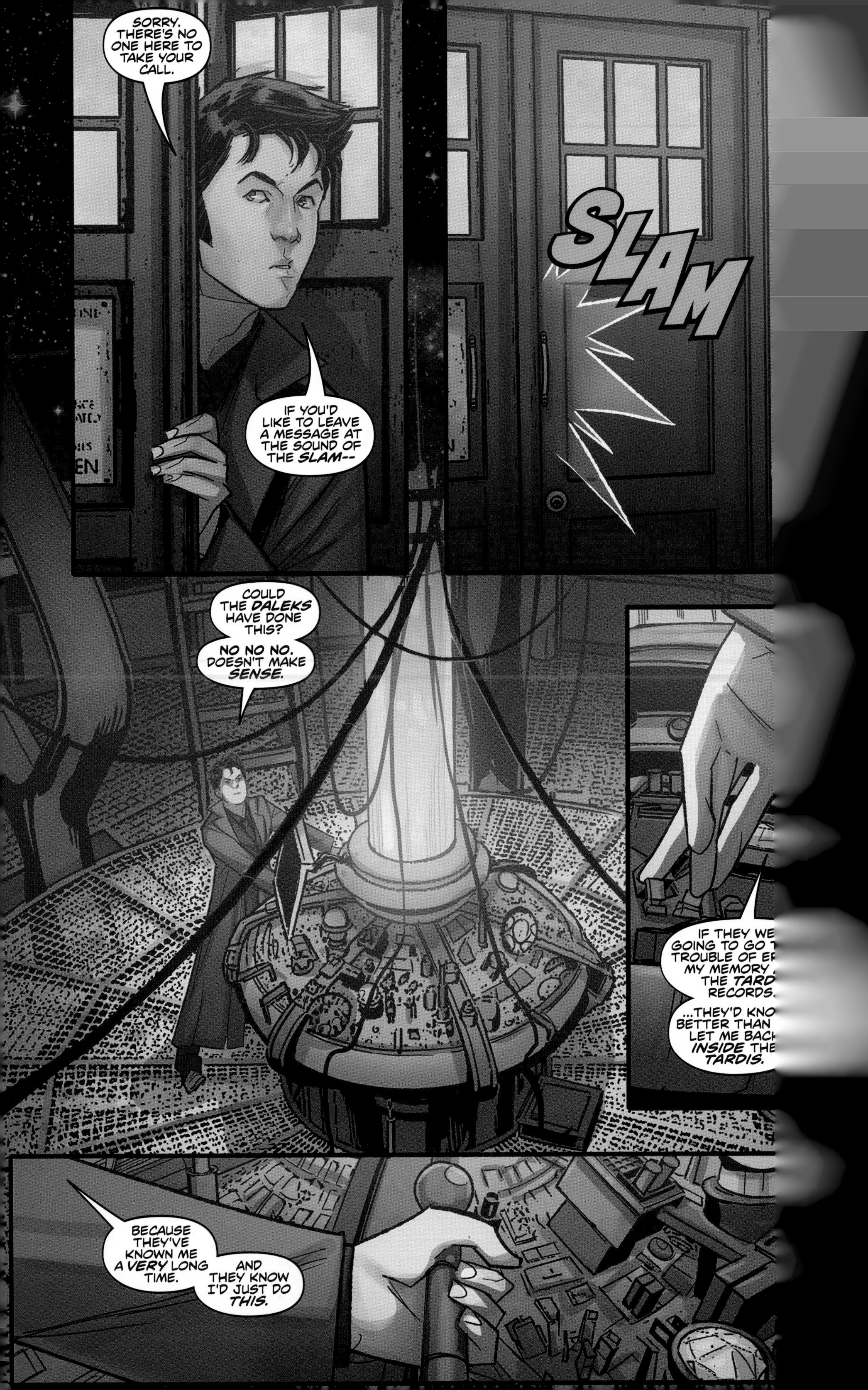
SORRY. THERE'S NO ONE HERE TO TAKE YOUR CALL.
IF YOU'D LIKE TO LEAVE A MESSAGE AT THE SOUND OF THE SLAM--
SLAM
COULD THE DALEKS HAVE DONE THIS?
NO NO NO. DOESN'T MAKE SENSE.
BECAUSE THEY'VE KNOWN ME A VERY LONG TIME.
AND THEY KNOW I'D JUST DO THIS.

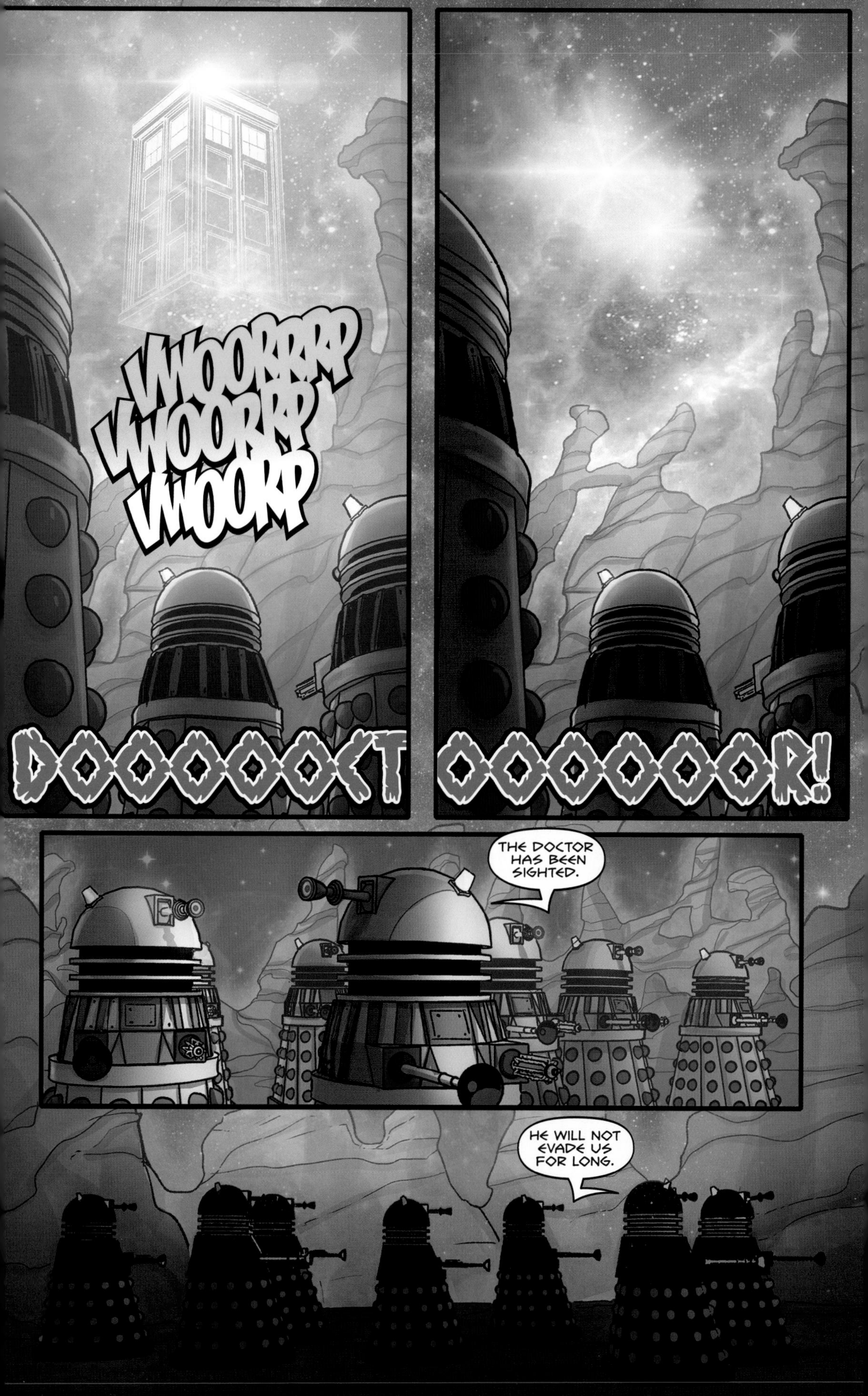
VWOORRRP
VWOORRP
VWOORP
DOOOOOCT
OOOOOOOR!
THE DOCTOR HAS BEEN SIGHTED.
HE WILL NOT EVADE US FOR LONG.

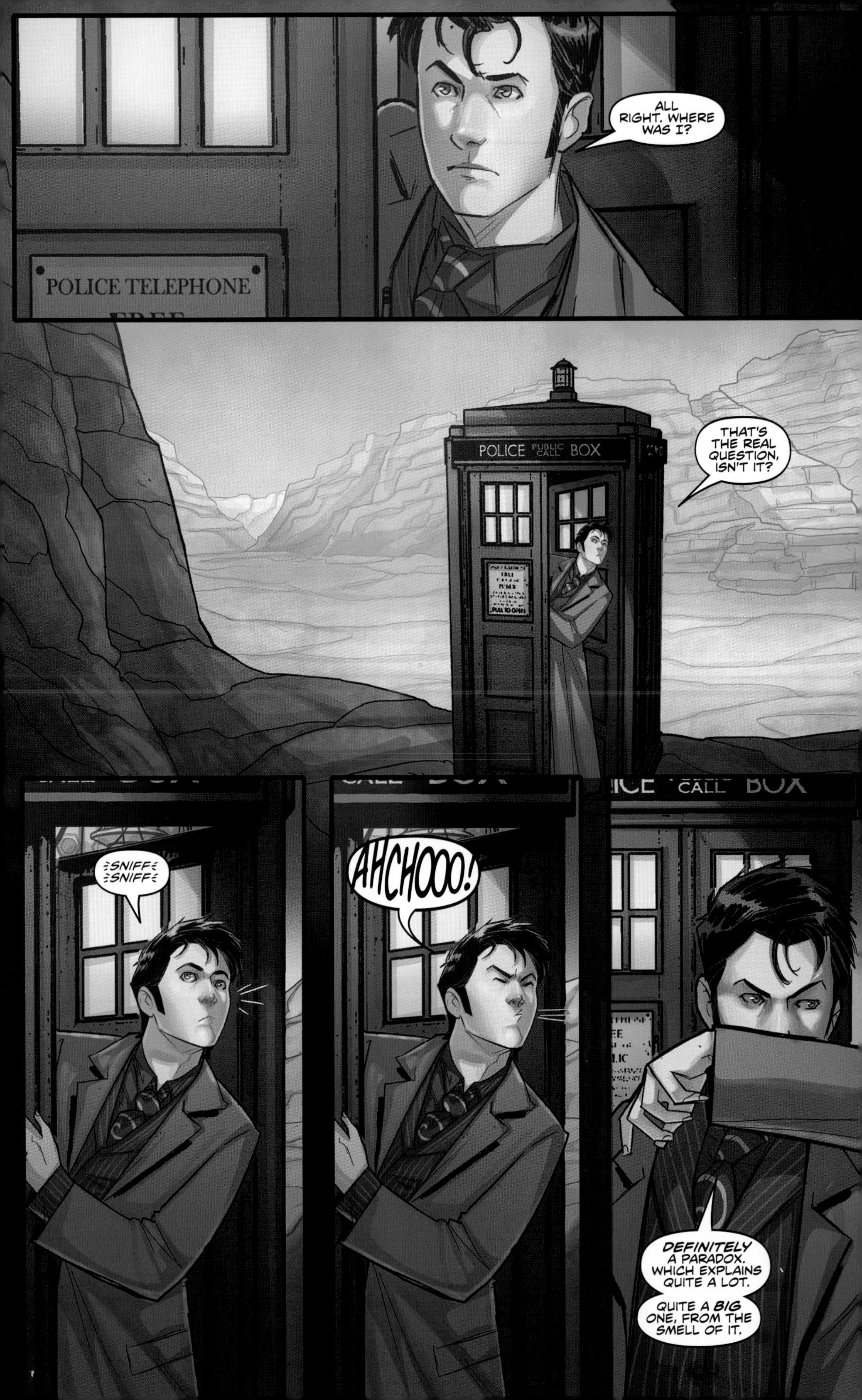
POLICE TELEPHONE
ALL RIGHT. WHERE WAS I?
POLICE PUBLIC CALL BOX
THAT'S THE REAL QUESTION, ISN'T IT?
SNIFF SNIFF
AHCHOOO!
*DEFINITELY* A PARADOX. WHICH EXPLAINS QUITE A LOT.
QUITE A *BIG* ONE, FROM THE SMELL OF IT.

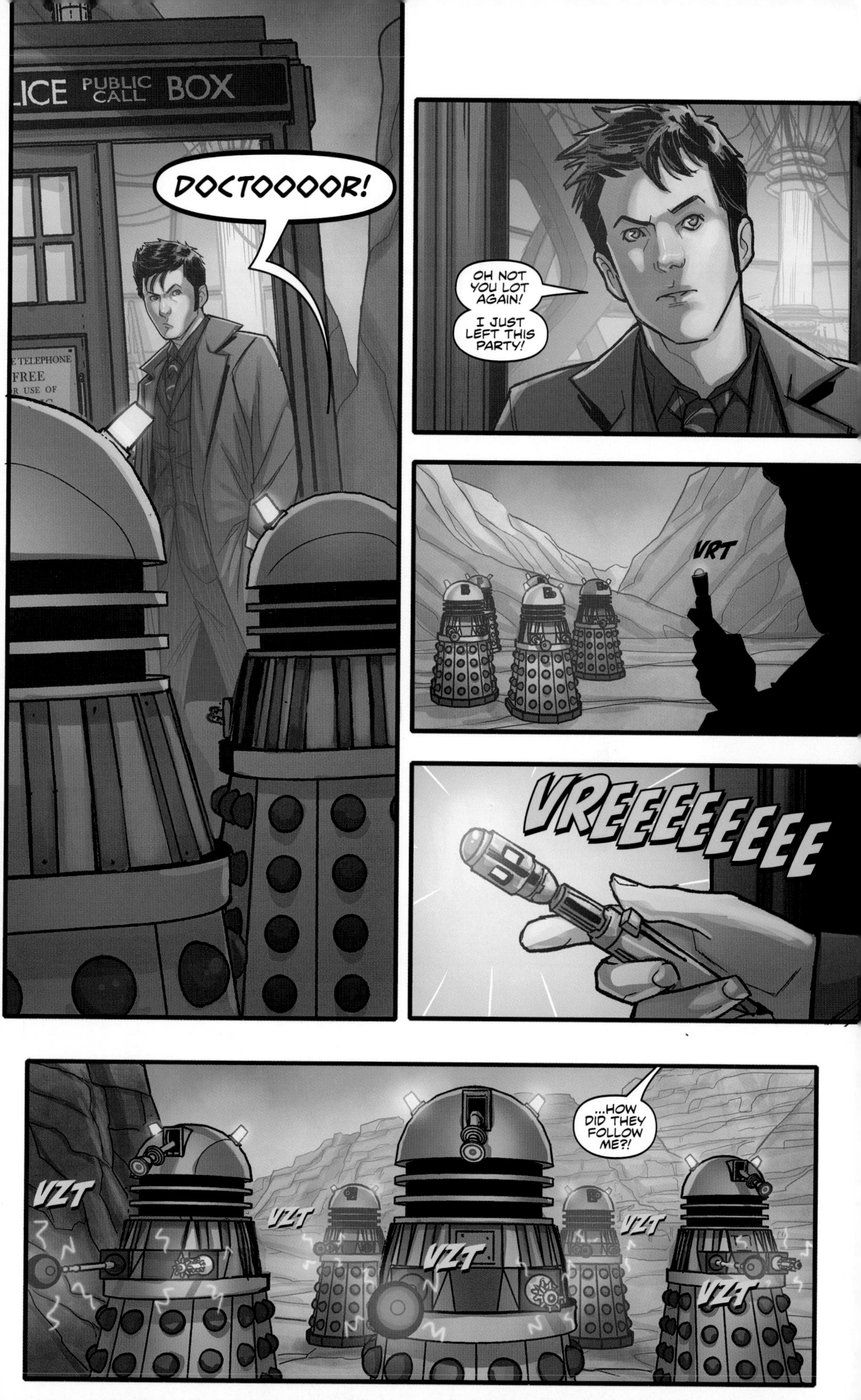

LICE PUBLIC CALL BOX
DOCTOOOOR!
OH NOT YOU LOT AGAIN!
I JUST LEFT THIS PARTY!
VRT
VREEEEEEEEE
VZT
VZT
VZT
VZT
VZT
...HOW DID THEY FOLLOW ME?!

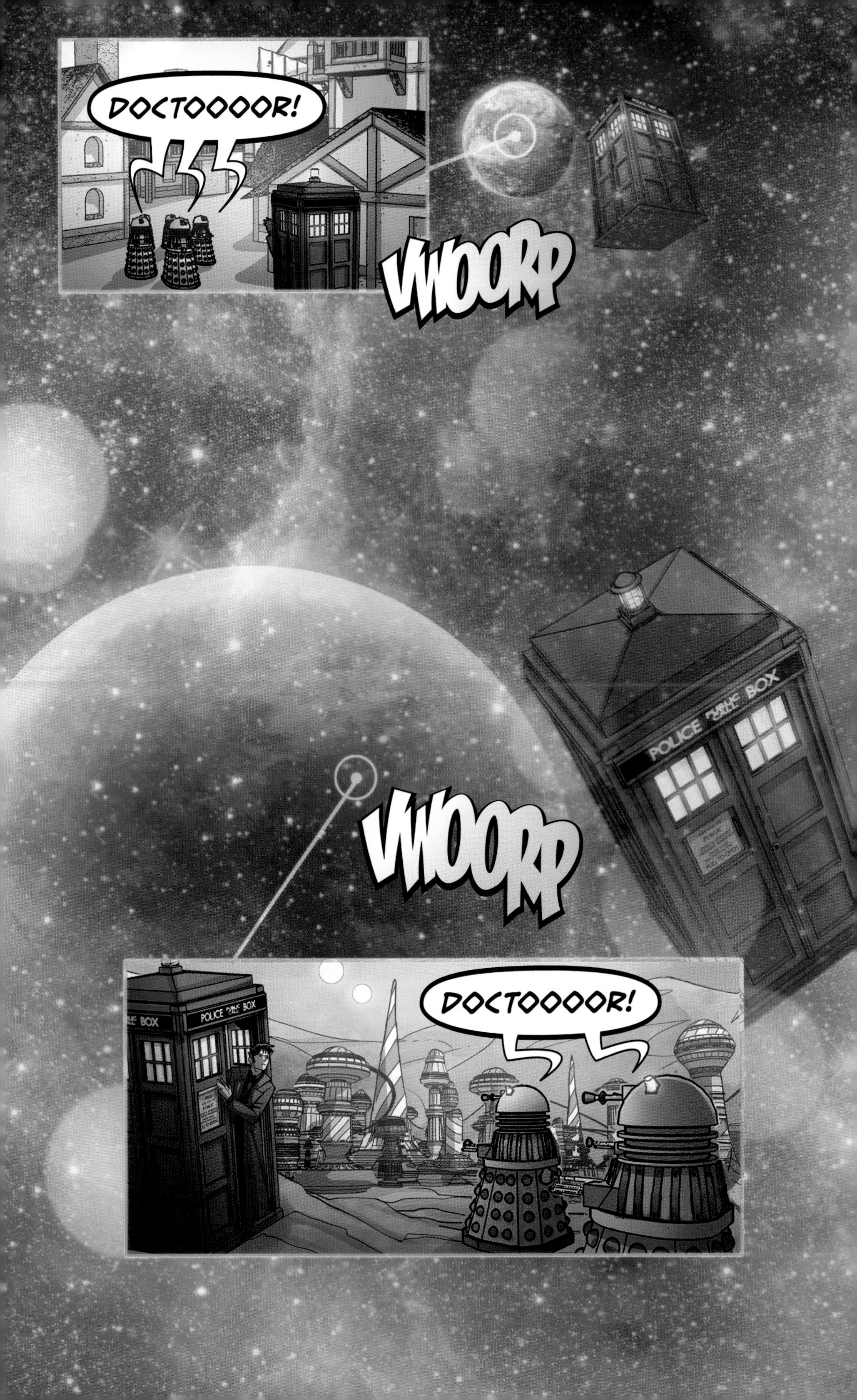
DOCTOOOOR!
VWOORP
POLICE PUBLIC CALL BOX
VWOORP
POLICE PUBLIC CALL BOX
DOCTOOOOR!

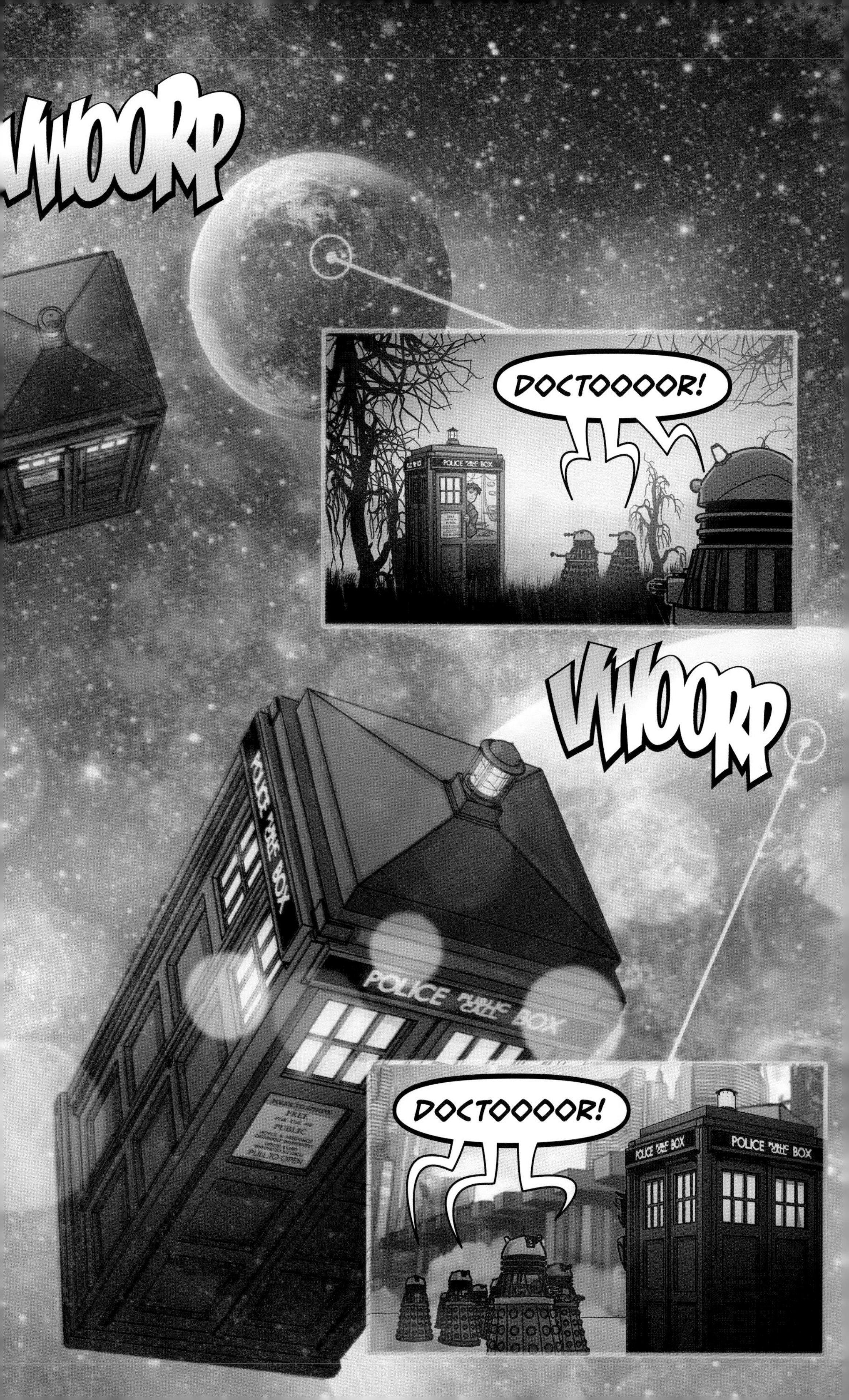

VWOORP
DOCTOOOOR!
VWOORP
DOCTOOOOR!

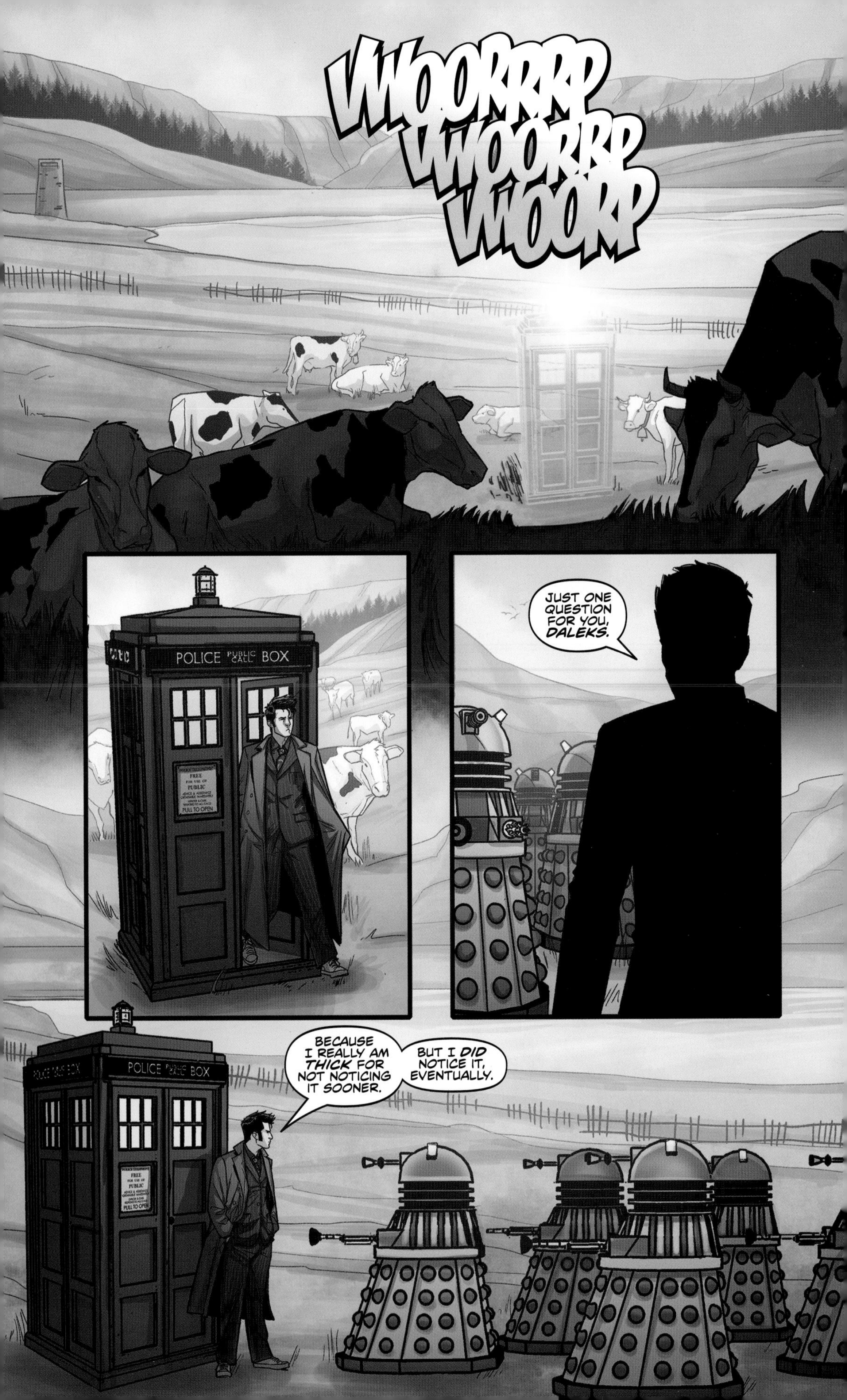
VWOORRRP VWOORRP VWOORP
POLICE PUBLIC CALL BOX
JUST ONE QUESTION FOR YOU, DALEKS.
BECAUSE I REALLY AM THICK FOR NOT NOTICING IT SOONER.
BUT I DID NOTICE IT, EVENTUALLY.
POLICE PUBLIC CALL BOX

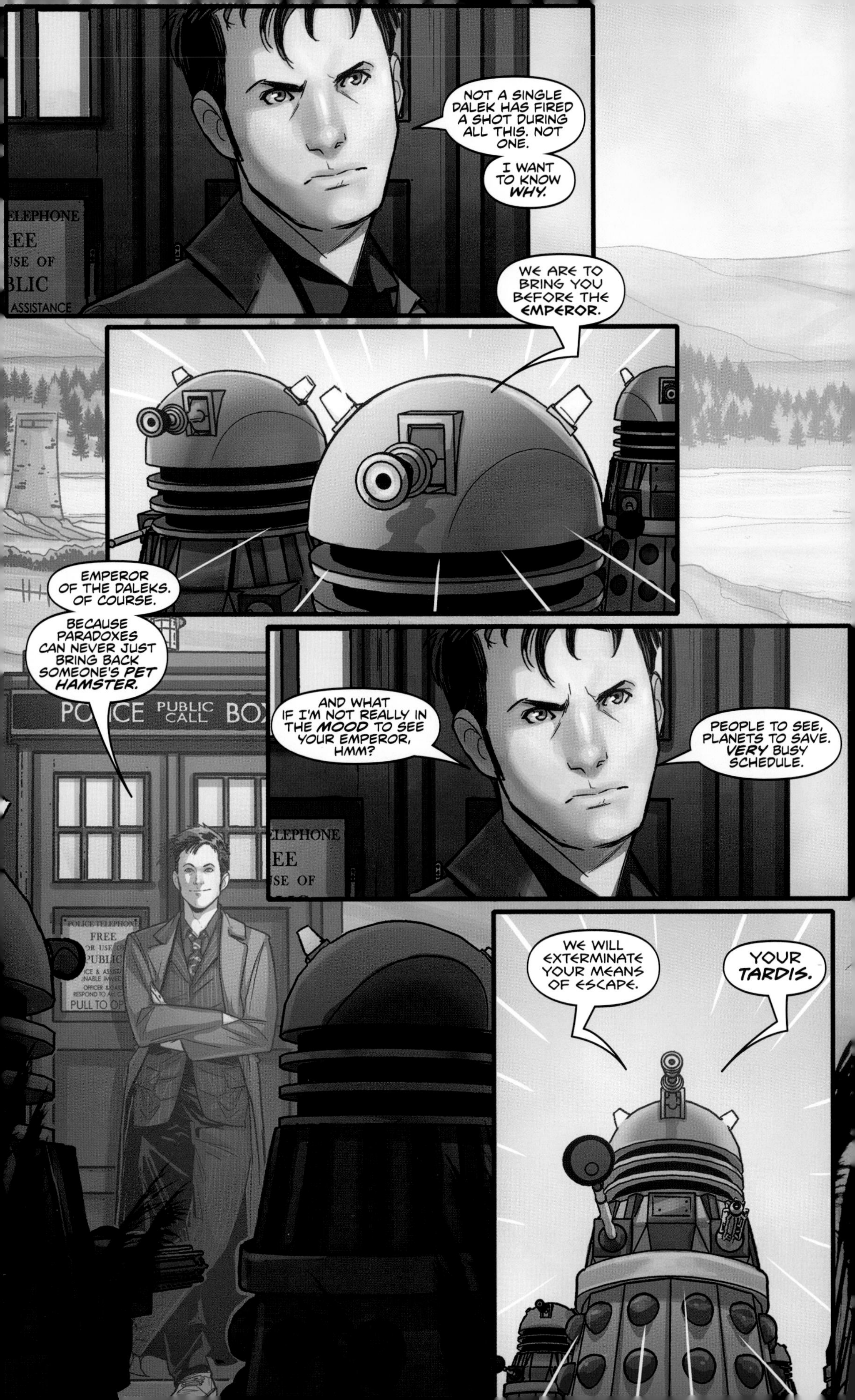
NOT A SINGLE DALEK HAS FIRED A SHOT DURING ALL THIS. NOT ONE.
I WANT TO KNOW WHY.
ELEPHONE
EE
USE OF
BLIC
ASSISTANCE
WE ARE TO BRING YOU BEFORE THE EMPEROR.
EMPEROR OF THE DALEKS. OF COURSE.
BECAUSE PARADOXES CAN NEVER JUST BRING BACK SOMEONE'S PET HAMSTER.
POLICE PUBLIC CALL BOX
AND WHAT IF I'M NOT REALLY IN THE MOOD TO SEE YOUR EMPEROR, HMM?
PEOPLE TO SEE, PLANETS TO SAVE. VERY BUSY SCHEDULE.
ELEPHONE
EE
USE OF
FREE
PULL TO OP
WE WILL EXTERMINATE YOUR MEANS OF ESCAPE.
YOUR TARDIS.

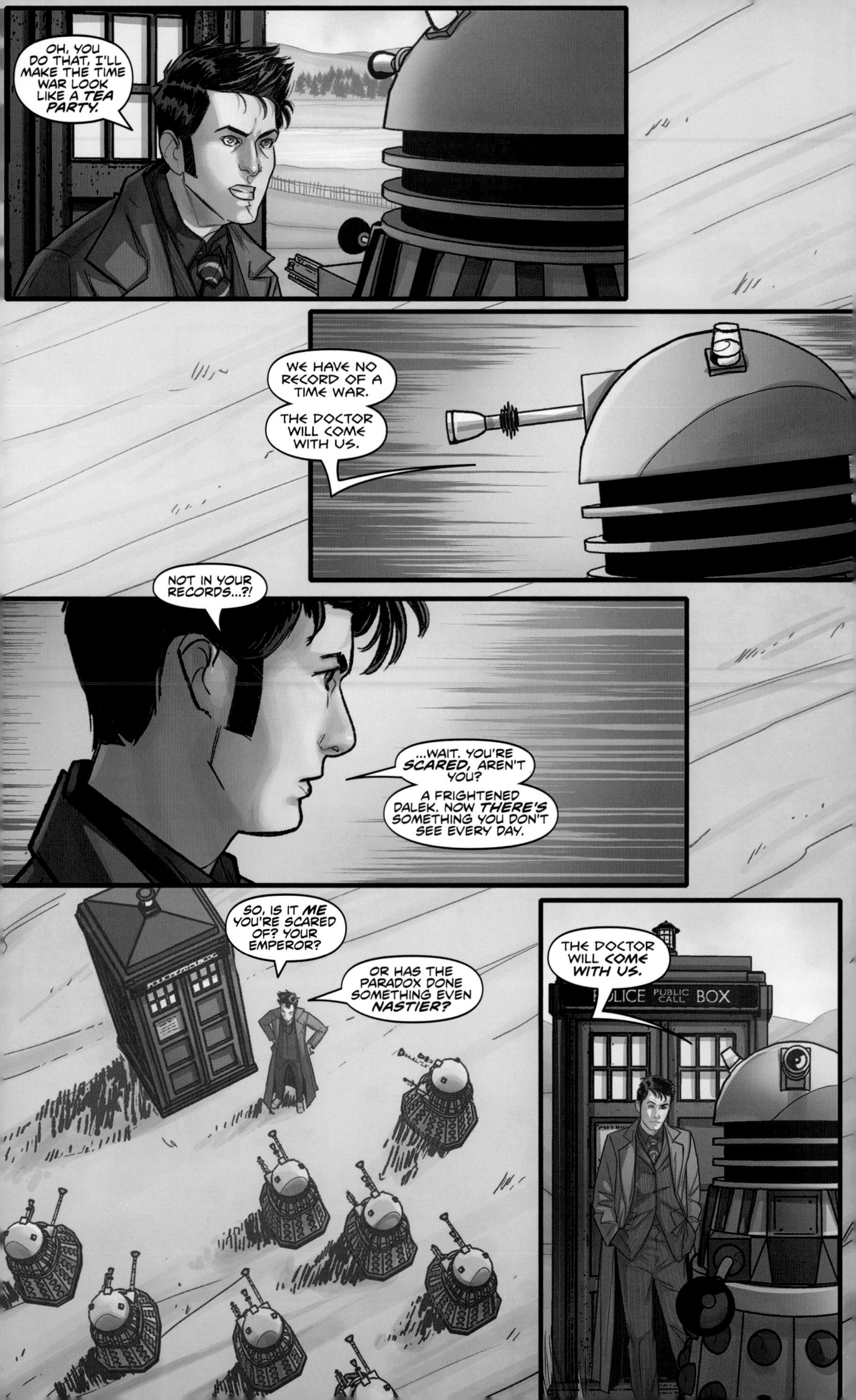
OH, YOU DO THAT, I'LL MAKE THE TIME WAR LOOK LIKE A *TEA PARTY.*
WE HAVE NO RECORD OF A TIME WAR.
THE DOCTOR WILL COME WITH US.
NOT IN YOUR RECORDS...?!
...WAIT. YOU'RE *SCARED,* AREN'T YOU?
A FRIGHTENED DALEK. NOW *THERE'S* SOMETHING YOU DON'T SEE EVERY DAY.
SO, IS IT *ME* YOU'RE SCARED OF? YOUR EMPEROR?
OR HAS THE PARADOX DONE SOMETHING EVEN *NASTIER?*
THE DOCTOR WILL *COME WITH US.*
POLICE PUBLIC CALL BOX

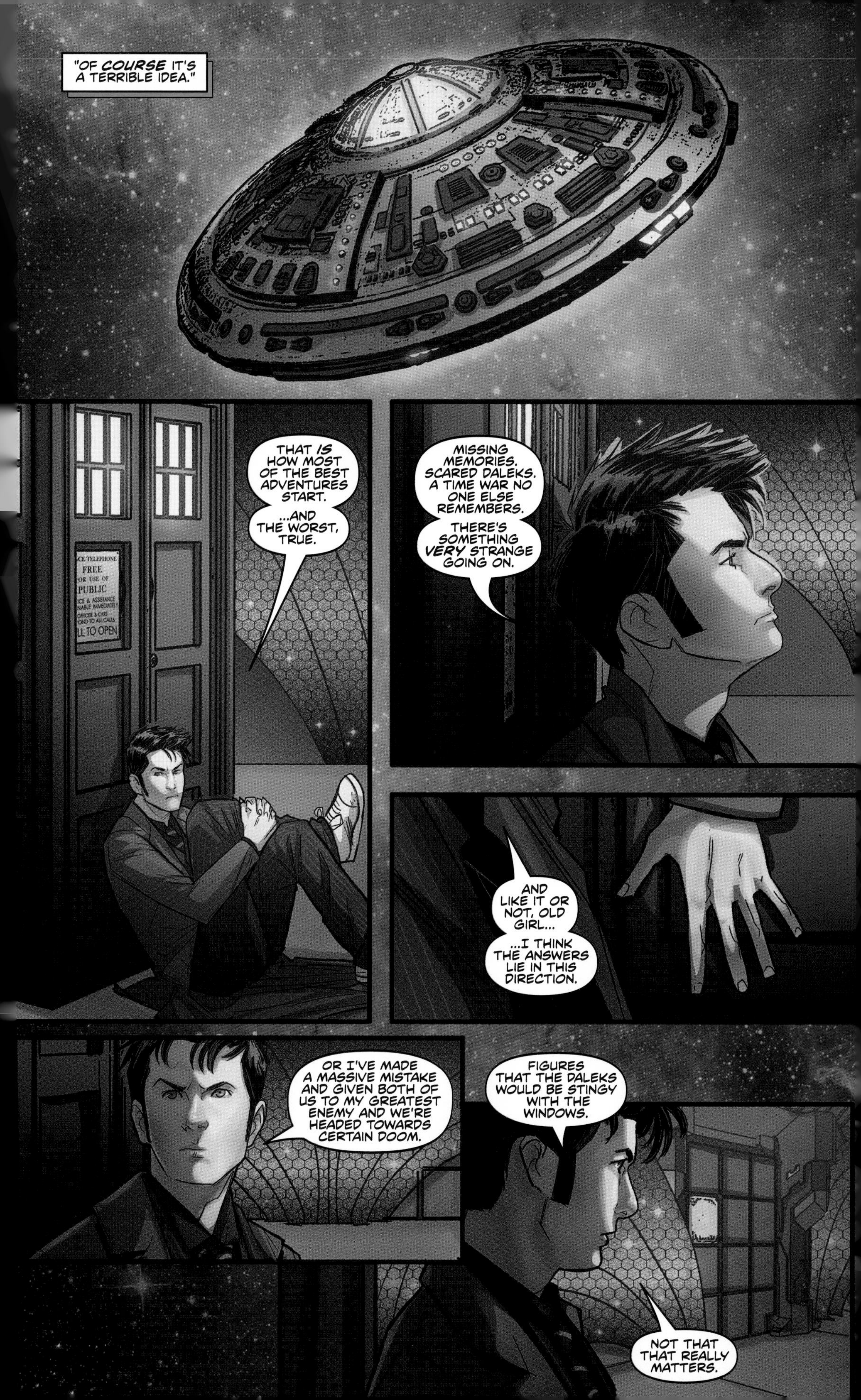
"OF COURSE IT'S A TERRIBLE IDEA."
THAT IS HOW MOST OF THE BEST ADVENTURES START.
...AND THE WORST, TRUE.
MISSING MEMORIES. SCARED DALEKS. A TIME WAR NO ONE ELSE REMEMBERS.
THERE'S SOMETHING VERY STRANGE GOING ON.
AND LIKE IT OR NOT, OLD GIRL...
...I THINK THE ANSWERS LIE IN THIS DIRECTION.
OR I'VE MADE A MASSIVE MISTAKE AND GIVEN BOTH OF US TO MY GREATEST ENEMY AND WE'RE HEADED TOWARDS CERTAIN DOOM.
FIGURES THAT THE DALEKS WOULD BE STINGY WITH THE WINDOWS.
NOT THAT THAT REALLY MATTERS.

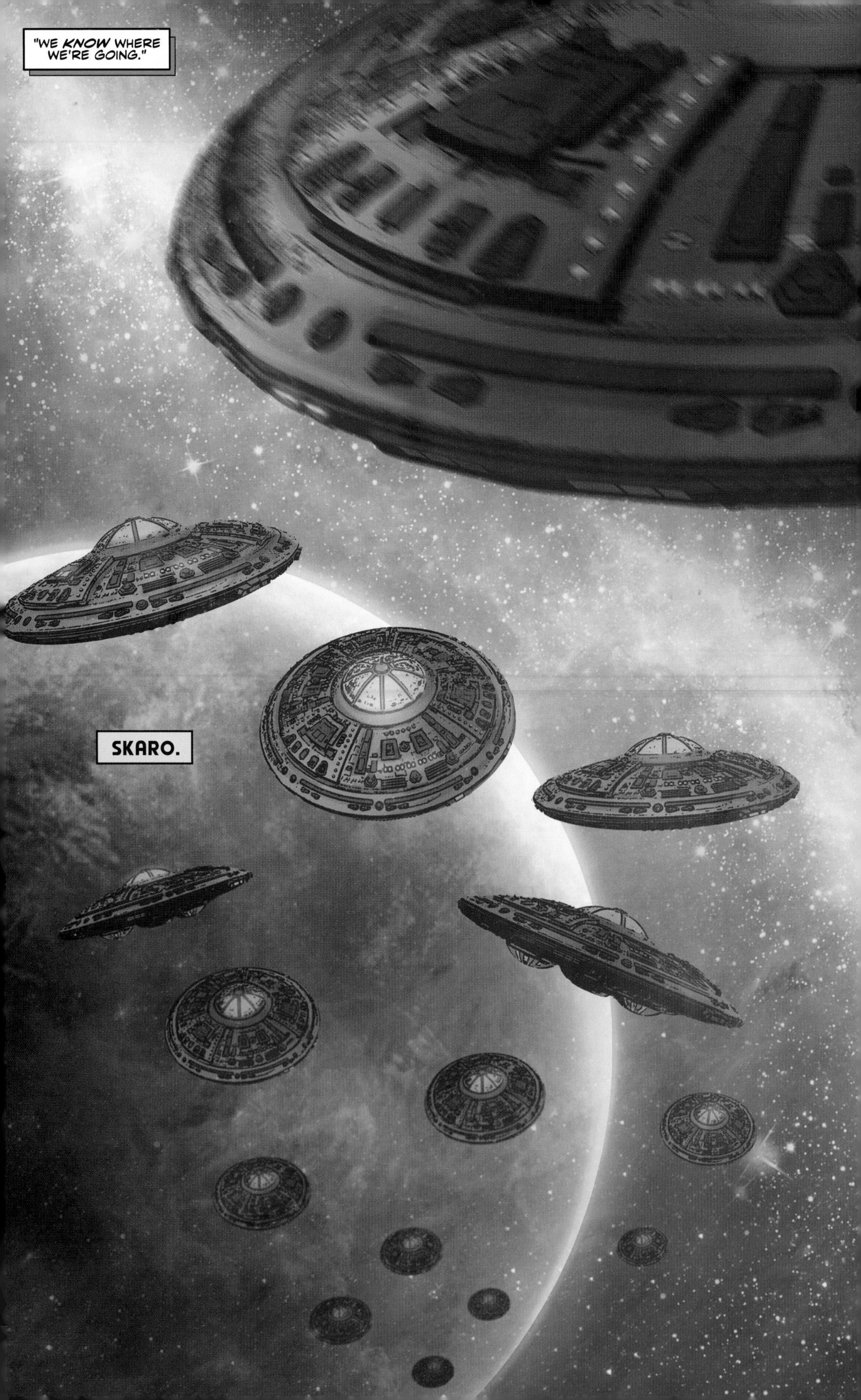
"WE KNOW WHERE WE'RE GOING."
SKARO.

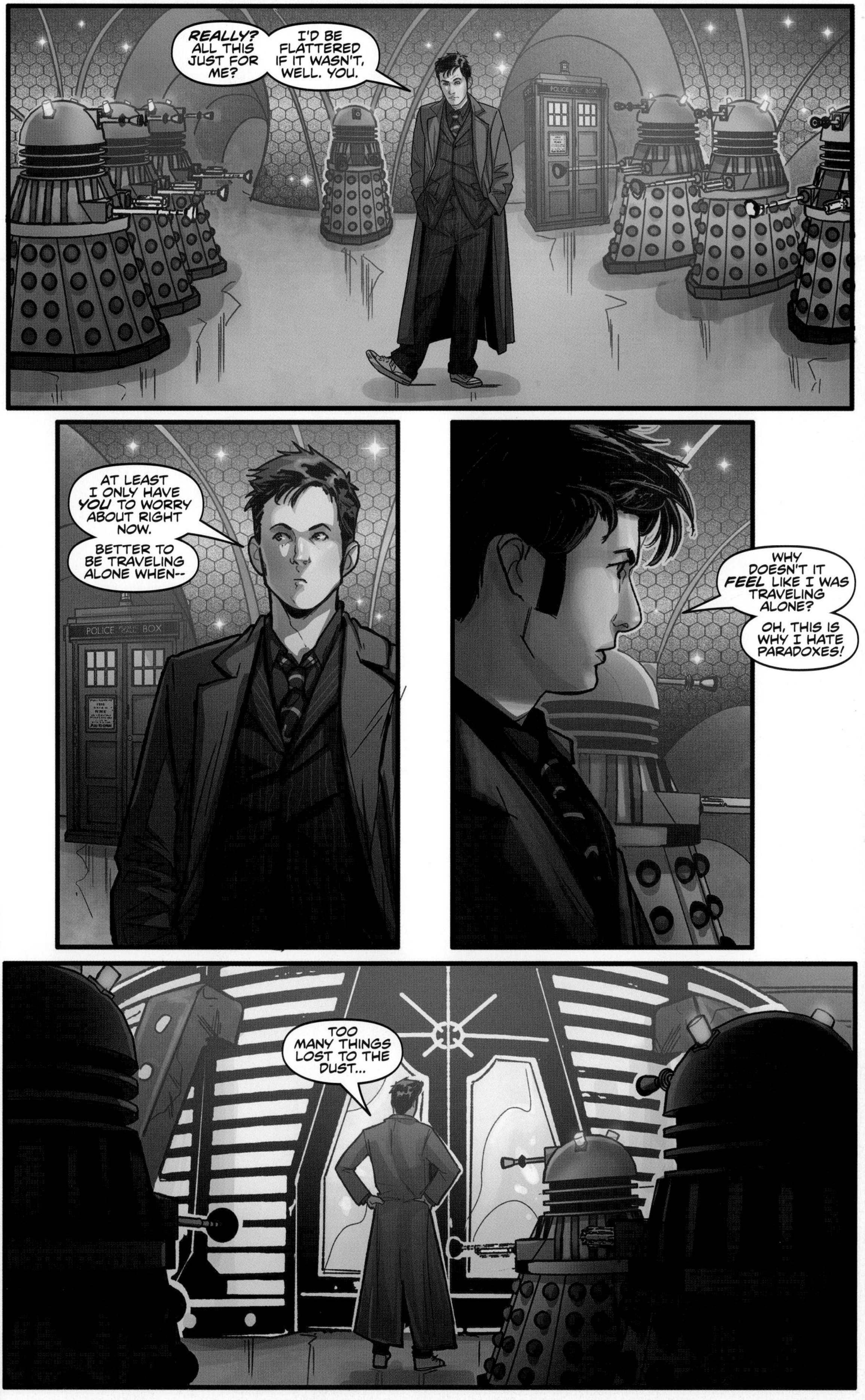

REALLY? ALL THIS JUST FOR ME?
I'D BE FLATTERED IF IT WASN'T, WELL. YOU.
POLICE BOX
AT LEAST I ONLY HAVE YOU TO WORRY ABOUT RIGHT NOW.
BETTER TO BE TRAVELING ALONE WHEN--
WHY DOESN'T IT FEEL LIKE I WAS TRAVELING ALONE?
OH, THIS IS WHY I HATE PARADOXES!
TOO MANY THINGS LOST TO THE DUST...

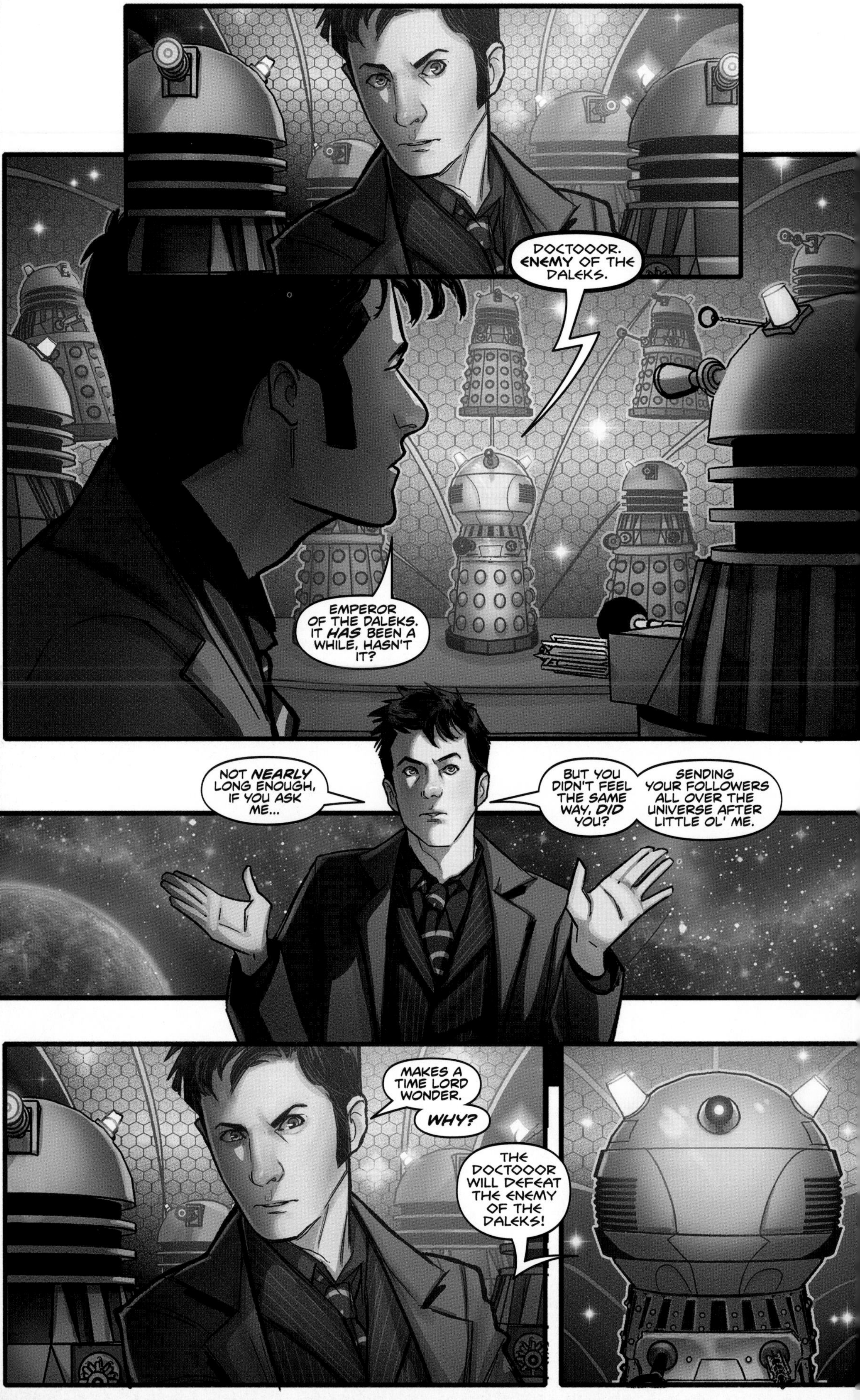
DOCTOOOR. ENEMY OF THE DALEKS.
EMPEROR OF THE DALEKS. IT HAS BEEN A WHILE, HASN'T IT?
NOT NEARLY LONG ENOUGH, IF YOU ASK ME...
BUT YOU DIDN'T FEEL THE SAME WAY, DID YOU?
SENDING YOUR FOLLOWERS ALL OVER THE UNIVERSE AFTER LITTLE OL' ME.
MAKES A TIME LORD WONDER.
WHY?
THE DOCTOOOR WILL DEFEAT THE ENEMY OF THE DALEKS!

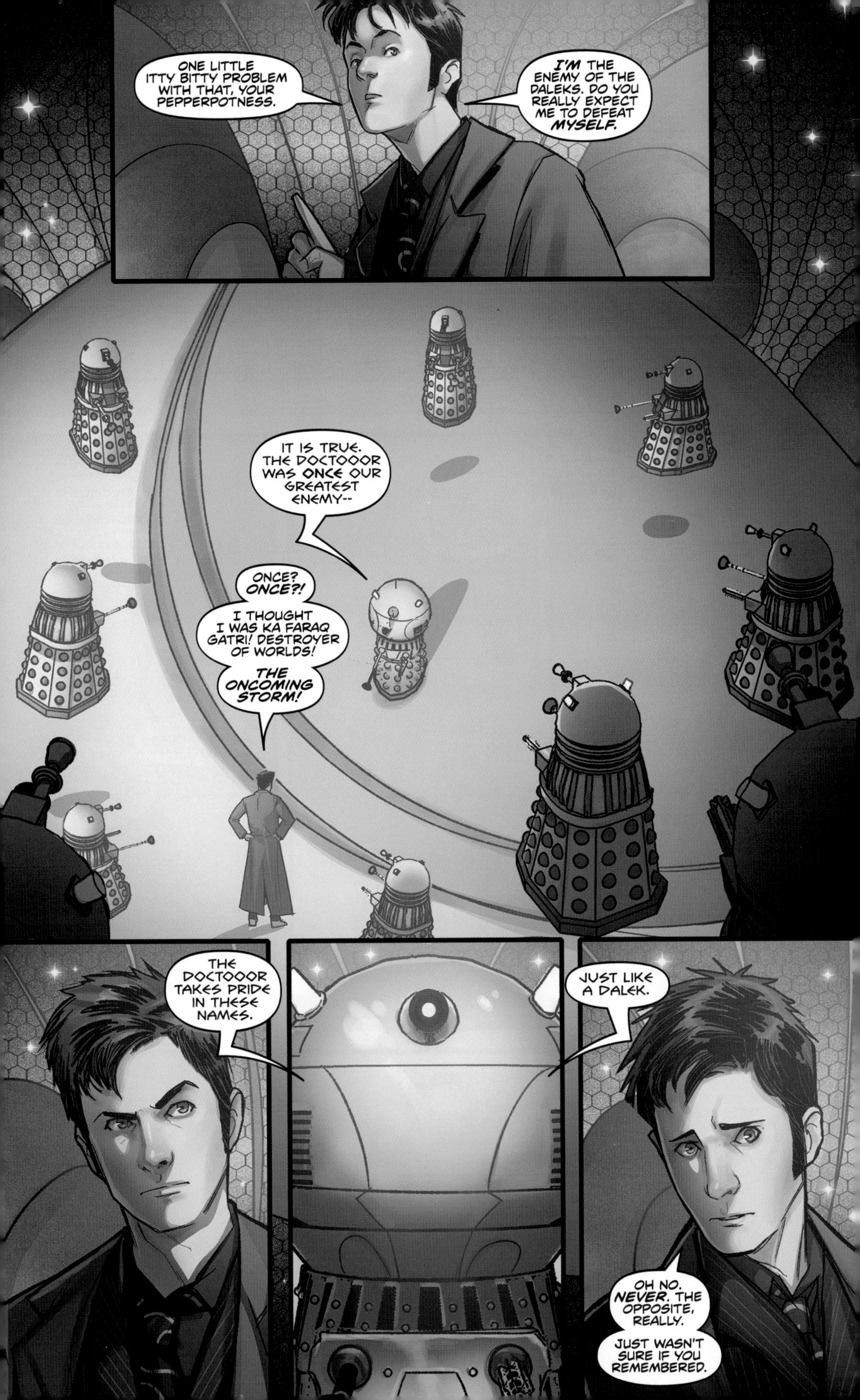
ONE LITTLE ITTY BITTY PROBLEM WITH THAT, YOUR PEPPERPOTNESS.
I'M THE ENEMY OF THE DALEKS. DO YOU REALLY EXPECT ME TO DEFEAT MYSELF.
IT IS TRUE. THE DOCTOOOR WAS ONCE OUR GREATEST ENEMY--
ONCE? ONCE?!
I THOUGHT I WAS KA FARAQ GATRI! DESTROYER OF WORLDS!
THE ONCOMING STORM!
THE DOCTOOOR TAKES PRIDE IN THESE NAMES.
JUST LIKE A DALEK.
OH NO. NEVER. THE OPPOSITE, REALLY.
JUST WASN'T SURE IF YOU REMEMBERED.

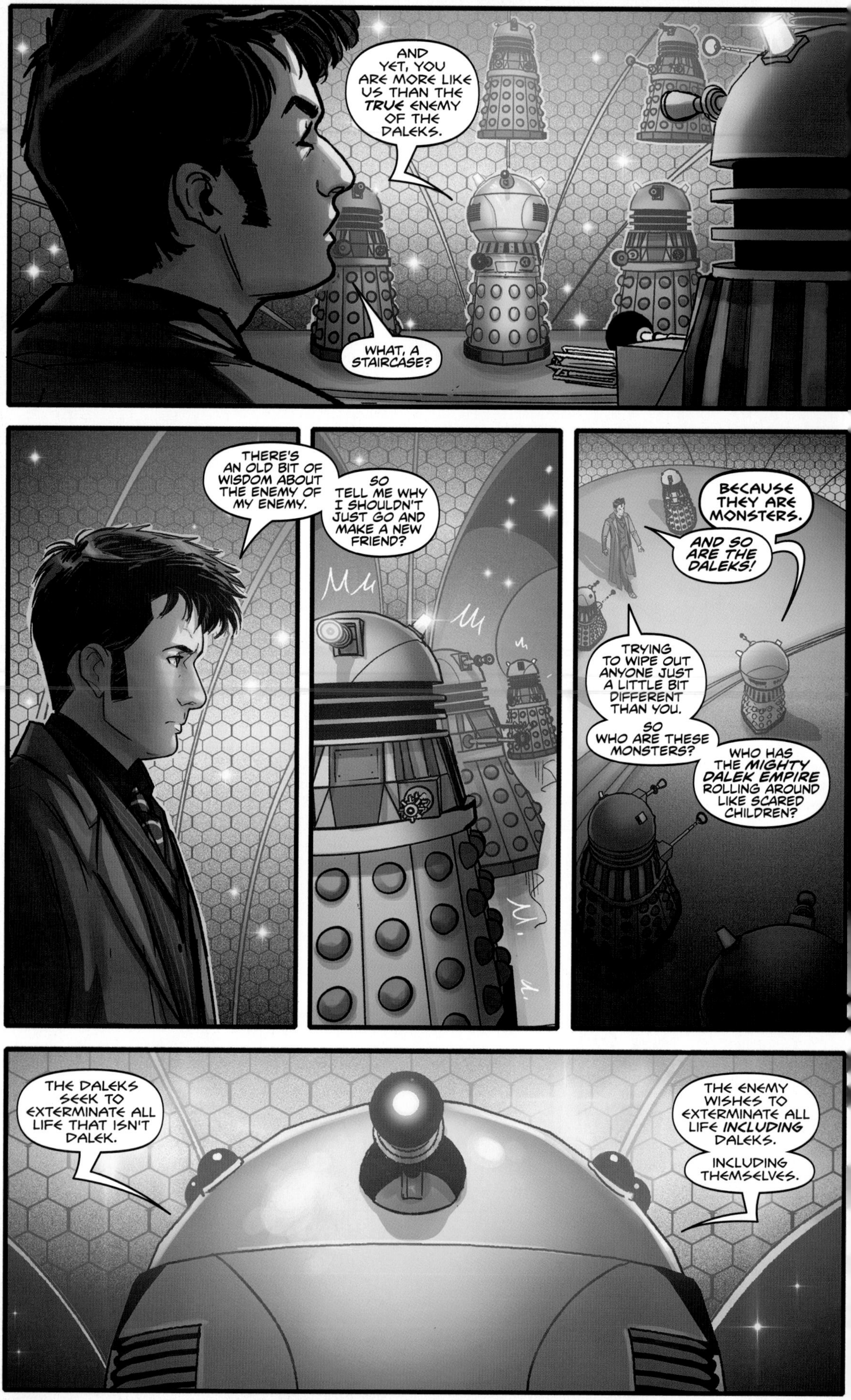
AND YET, YOU ARE MORE LIKE US THAN THE *TRUE* ENEMY OF THE DALEKS.
WHAT, A STAIRCASE?
THERE'S AN OLD BIT OF WISDOM ABOUT THE ENEMY OF MY ENEMY.
SO TELL ME WHY I SHOULDN'T JUST GO AND MAKE A NEW FRIEND?
**BECAUSE THEY ARE MONSTERS.**
***AND SO ARE THE DALEKS!***
TRYING TO WIPE OUT ANYONE JUST A LITTLE BIT DIFFERENT THAN YOU.
SO WHO ARE THESE MONSTERS?
WHO HAS THE ***MIGHTY DALEK EMPIRE*** ROLLING AROUND LIKE SCARED CHILDREN?
THE DALEKS SEEK TO EXTERMINATE ALL LIFE THAT ISN'T DALEK.
THE ENEMY WISHES TO EXTERMINATE ALL LIFE *INCLUDING* DALEKS.
INCLUDING THEMSELVES.

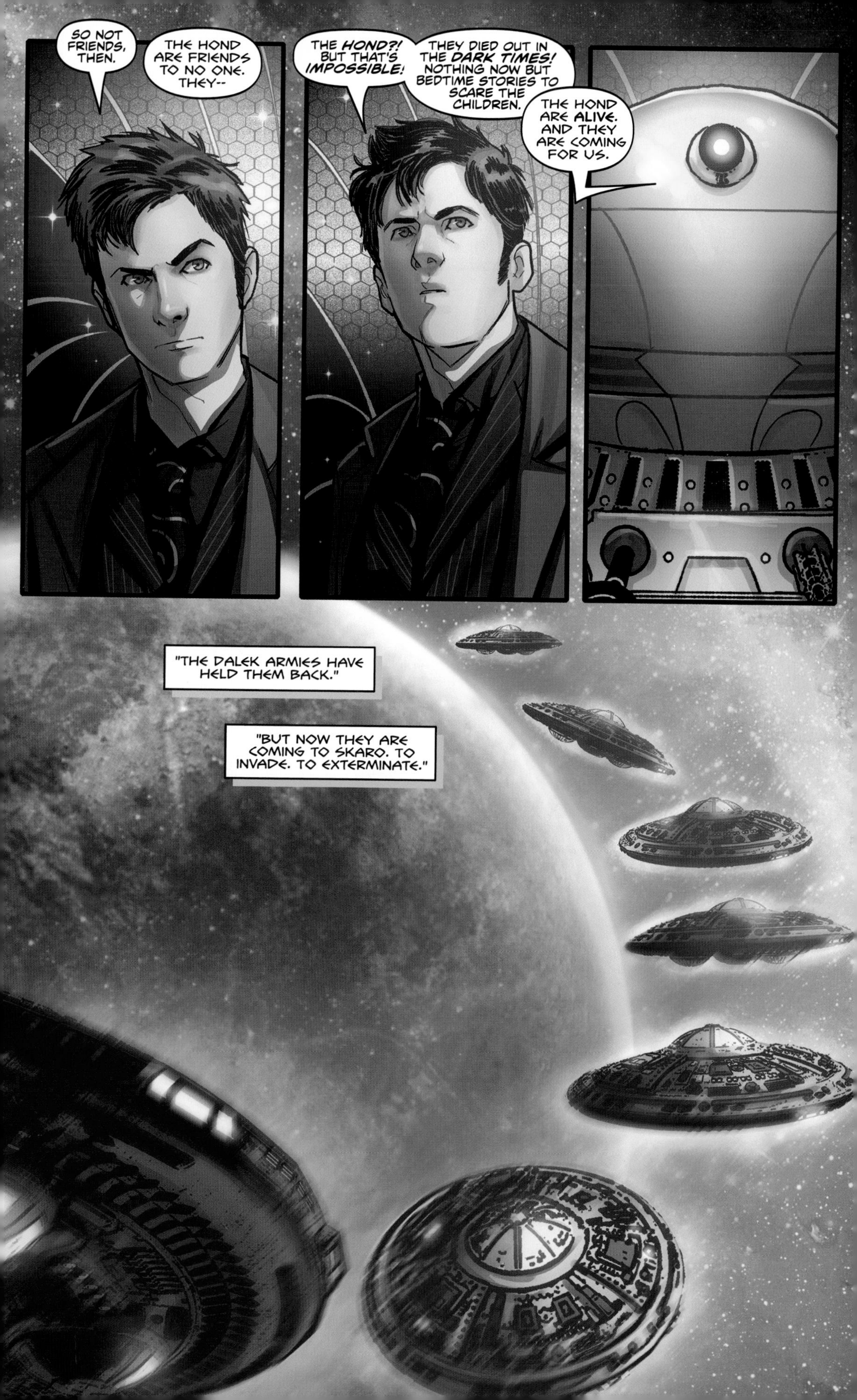
SO NOT FRIENDS, THEN.
THE HOND ARE FRIENDS TO NO ONE. THEY--
THE HOND?! BUT THAT'S IMPOSSIBLE!
THEY DIED OUT IN THE DARK TIMES! NOTHING NOW BUT BEDTIME STORIES TO SCARE THE CHILDREN.
THE HOND ARE ALIVE. AND THEY ARE COMING FOR US.
"THE DALEK ARMIES HAVE HELD THEM BACK."
"BUT NOW THEY ARE COMING TO SKARO. TO INVADE. TO EXTERMINATE."

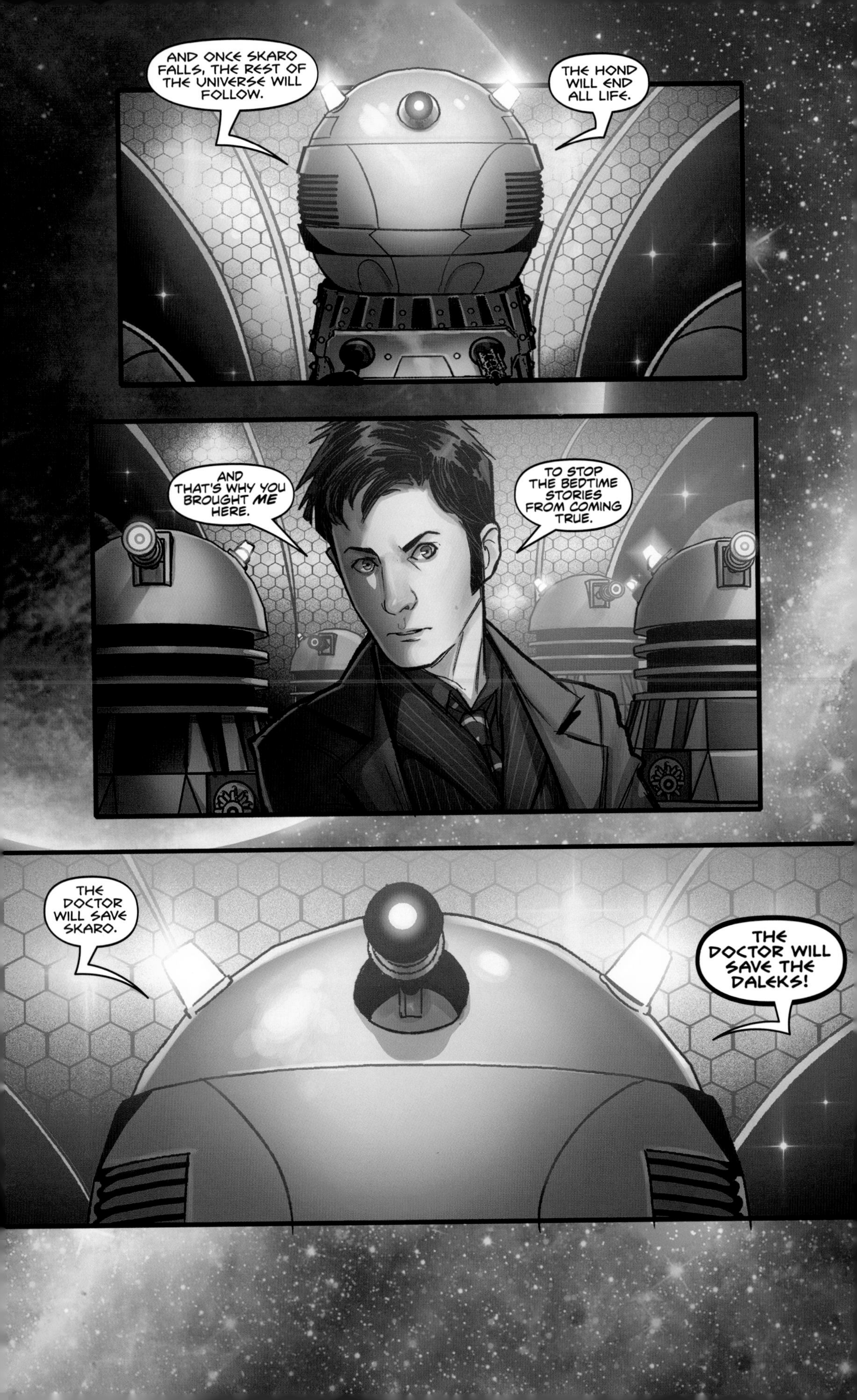
AND ONCE SKARO FALLS, THE REST OF THE UNIVERSE WILL FOLLOW.
THE HOND WILL END ALL LIFE.
AND THAT'S WHY YOU BROUGHT *ME* HERE.
TO STOP THE BEDTIME STORIES FROM COMING TRUE.
THE DOCTOR WILL SAVE SKARO.
THE DOCTOR WILL SAVE THE DALEKS!

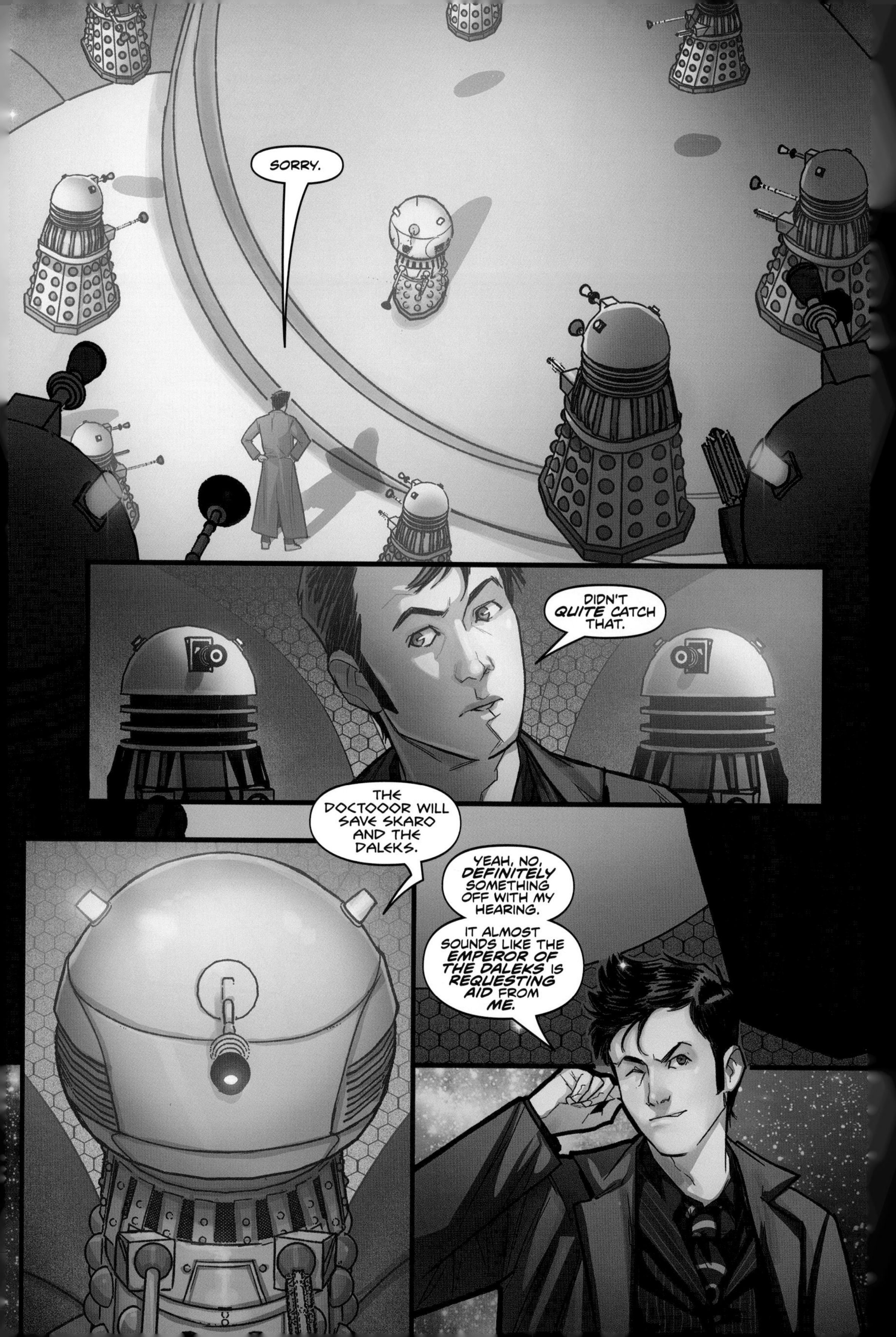
SORRY.
DIDN'T QUITE CATCH THAT.
THE DOCTOOOR WILL SAVE SKARO AND THE DALEKS.
YEAH, NO, DEFINITELY SOMETHING OFF WITH MY HEARING.
IT ALMOST SOUNDS LIKE THE EMPEROR OF THE DALEKS IS REQUESTING AID FROM ME.

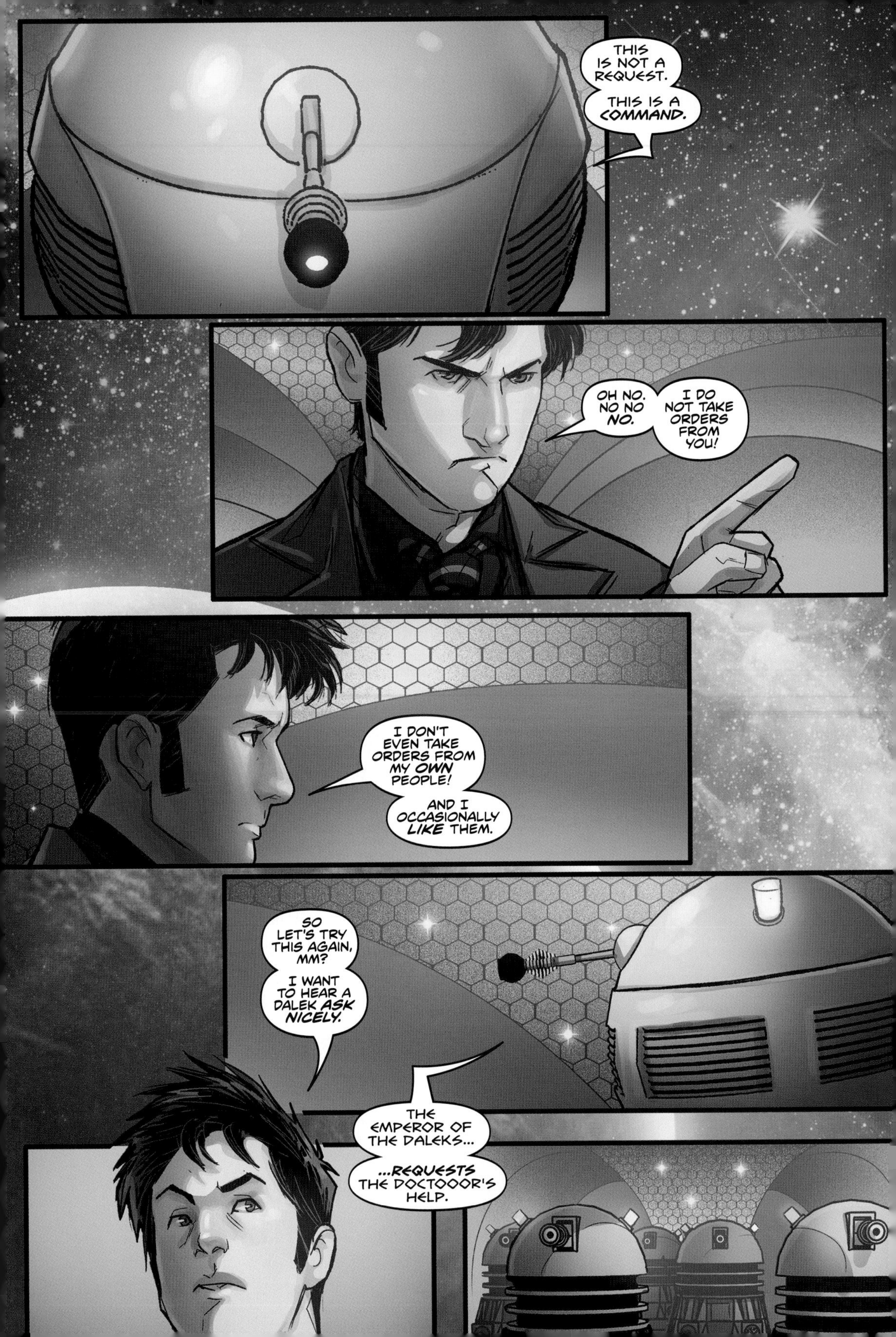
THIS IS NOT A REQUEST.
THIS IS A COMMAND.
OH NO. NO NO NO.
I DO NOT TAKE ORDERS FROM YOU!
I DON'T EVEN TAKE ORDERS FROM MY OWN PEOPLE!
AND I OCCASIONALLY LIKE THEM.
SO LET'S TRY THIS AGAIN, MM?
I WANT TO HEAR A DALEK ASK NICELY.
THE EMPEROR OF THE DALEKS...
...REQUESTS THE DOCTOOOR'S HELP.

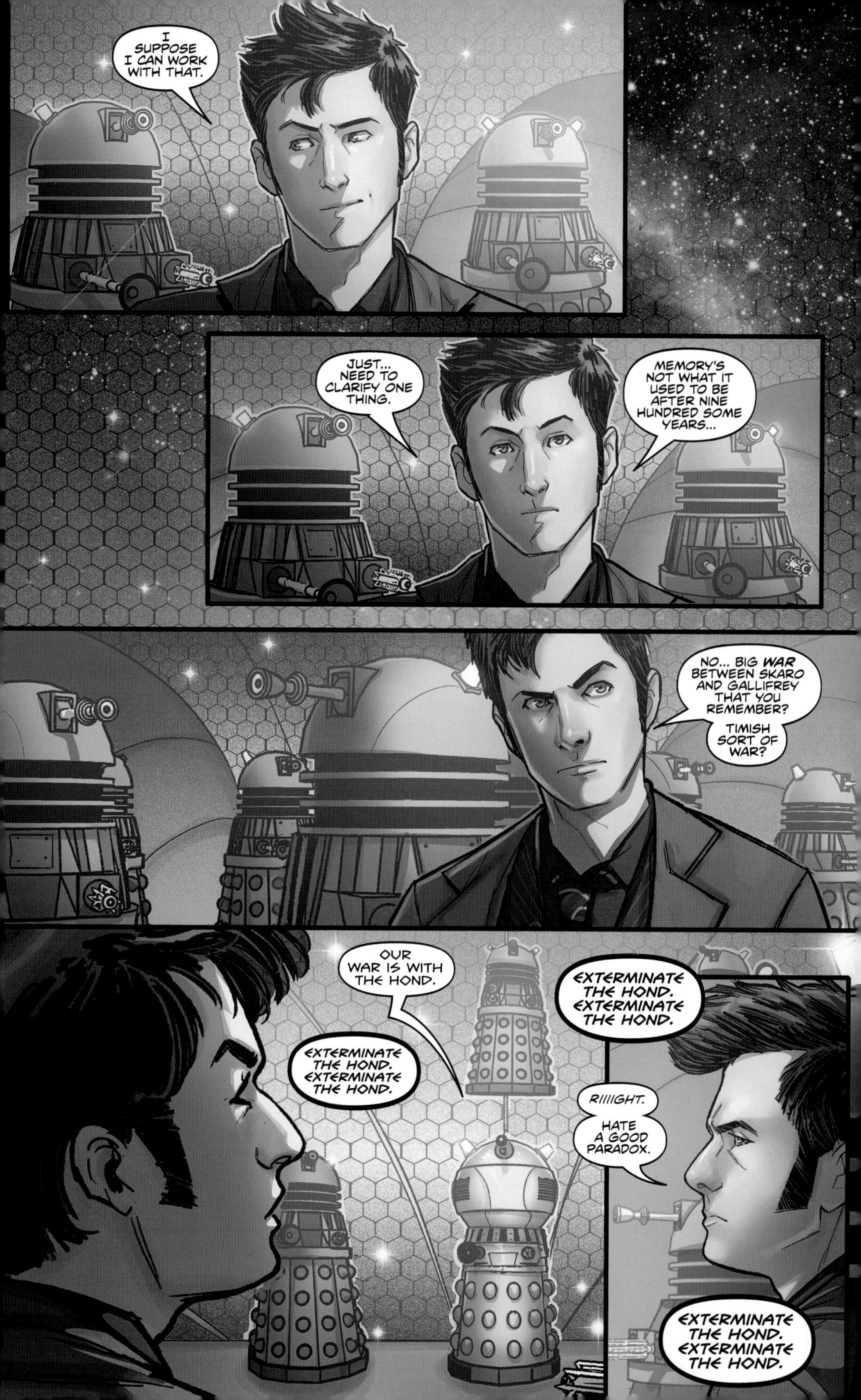
I SUPPOSE I CAN WORK WITH THAT.
JUST... NEED TO CLARIFY ONE THING.
MEMORY'S NOT WHAT IT USED TO BE AFTER NINE HUNDRED SOME YEARS...
NO... BIG WAR BETWEEN SKARO AND GALLIFREY THAT YOU REMEMBER?
TIMISH SORT OF WAR?
OUR WAR IS WITH THE HOND.
EXTERMINATE THE HOND. EXTERMINATE THE HOND.
EXTERMINATE THE HOND. EXTERMINATE THE HOND.
RIIIIGHT.
HATE A GOOD PARADOX.
EXTERMINATE THE HOND. EXTERMINATE THE HOND.

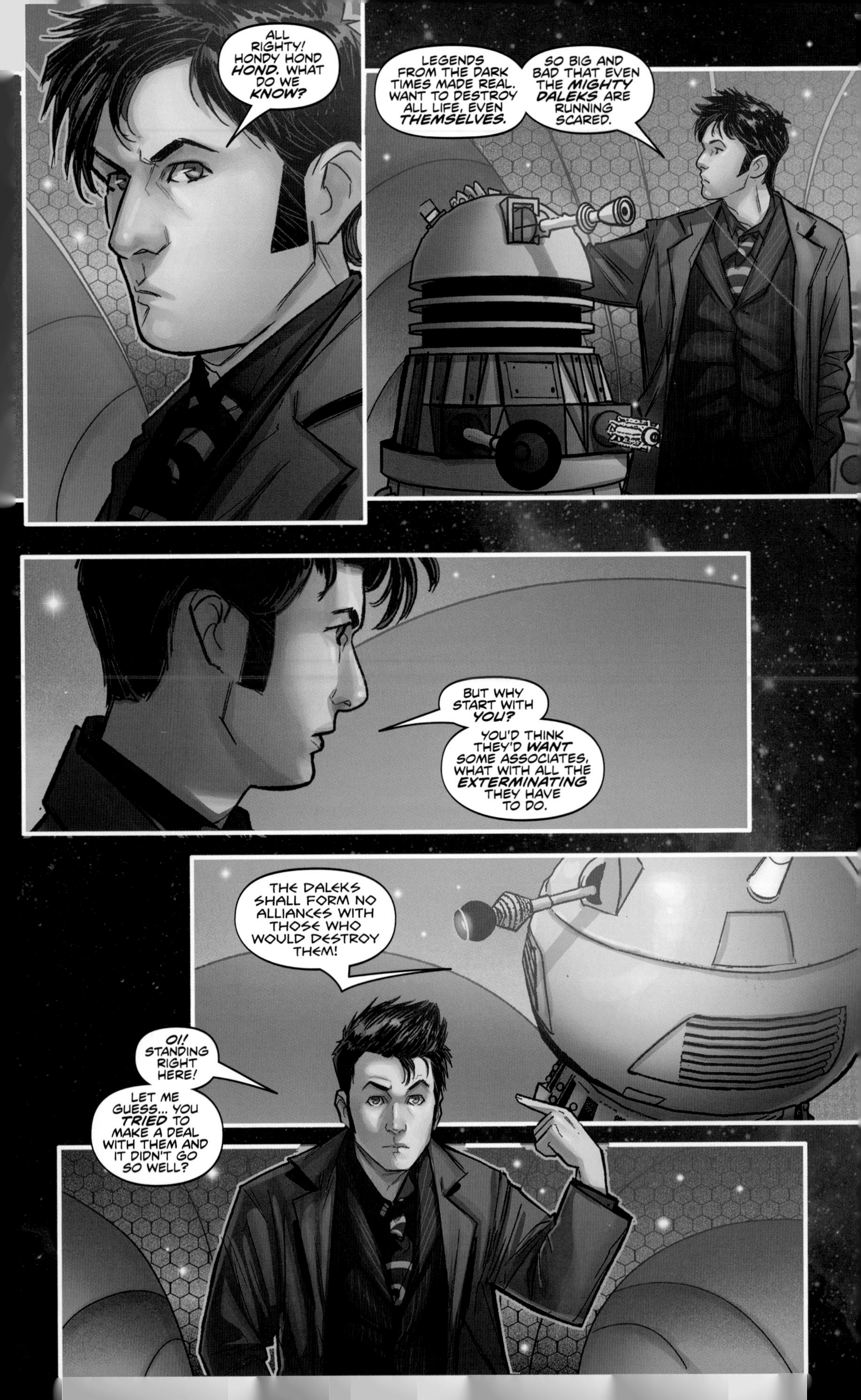
ALL RIGHTY! HONDY HOND HOND. WHAT DO WE KNOW?
LEGENDS FROM THE DARK TIMES MADE REAL. WANT TO DESTROY ALL LIFE, EVEN THEMSELVES.
SO BIG AND BAD THAT EVEN THE MIGHTY DALEKS ARE RUNNING SCARED.
BUT WHY START WITH YOU?
YOU'D THINK THEY'D WANT SOME ASSOCIATES, WHAT WITH ALL THE EXTERMINATING THEY HAVE TO DO.
THE DALEKS SHALL FORM NO ALLIANCES WITH THOSE WHO WOULD DESTROY THEM!
OI! STANDING RIGHT HERE!
LET ME GUESS... YOU TRIED TO MAKE A DEAL WITH THEM AND IT DIDN'T GO SO WELL?

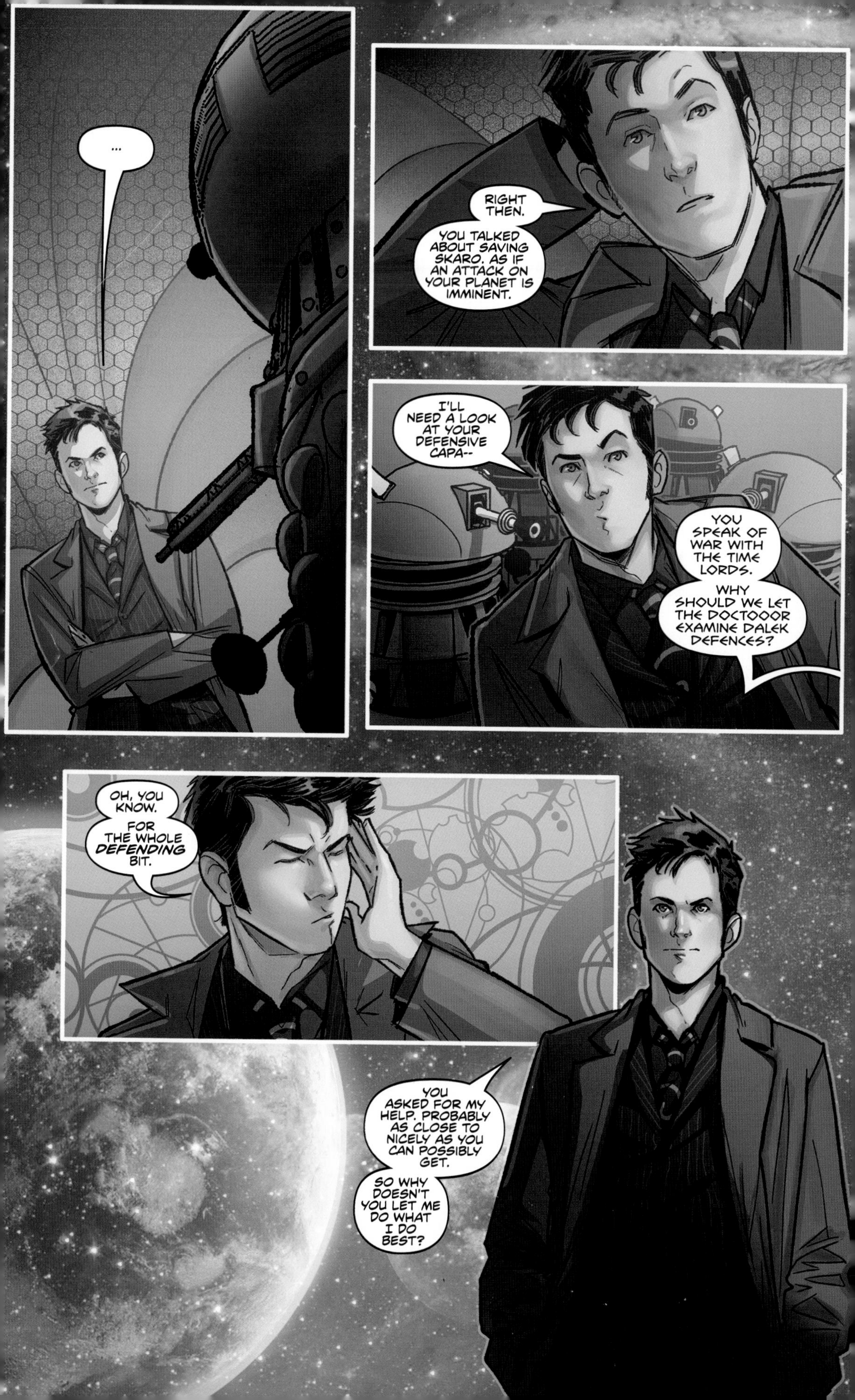
...
RIGHT THEN.
YOU TALKED ABOUT SAVING SKARO, AS IF AN ATTACK ON YOUR PLANET IS IMMINENT.
I'LL NEED A LOOK AT YOUR DEFENSIVE CAPA--
YOU SPEAK OF WAR WITH THE TIME LORDS.
WHY SHOULD WE LET THE DOCTOOOR EXAMINE DALEK DEFENCES?
OH, YOU KNOW.
FOR THE WHOLE *DEFENDING* BIT.
YOU ASKED FOR MY HELP. PROBABLY AS CLOSE TO NICELY AS YOU CAN POSSIBLY GET.
SO WHY DOESN'T YOU LET ME DO WHAT I DO BEST?

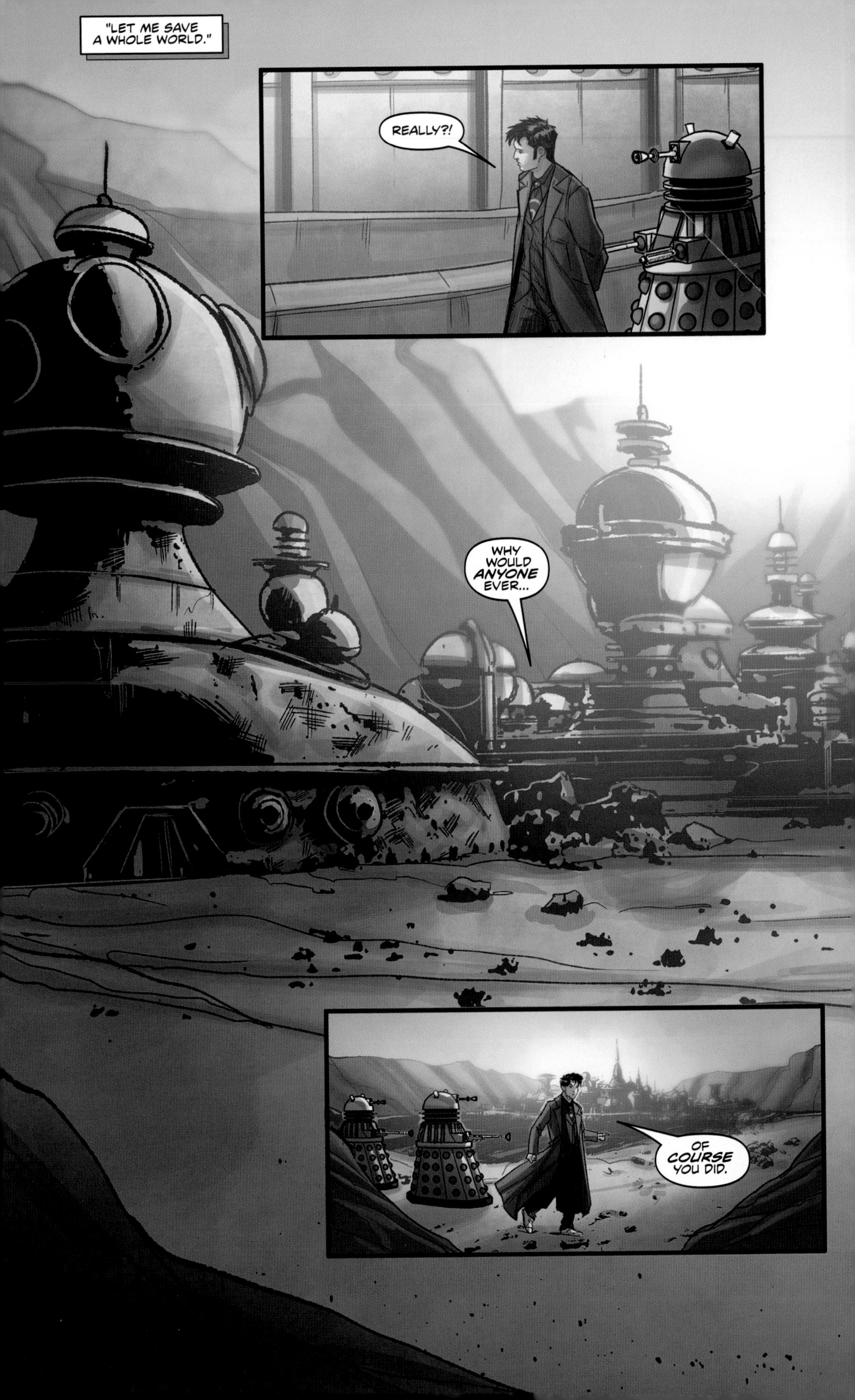
"LET ME SAVE A WHOLE WORLD."
REALLY?!
WHY WOULD ANYONE EVER...
OF COURSE YOU DID.

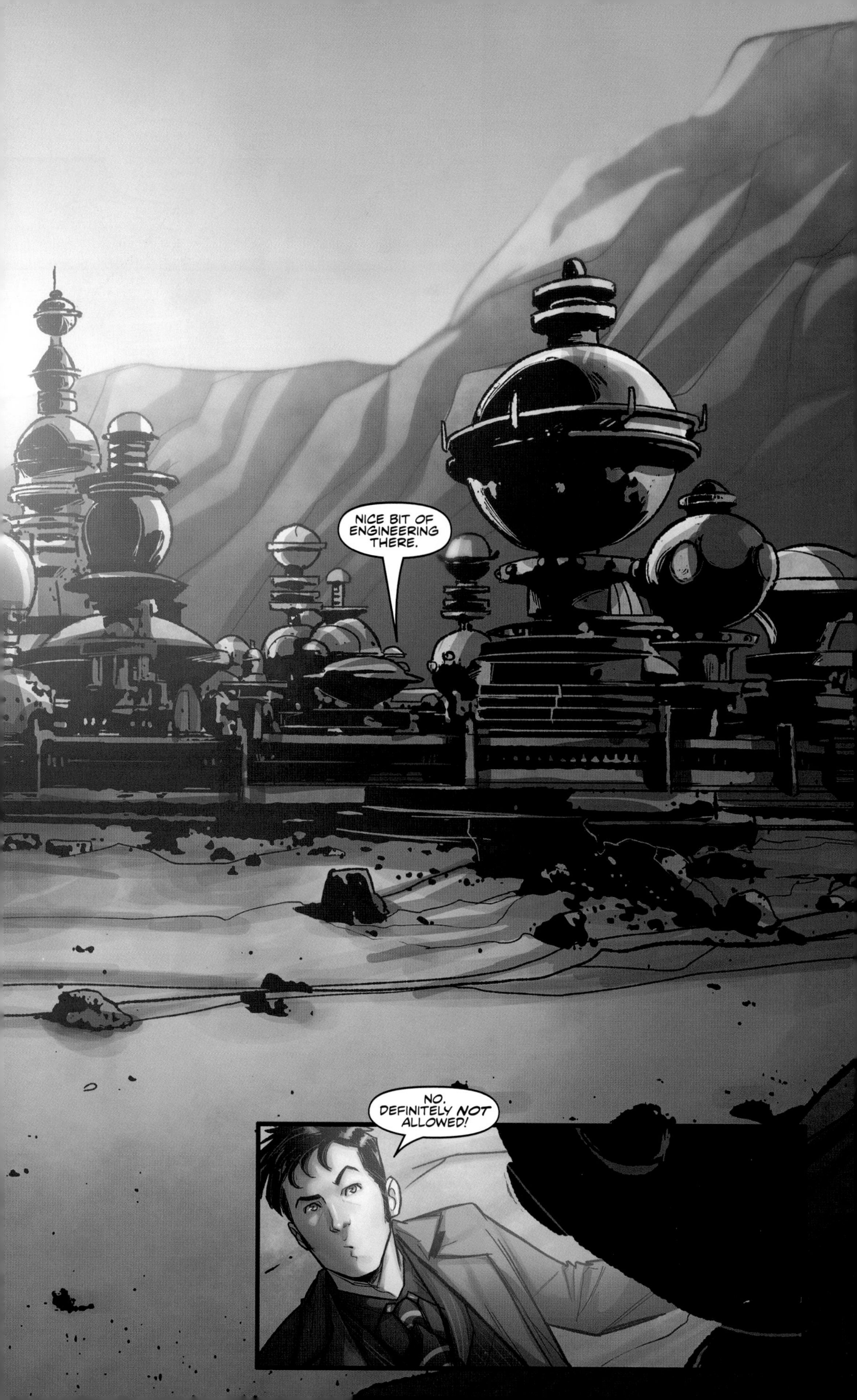
NICE BIT OF ENGINEERING THERE.
NO. DEFINITELY NOT ALLOWED!

AND THAT'S NOT HERE EITHER...

YOU HAVEN'T SHOWN ME EVERYTHING, HAVE YOU?

WE HAVE SHOWN THE DOCTOOOR WHAT HE NEEDED.

I KNOW YOUR PEOPLE. I *KNOW* WHAT YOU'RE CAPABLE OF.

PERHAPS EVEN BETTER THAN *YOU* DO.

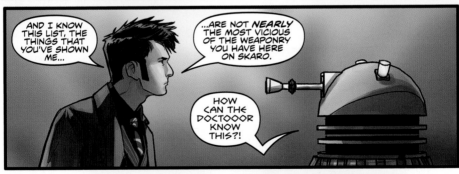

AND I KNOW THIS LIST, THE THINGS THAT YOU'VE SHOWN ME...

...ARE NOT *NEARLY* THE MOST VICIOUS OF THE WEAPONRY YOU HAVE HERE ON SKARO.

HOW CAN THE DOCTOOOR KNOW THIS?!

JUST BELIEVE ME WHEN I SAY I KNOW.

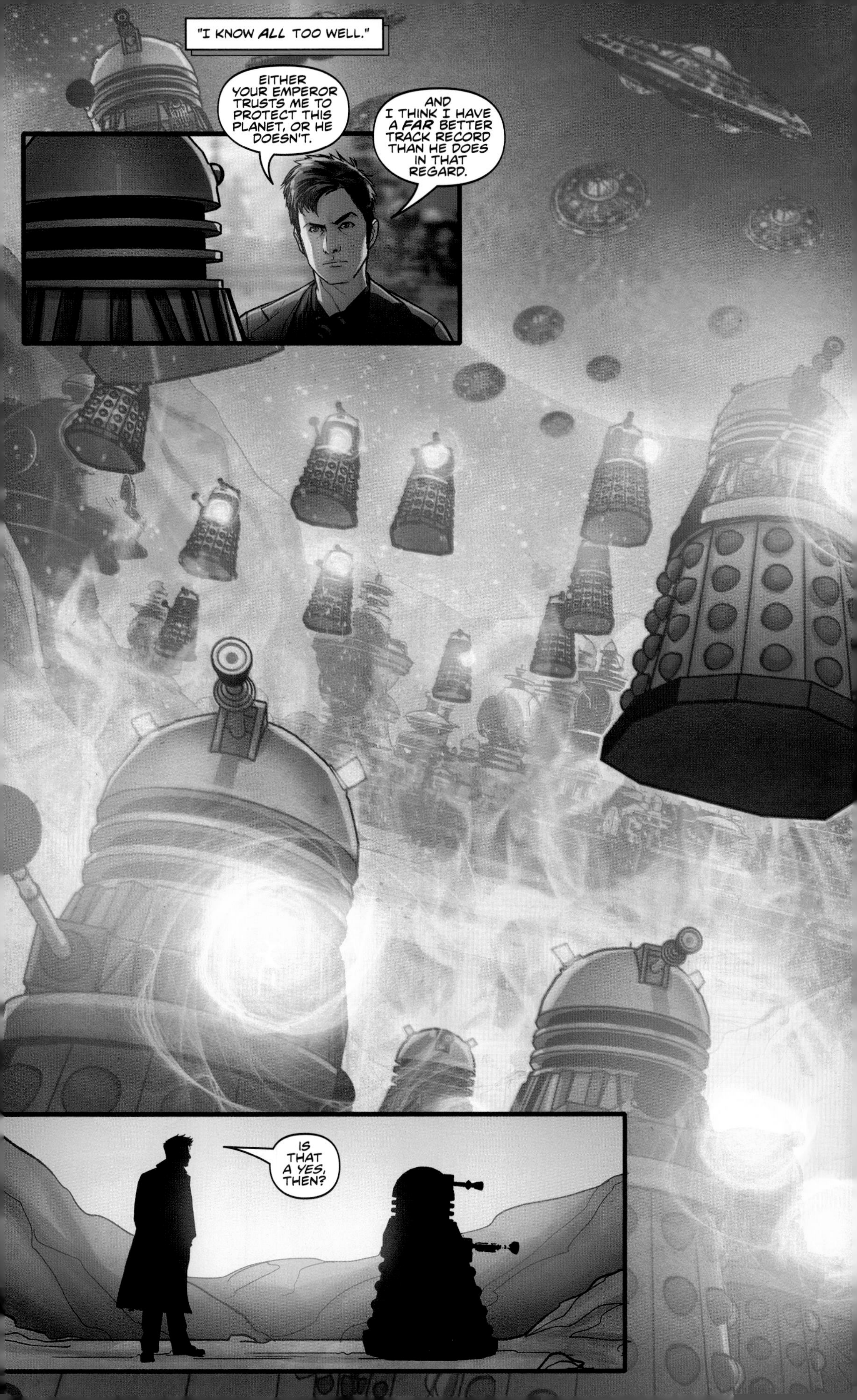
"I KNOW ALL TOO WELL."
EITHER YOUR EMPEROR TRUSTS ME TO PROTECT THIS PLANET, OR HE DOESN'T.
AND I THINK I HAVE A FAR BETTER TRACK RECORD THAN HE DOES IN THAT REGARD.
IS THAT A YES, THEN?

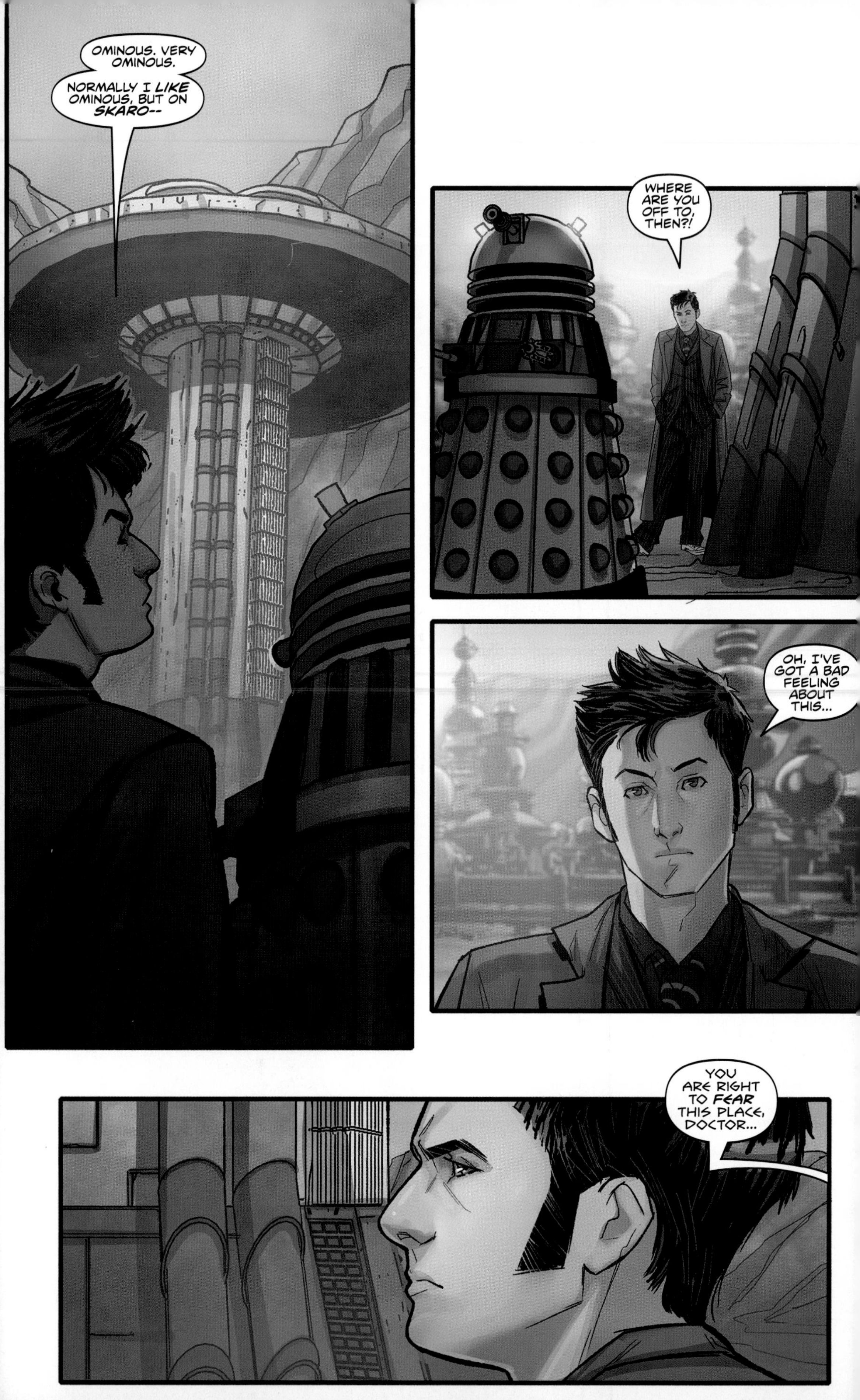
OMINOUS. VERY OMINOUS.
NORMALLY I LIKE OMINOUS, BUT ON SKARO--
WHERE ARE YOU OFF TO, THEN?!
OH, I'VE GOT A BAD FEELING ABOUT THIS...
YOU ARE RIGHT TO FEAR THIS PLACE, DOCTOR...

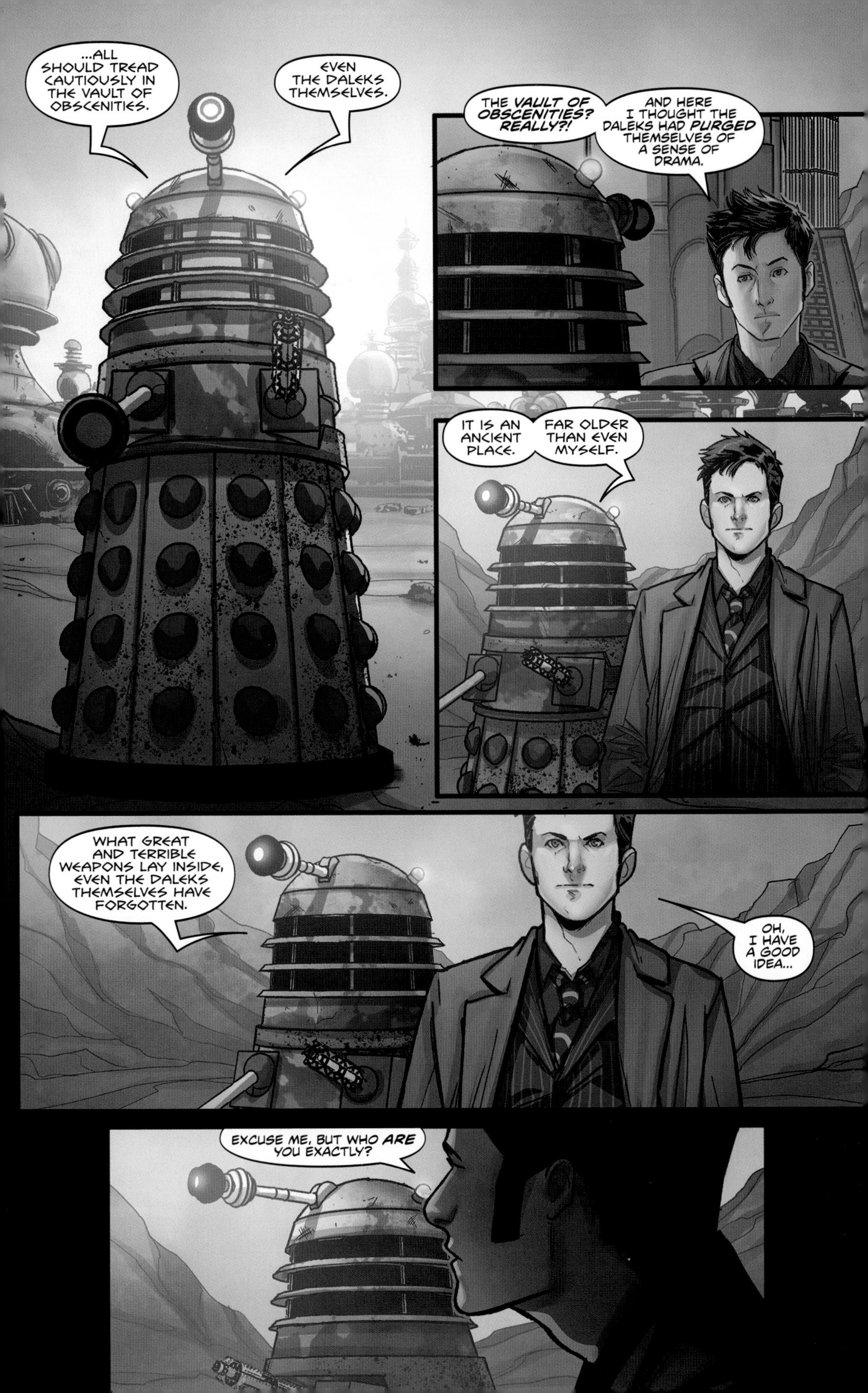
...ALL SHOULD TREAD CAUTIOUSLY IN THE VAULT OF OBSCENITIES.
EVEN THE DALEKS THEMSELVES.
THE VAULT OF OBSCENITIES? REALLY?!
AND HERE I THOUGHT THE DALEKS HAD PURGED THEMSELVES OF A SENSE OF DRAMA.
IT IS AN ANCIENT PLACE.
FAR OLDER THAN EVEN MYSELF.
WHAT GREAT AND TERRIBLE WEAPONS LAY INSIDE, EVEN THE DALEKS THEMSELVES HAVE FORGOTTEN.
OH, I HAVE A GOOD IDEA...
EXCUSE ME, BUT WHO ARE YOU EXACTLY?

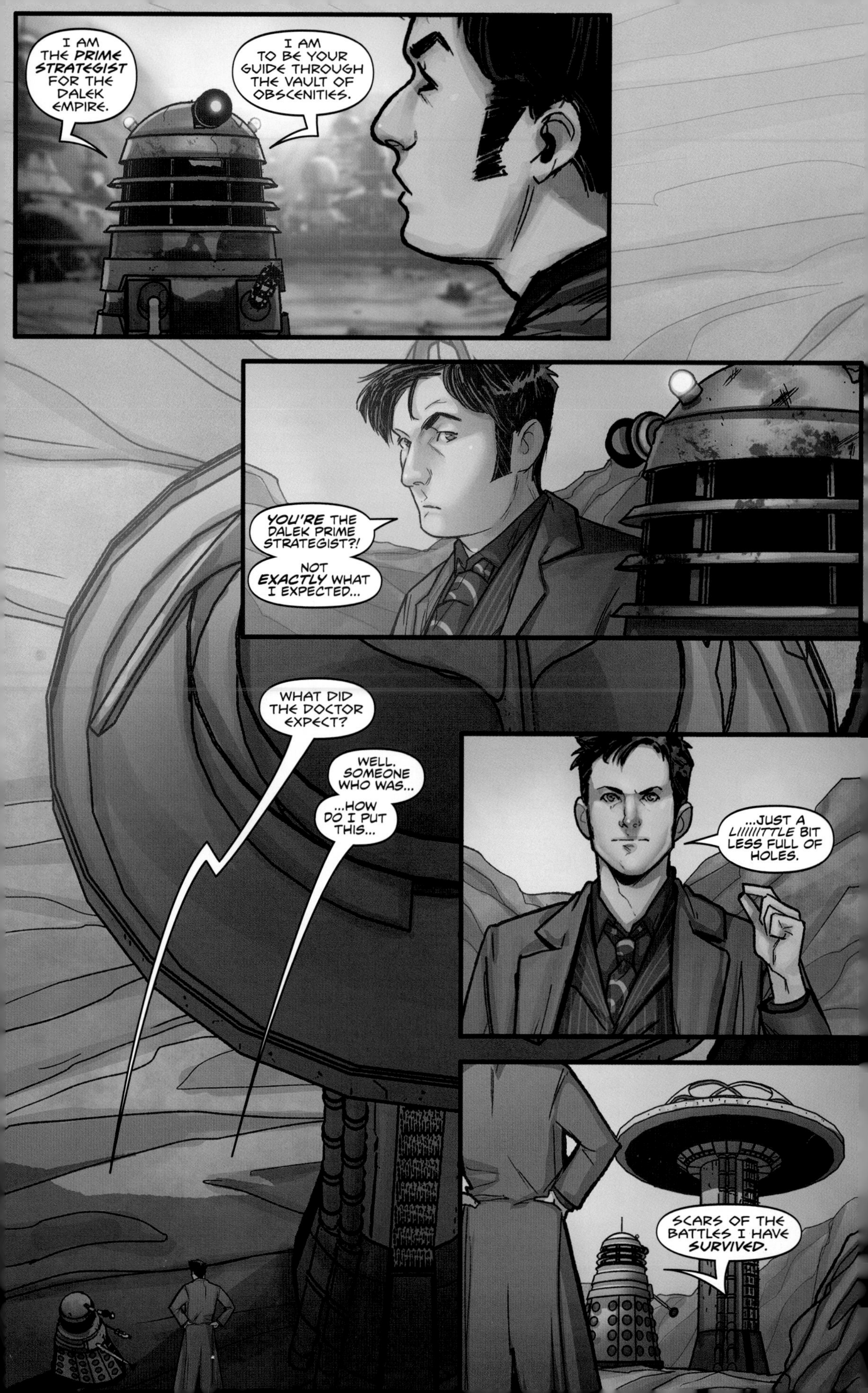
I AM THE PRIME STRATEGIST FOR THE DALEK EMPIRE.
I AM TO BE YOUR GUIDE THROUGH THE VAULT OF OBSCENITIES.
YOU'RE THE DALEK PRIME STRATEGIST?!
NOT EXACTLY WHAT I EXPECTED...
WHAT DID THE DOCTOR EXPECT?
WELL. SOMEONE WHO WAS...
...HOW DO I PUT THIS...
...JUST A LIIIIIITTLE BIT LESS FULL OF HOLES.
SCARS OF THE BATTLES I HAVE SURVIVED.

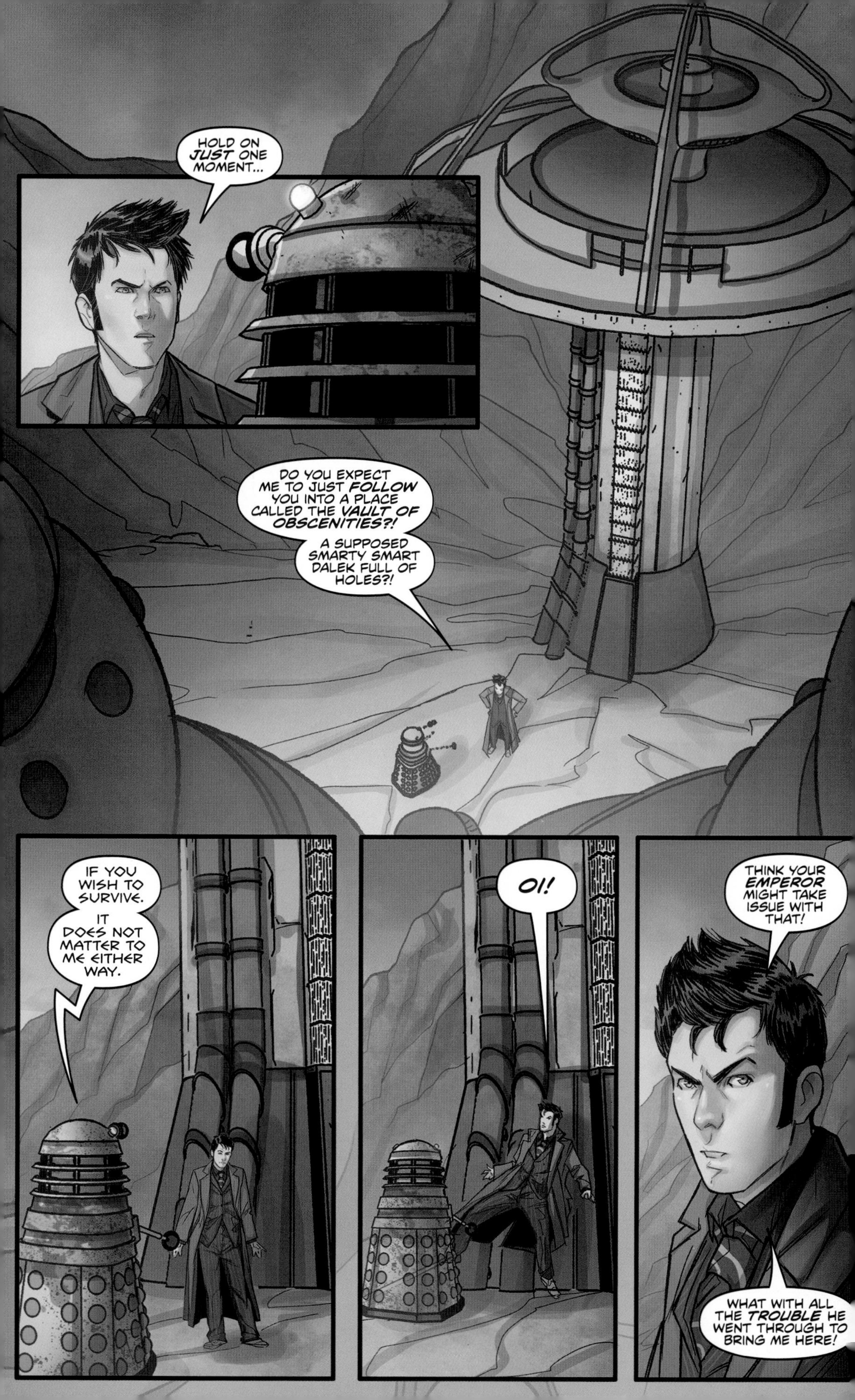
HOLD ON JUST ONE MOMENT...
DO YOU EXPECT ME TO JUST FOLLOW YOU INTO A PLACE CALLED THE VAULT OF OBSCENITIES?!
A SUPPOSED SMARTY SMART DALEK FULL OF HOLES?!
IF YOU WISH TO SURVIVE.
IT DOES NOT MATTER TO ME EITHER WAY.
OI!
THINK YOUR EMPEROR MIGHT TAKE ISSUE WITH THAT!
WHAT WITH ALL THE TROUBLE HE WENT THROUGH TO BRING ME HERE!

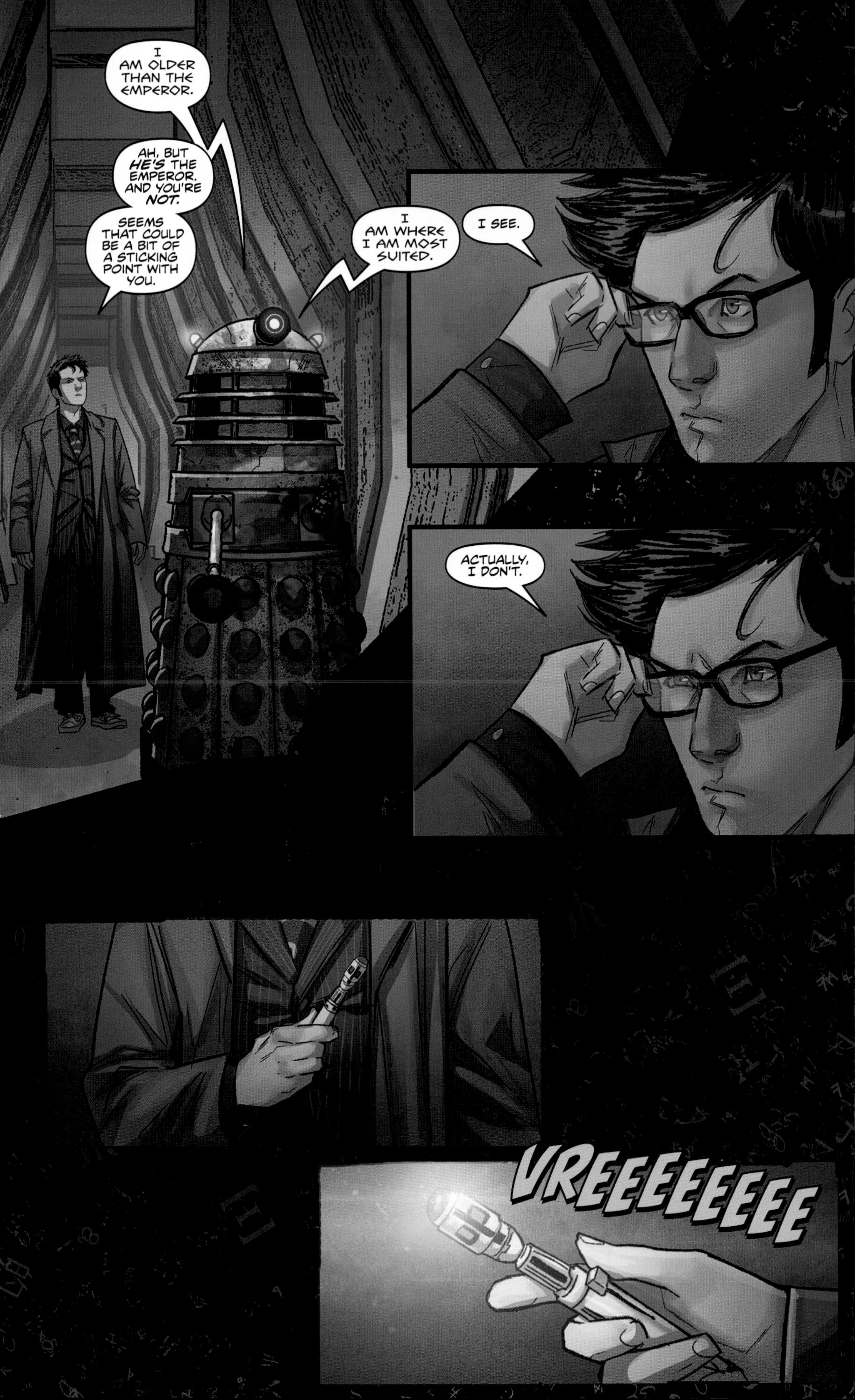
I AM OLDER THAN THE EMPEROR.
AH, BUT HE'S THE EMPEROR. AND YOU'RE NOT.
SEEMS THAT COULD BE A BIT OF A STICKING POINT WITH YOU.
I AM WHERE I AM MOST SUITED.
I SEE.
ACTUALLY, I DON'T.
VREEEEEEEEE

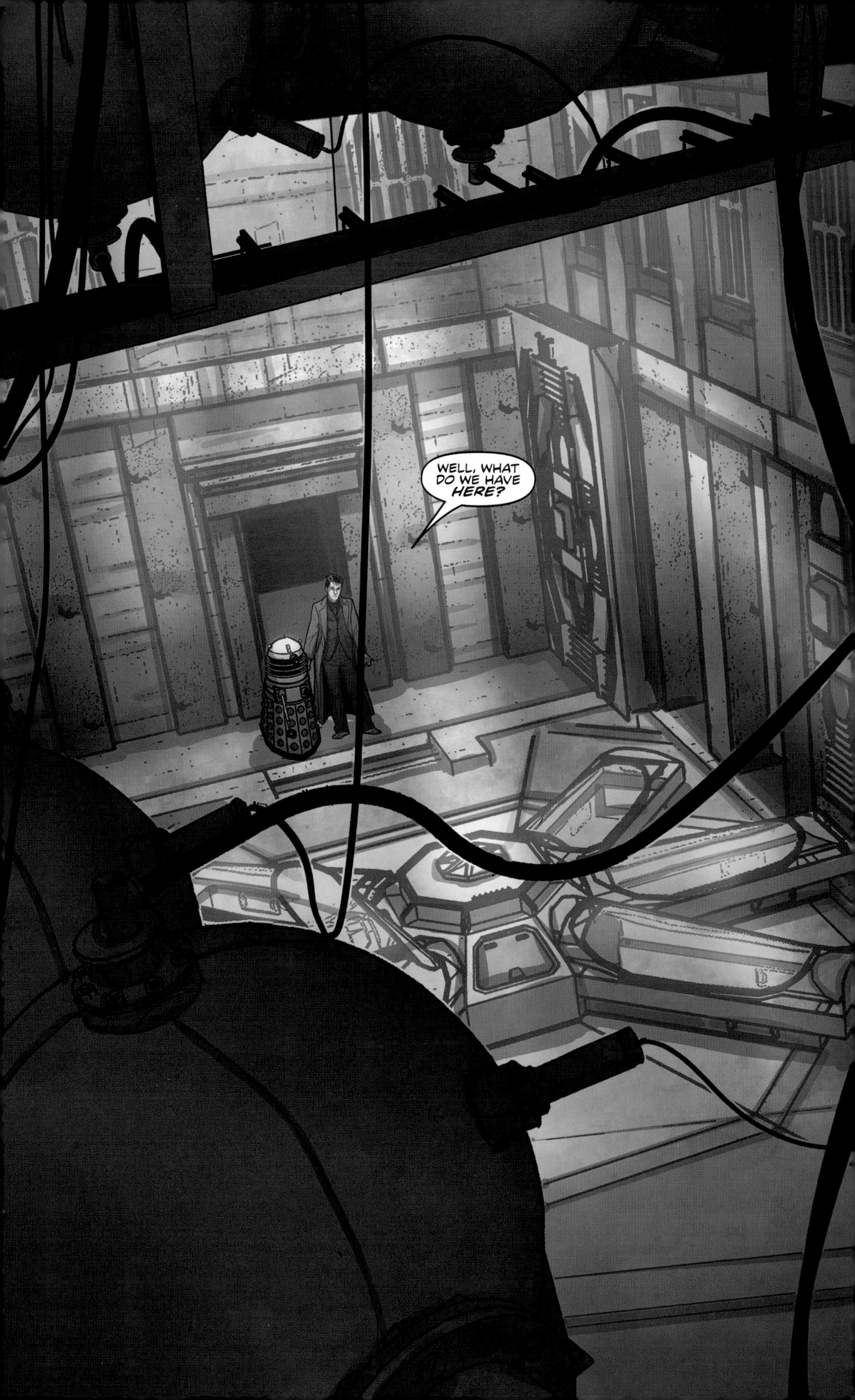
WELL, WHAT DO WE HAVE *HERE?*

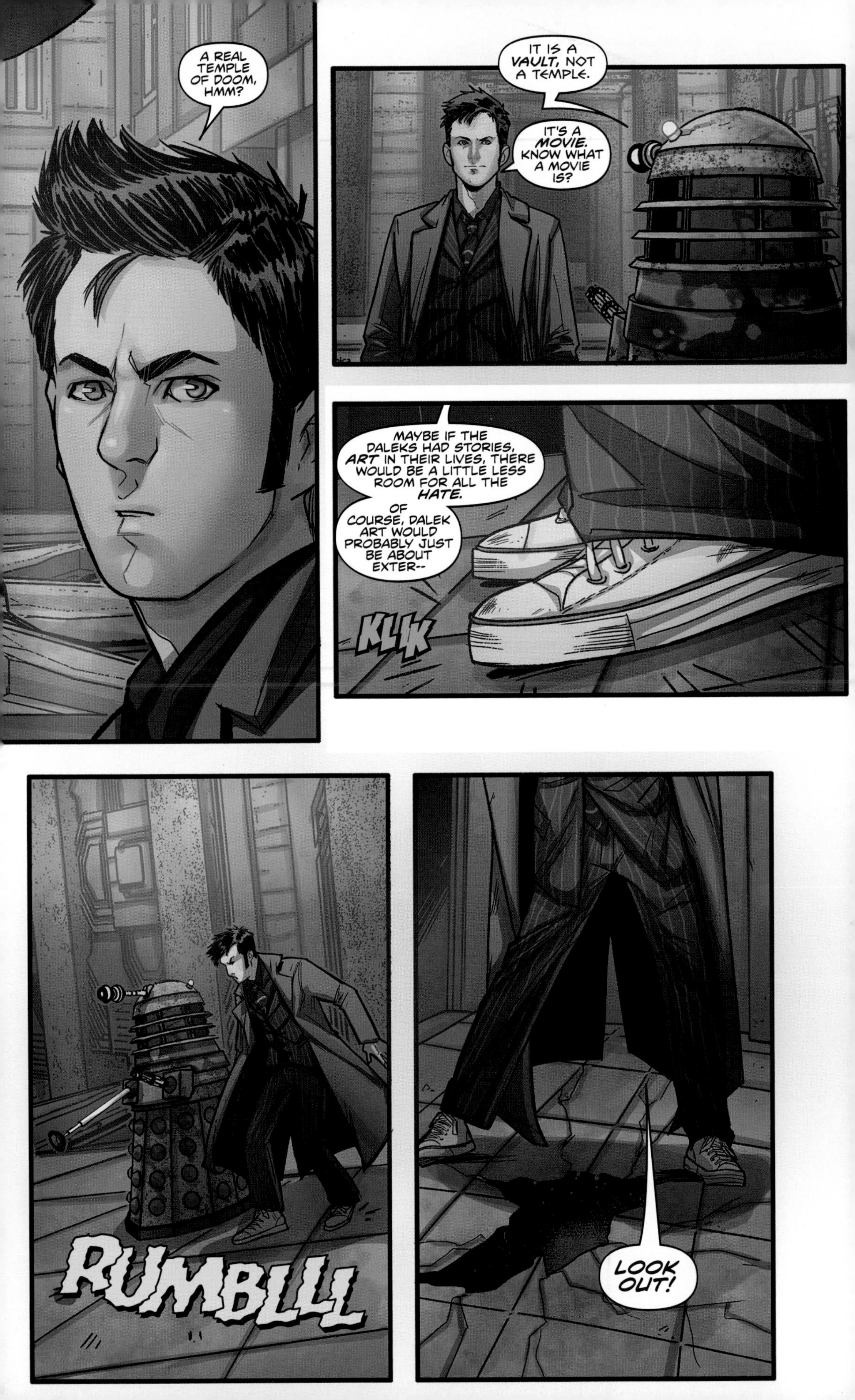
A REAL TEMPLE OF DOOM, HMM?
IT IS A VAULT, NOT A TEMPLE.
IT'S A MOVIE. KNOW WHAT A MOVIE IS?
MAYBE IF THE DALEKS HAD STORIES, ART IN THEIR LIVES, THERE WOULD BE A LITTLE LESS ROOM FOR ALL THE HATE.
OF COURSE, DALEK ART WOULD PROBABLY JUST BE ABOUT EXTER--
KLIK
RUMBLLL
LOOK OUT!

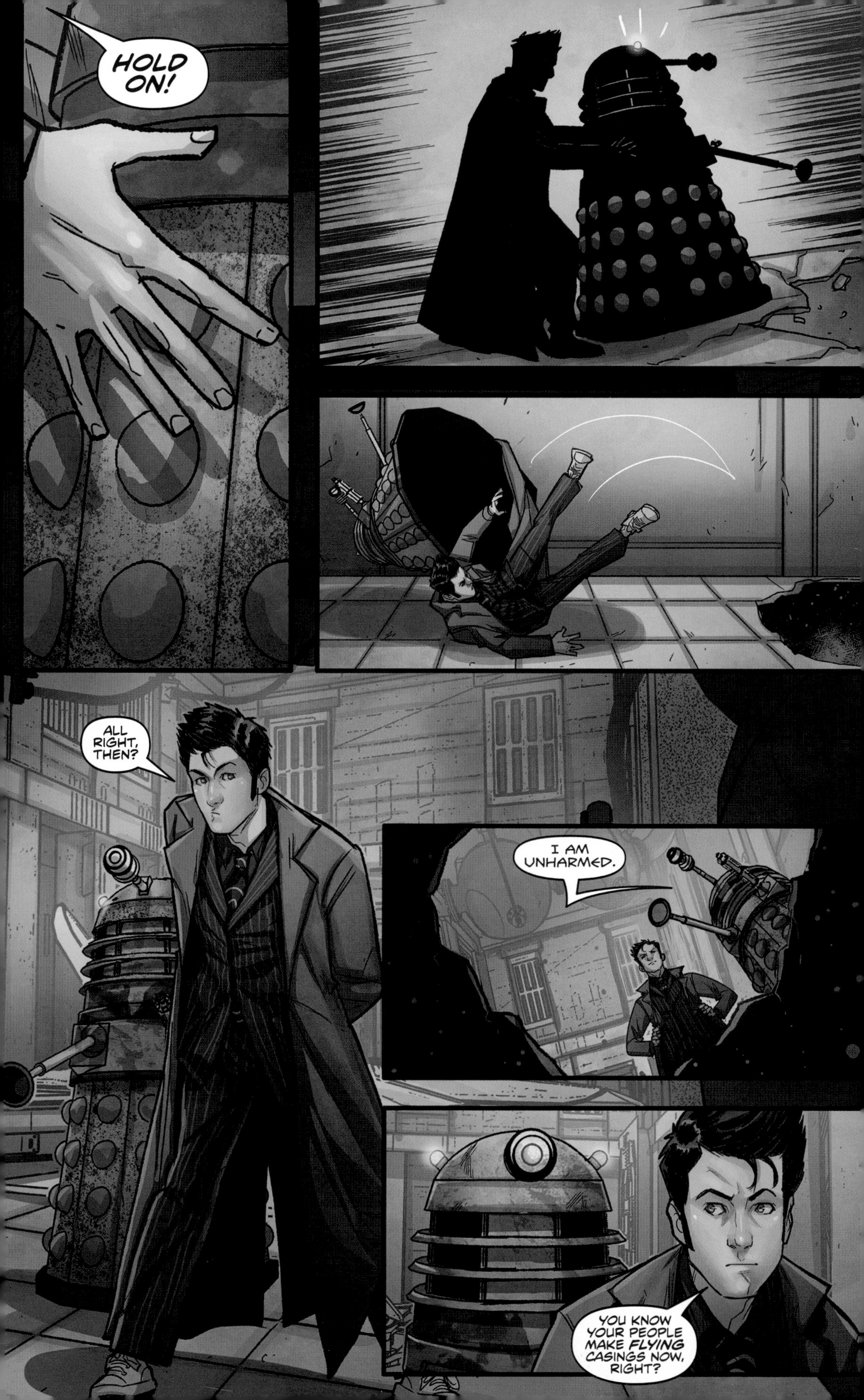
HOLD ON!
ALL RIGHT, THEN?
I AM UNHARMED.
YOU KNOW YOUR PEOPLE MAKE *FLYING* CASINGS NOW, RIGHT?

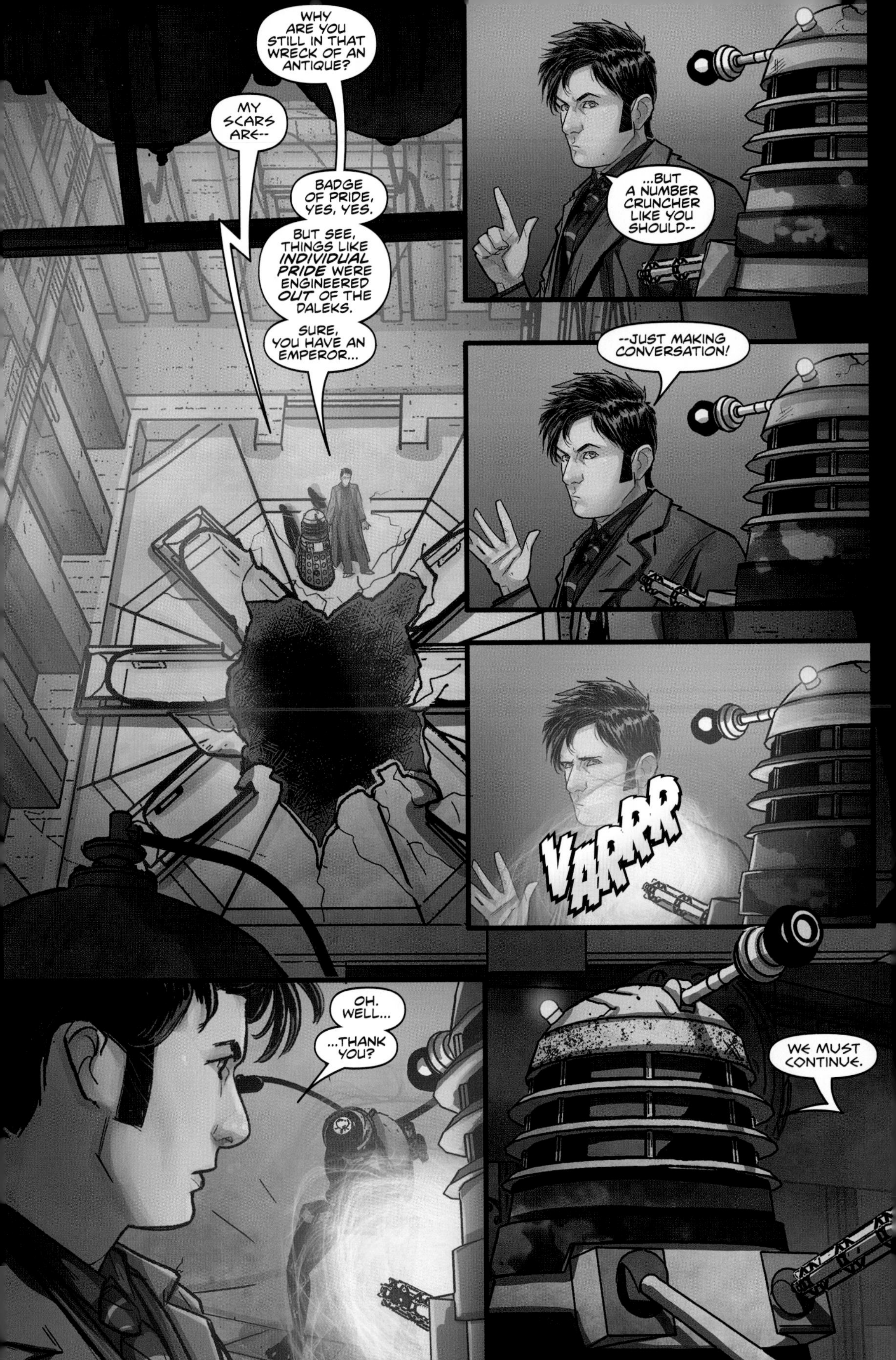
WHY ARE YOU STILL IN THAT WRECK OF AN ANTIQUE?
MY SCARS ARE--
BADGE OF PRIDE, YES, YES.
BUT SEE, THINGS LIKE *INDIVIDUAL PRIDE* WERE ENGINEERED *OUT* OF THE DALEKS.
SURE, YOU HAVE AN EMPEROR...
...BUT A NUMBER CRUNCHER LIKE YOU SHOULD--
--JUST MAKING CONVERSATION!
VARRR
OH. WELL...
...THANK YOU?
WE MUST CONTINUE.

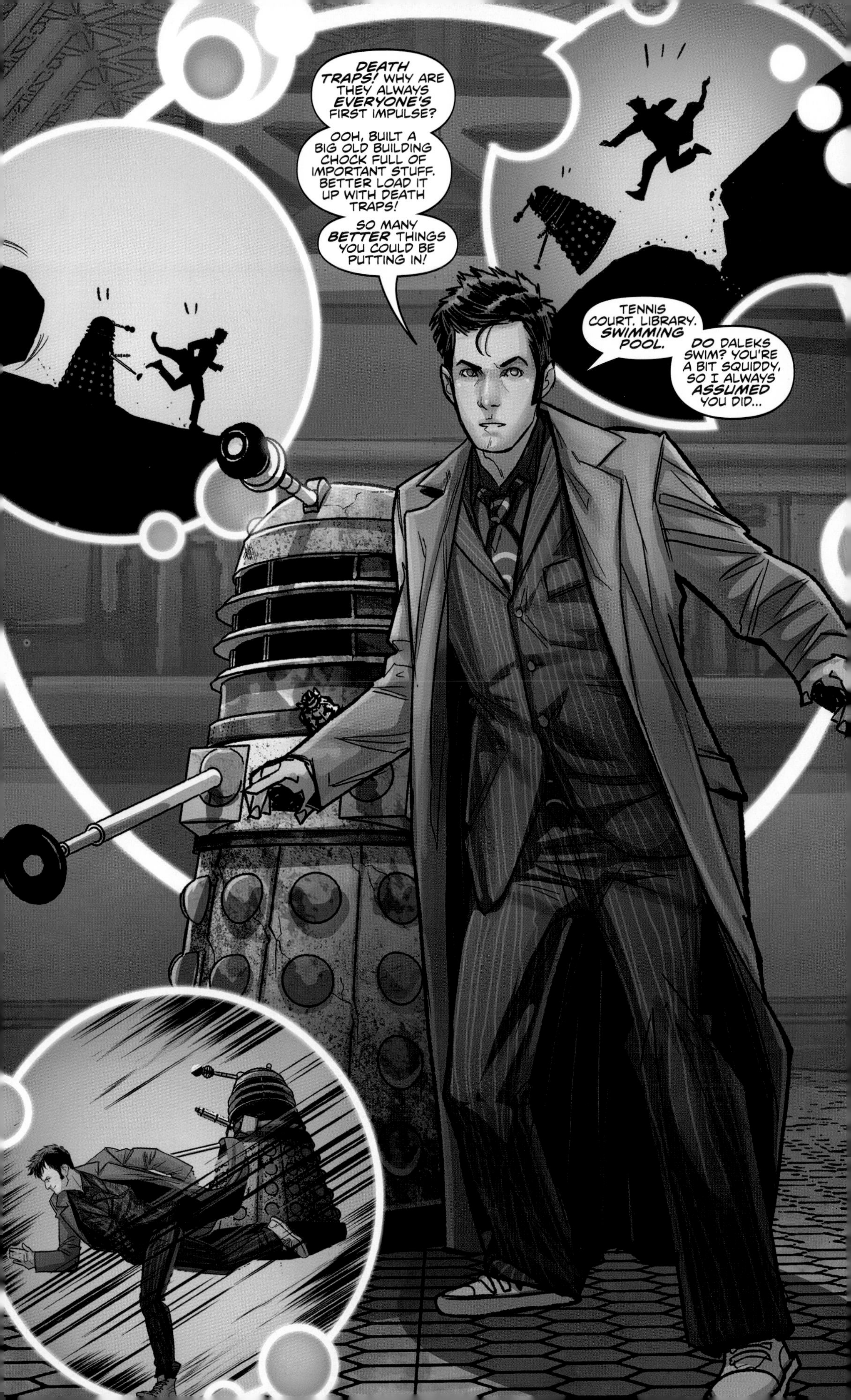
DEATH TRAPS! WHY ARE THEY ALWAYS EVERYONE'S FIRST IMPULSE?
OOH, BUILT A BIG OLD BUILDING CHOCK FULL OF IMPORTANT STUFF. BETTER LOAD IT UP WITH DEATH TRAPS!
SO MANY BETTER THINGS YOU COULD BE PUTTING IN!
TENNIS COURT. LIBRARY. SWIMMING POOL.
DO DALEKS SWIM? YOU'RE A BIT SQUIDDY, SO I ALWAYS ASSUMED YOU DID...

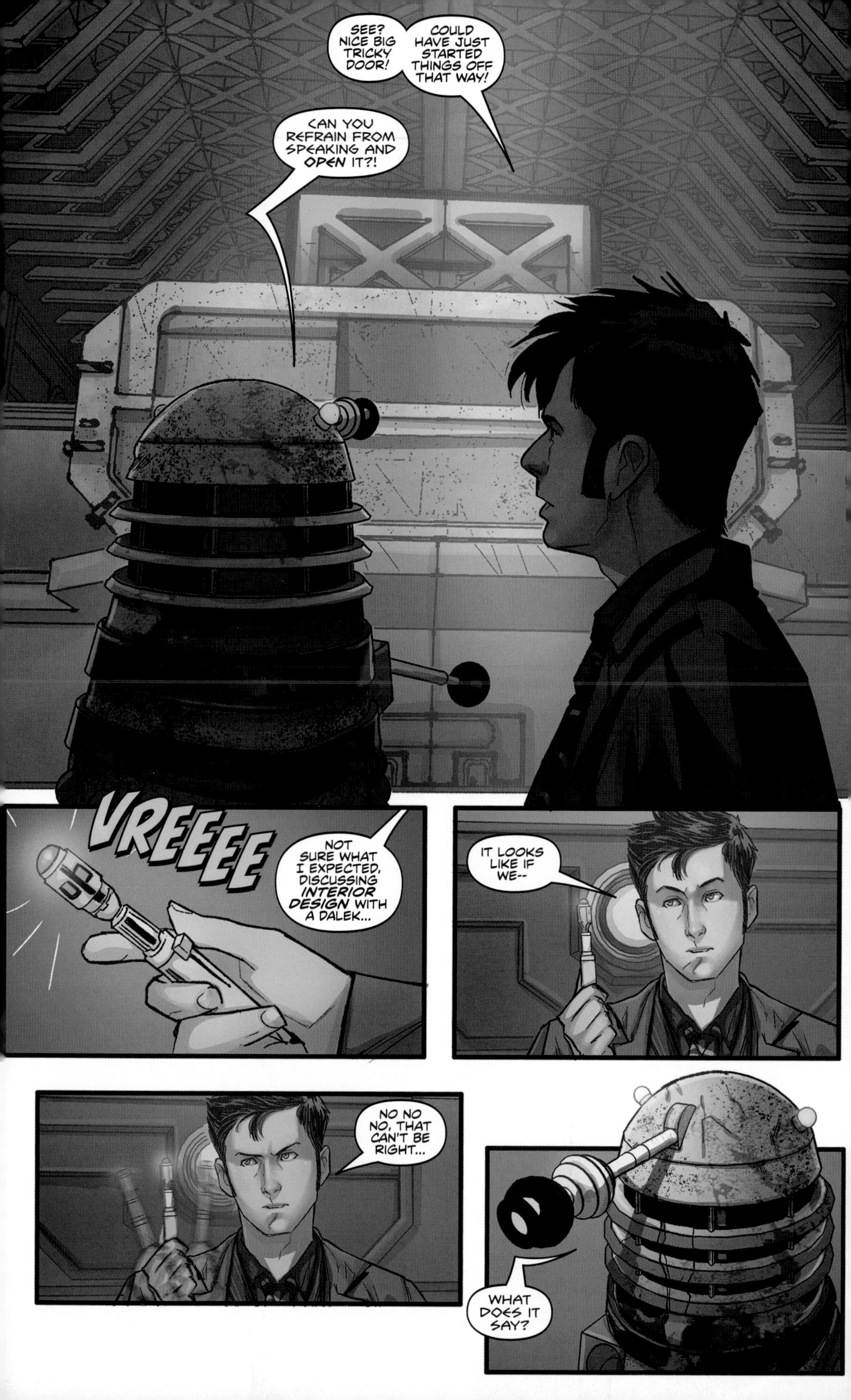
SEE? NICE BIG TRICKY DOOR!
COULD HAVE JUST STARTED THINGS OFF THAT WAY!
CAN YOU REFRAIN FROM SPEAKING AND OPEN IT?!
VREEEE
NOT SURE WHAT I EXPECTED, DISCUSSING INTERIOR DESIGN WITH A DALEK...
IT LOOKS LIKE IF WE--
NO NO NO, THAT CAN'T BE RIGHT...
WHAT DOES IT SAY?

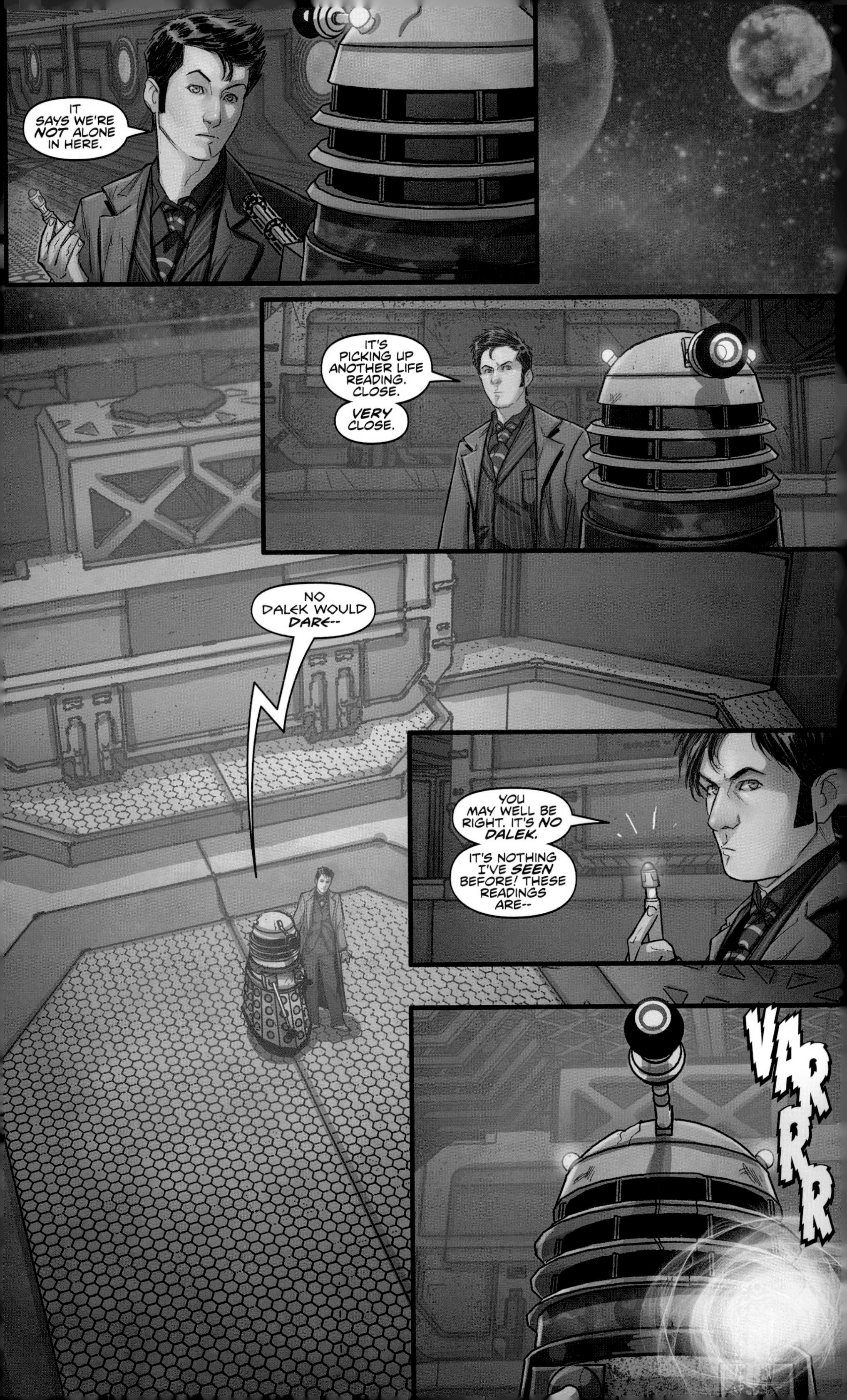
IT SAYS WE'RE NOT ALONE IN HERE.
IT'S PICKING UP ANOTHER LIFE READING. CLOSE.
VERY CLOSE.
NO DALEK WOULD DARE--
YOU MAY WELL BE RIGHT. IT'S NO DALEK.
IT'S NOTHING I'VE SEEN BEFORE! THESE READINGS ARE--
VARRR

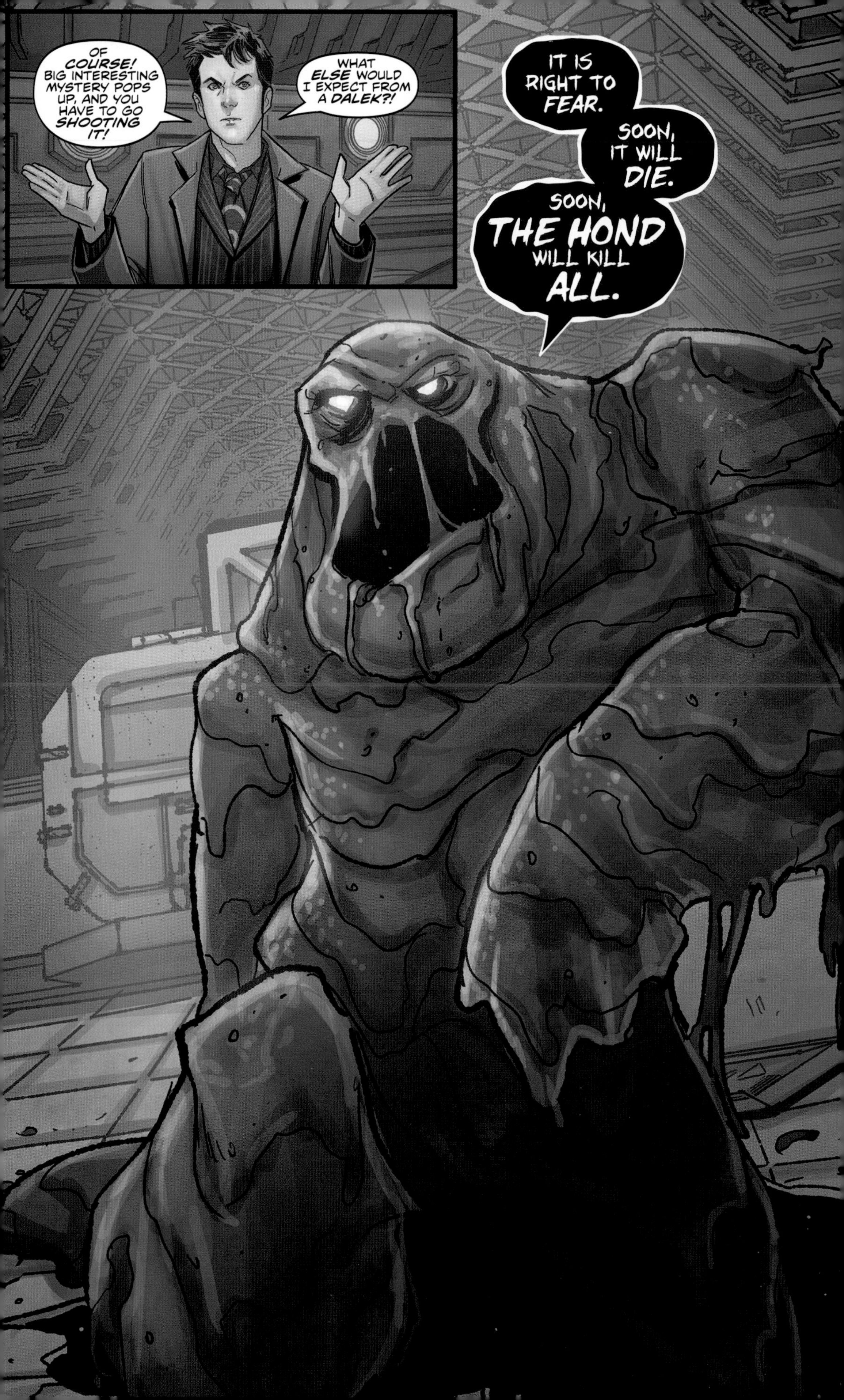
OF COURSE! BIG INTERESTING MYSTERY POPS UP, AND YOU HAVE TO GO SHOOTING IT!
WHAT ELSE WOULD I EXPECT FROM A DALEK?!
IT IS RIGHT TO FEAR.
SOON, IT WILL DIE.
SOON, THE HOND WILL KILL ALL.

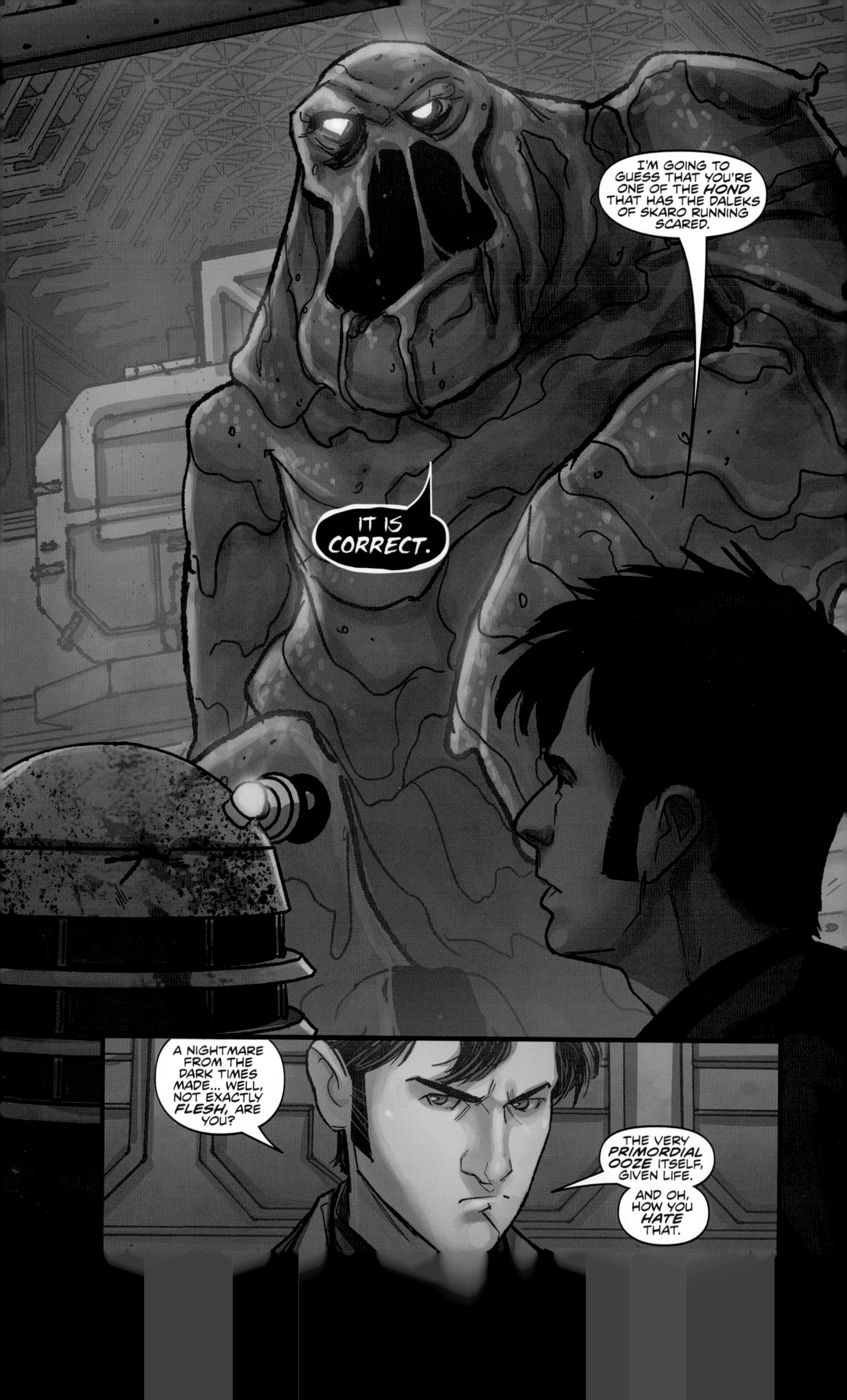
I'M GOING TO GUESS THAT YOU'RE ONE OF THE HOND THAT HAS THE DALEKS OF SKARO RUNNING SCARED.
IT IS CORRECT.
A NIGHTMARE FROM THE DARK TIMES MADE... WELL, NOT EXACTLY FLESH, ARE YOU?
THE VERY PRIMORDIAL OOZE ITSELF, GIVEN LIFE.
AND OH, HOW YOU HATE THAT.

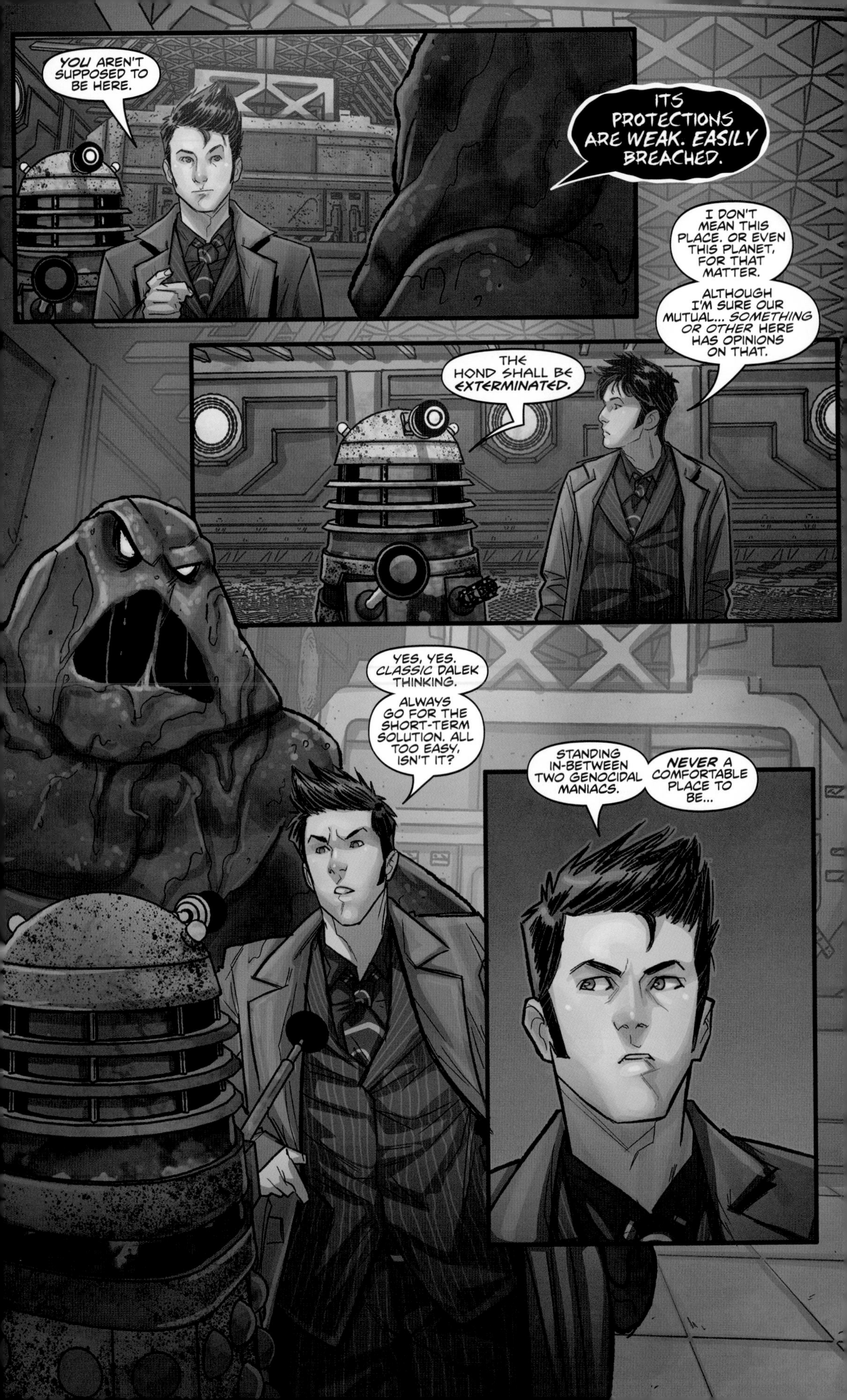
YOU AREN'T SUPPOSED TO BE HERE.
ITS PROTECTIONS ARE WEAK. EASILY BREACHED.
I DON'T MEAN THIS PLACE. OR EVEN THIS PLANET, FOR THAT MATTER.
ALTHOUGH I'M SURE OUR MUTUAL... SOMETHING OR OTHER HERE HAS OPINIONS ON THAT.
THE HOND SHALL BE EXTERMINATED.
YES, YES. CLASSIC DALEK THINKING.
ALWAYS GO FOR THE SHORT-TERM SOLUTION. ALL TOO EASY, ISN'T IT?
STANDING IN-BETWEEN TWO GENOCIDAL MANIACS.
NEVER A COMFORTABLE PLACE TO BE...

YOU. STOP. SIT. STAY.
GOOD DALEK.
AND YOU... HOW DID YOU GET HERE?
AND I DON'T MEAN THIS ROOM. I MEAN THIS TIME.
TIME?
WHAT DOES THE HOND CARE ABOUT TIME?
PERCEPTION OF TIME IS LIFE. ALL LIFE MUST END.
TIME WILL ONLY MATTER WHEN IT IS UNOBSERVED.
BUT WHY? WHY DO YOU WANT TO DESTROY EVERYONE? EVEN YOURSELVES?
LIFE HURTS.
WHEN ALL LIFE DIES, ALL PAIN DIES.

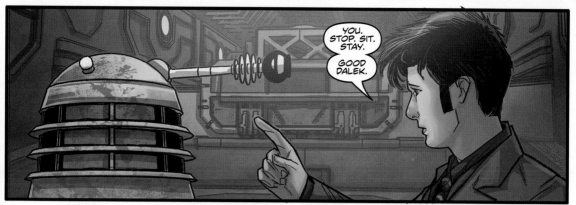

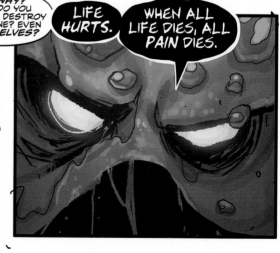

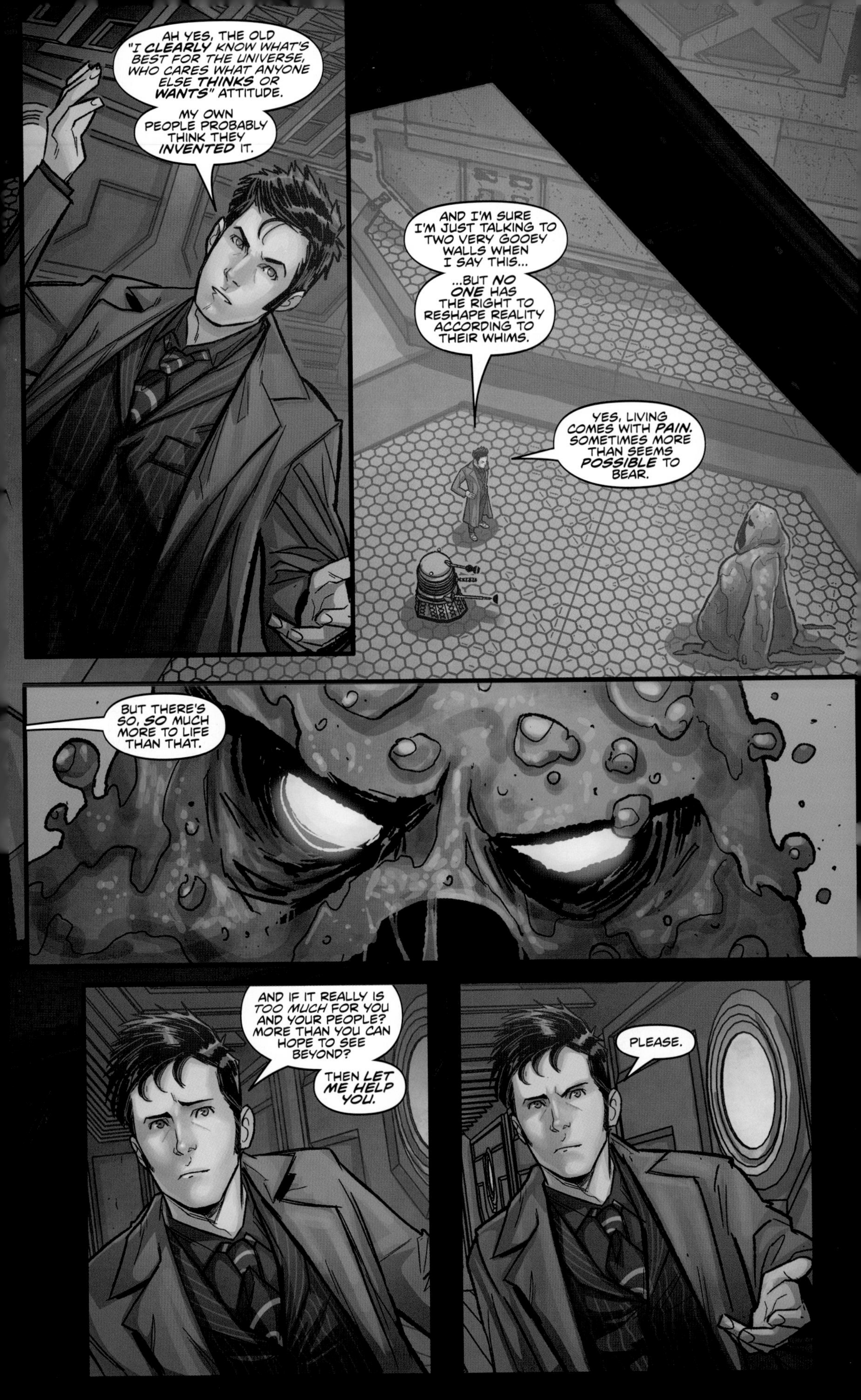
AH YES, THE OLD "I CLEARLY KNOW WHAT'S BEST FOR THE UNIVERSE, WHO CARES WHAT ANYONE ELSE THINKS OR WANTS" ATTITUDE.
MY OWN PEOPLE PROBABLY THINK THEY INVENTED IT.
AND I'M SURE I'M JUST TALKING TO TWO VERY GOOEY WALLS WHEN I SAY THIS...
...BUT NO ONE HAS THE RIGHT TO RESHAPE REALITY ACCORDING TO THEIR WHIMS.
YES, LIVING COMES WITH PAIN. SOMETIMES MORE THAN SEEMS POSSIBLE TO BEAR.
BUT THERE'S SO, SO MUCH MORE TO LIFE THAN THAT.
AND IF IT REALLY IS TOO MUCH FOR YOU AND YOUR PEOPLE? MORE THAN YOU CAN HOPE TO SEE BEYOND?
THEN LET ME HELP YOU.
PLEASE.

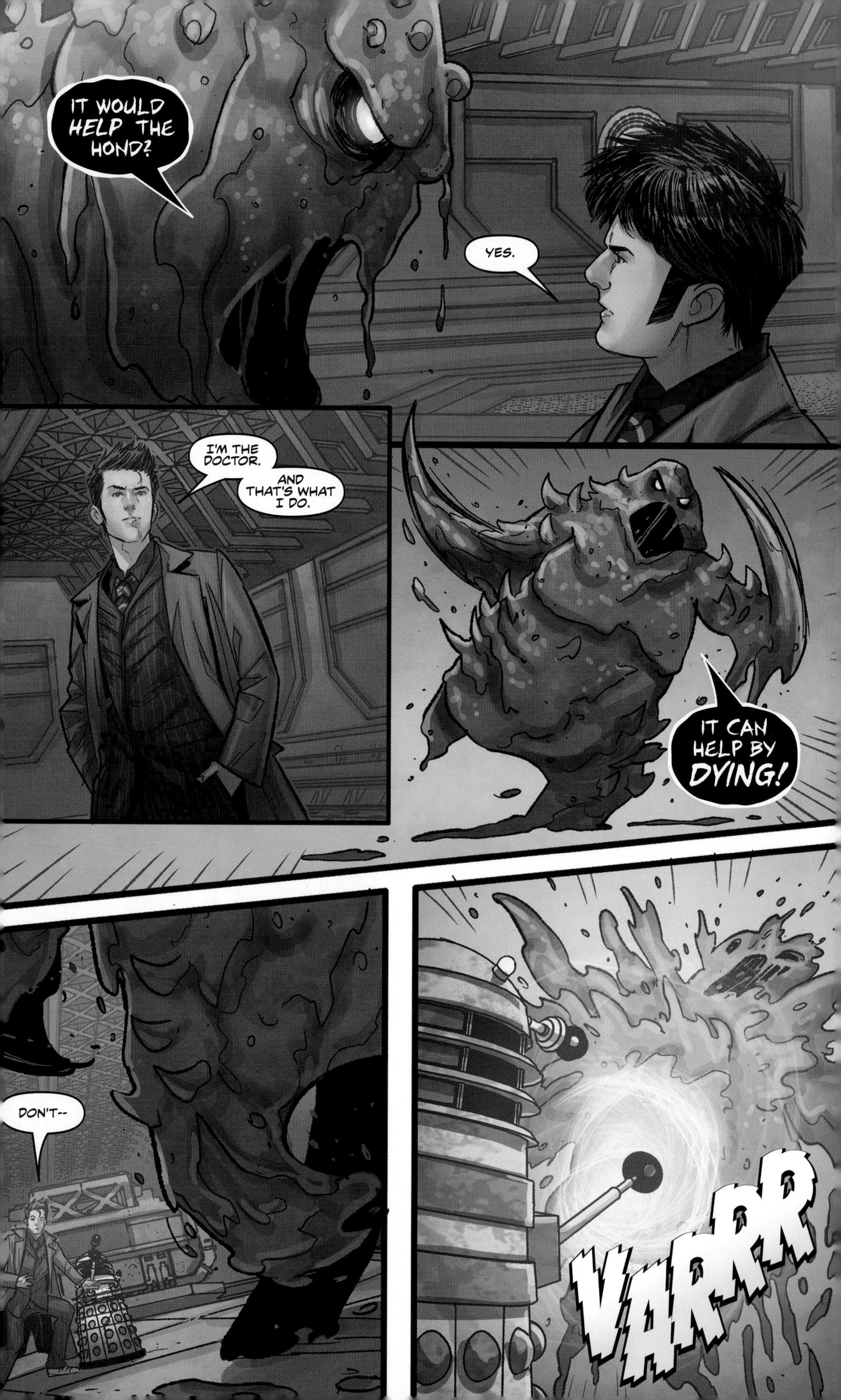
IT WOULD HELP THE HOND?
YES.
I'M THE DOCTOR.
AND THAT'S WHAT I DO.
IT CAN HELP BY DYING!
DON'T--
VARRR

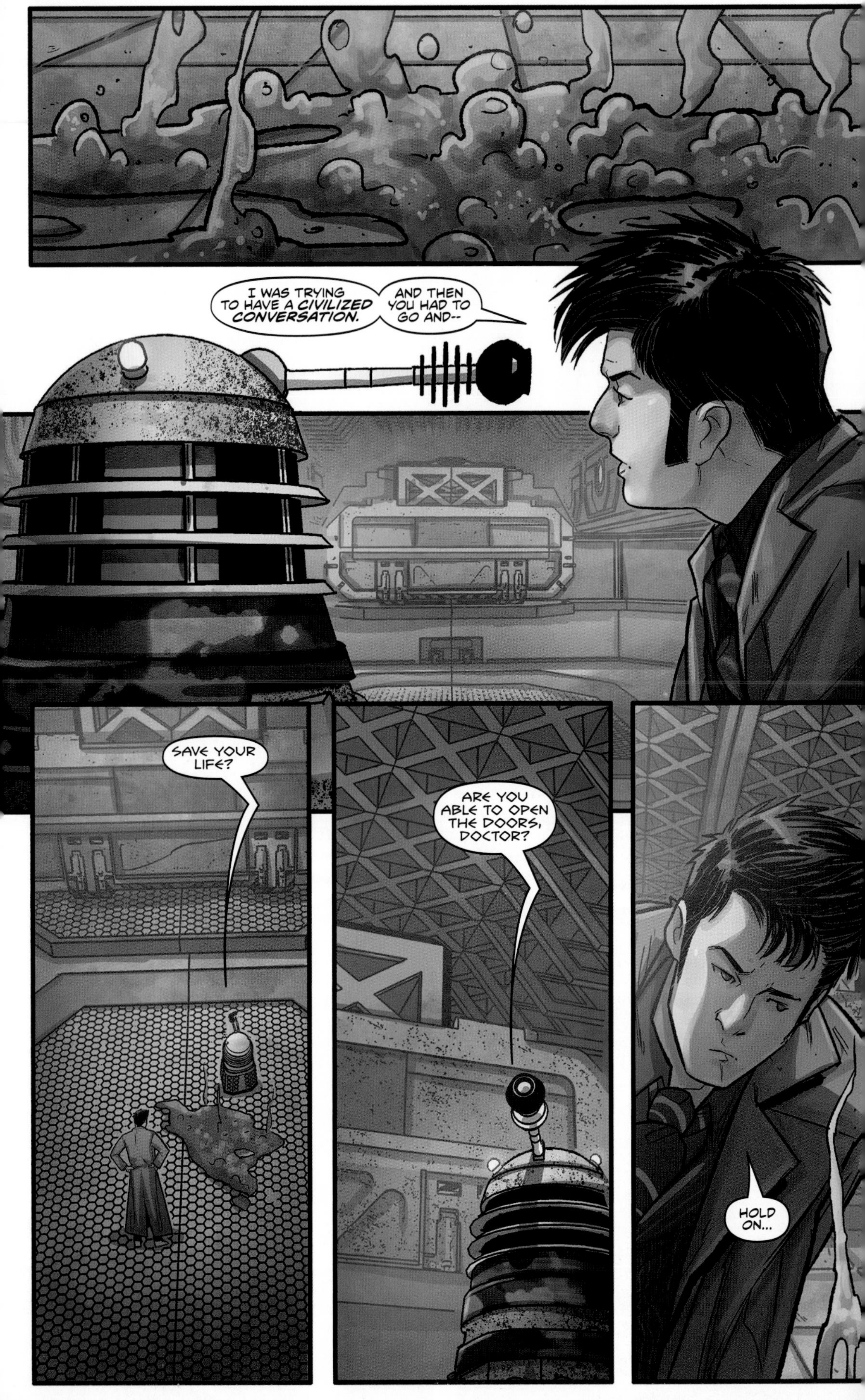
I WAS TRYING TO HAVE A *CIVILIZED* *CONVERSATION.*
AND THEN YOU HAD TO GO AND--
SAVE YOUR LIFE?
ARE YOU ABLE TO OPEN THE DOORS, DOCTOR?
HOLD ON...

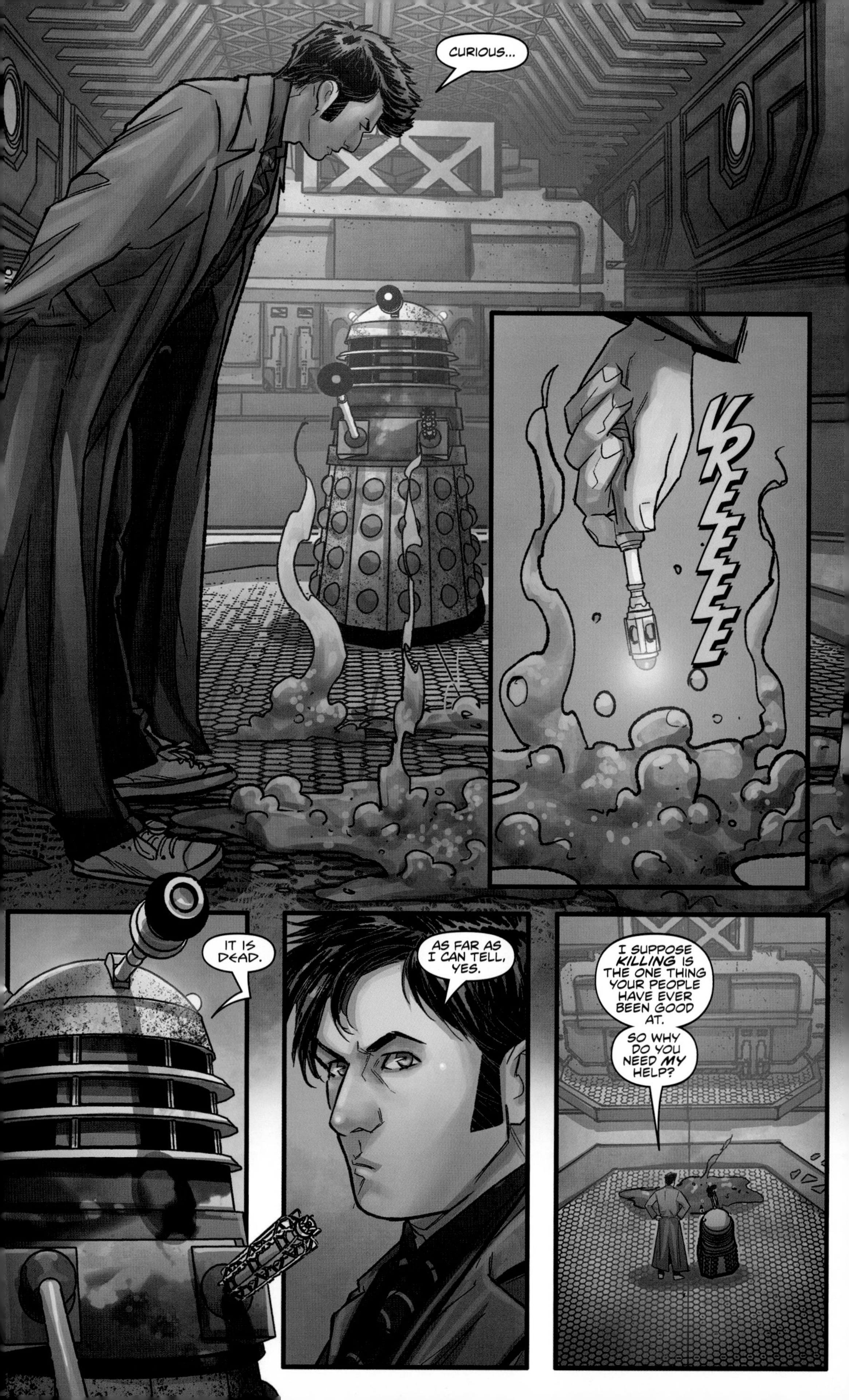
CURIOUS...
KREEEEE
IT IS DEAD.
AS FAR AS I CAN TELL, YES.
I SUPPOSE KILLING IS THE ONE THING YOUR PEOPLE HAVE EVER BEEN GOOD AT.
SO WHY DO YOU NEED MY HELP?

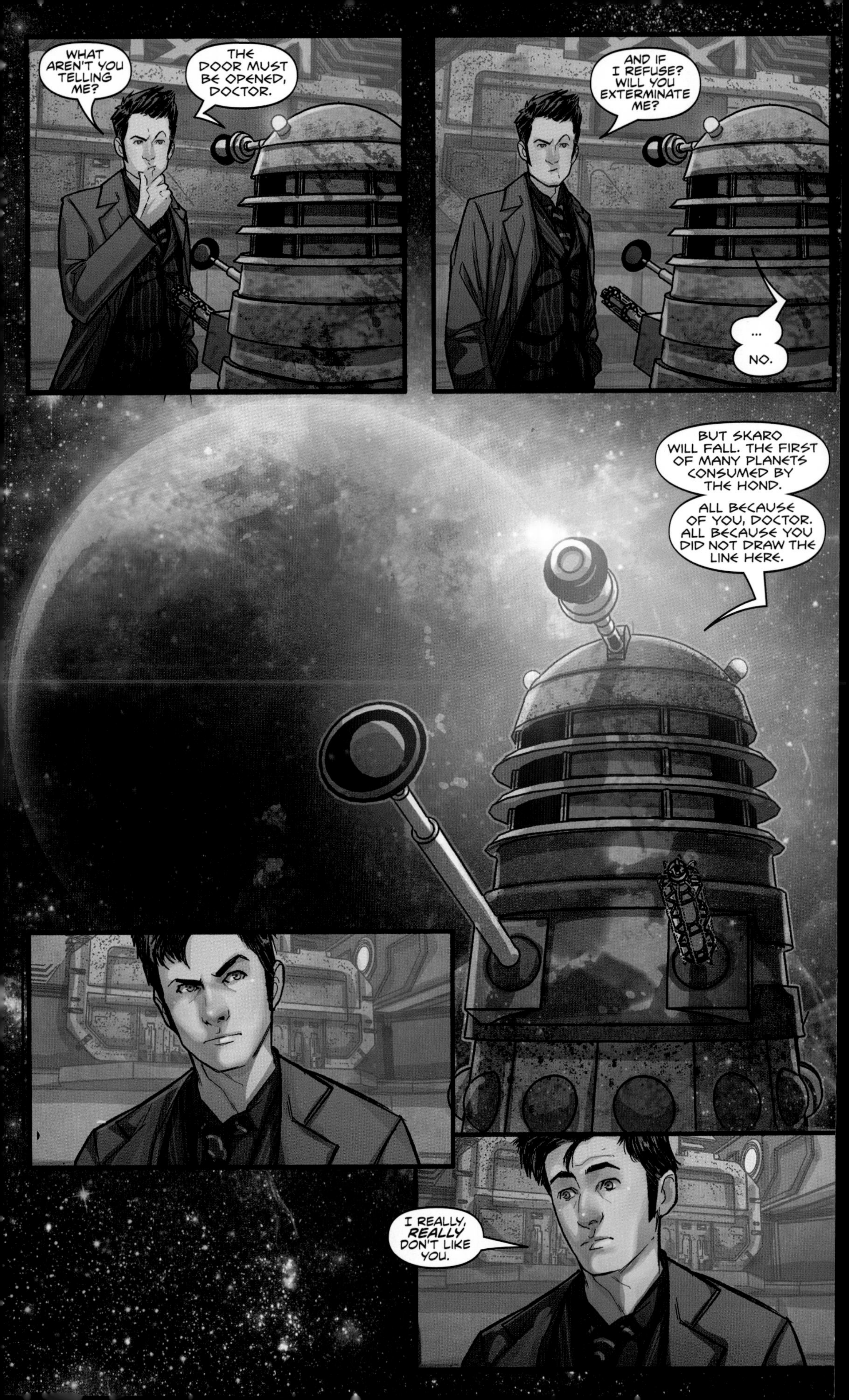
WHAT AREN'T YOU TELLING ME?
THE DOOR MUST BE OPENED, DOCTOR.
AND IF I REFUSE? WILL YOU EXTERMINATE ME?
...
NO.
BUT SKARO WILL FALL. THE FIRST OF MANY PLANETS CONSUMED BY THE HOND.
ALL BECAUSE OF YOU, DOCTOR. ALL BECAUSE YOU DID NOT DRAW THE LINE HERE.
I REALLY, *REALLY* DON'T LIKE YOU.

AND I DON'T *TRUST* YOU.

BUT... YOU'RE NOT WRONG ABOUT THE THREAT THE HOND POSE.

I AM NOT.

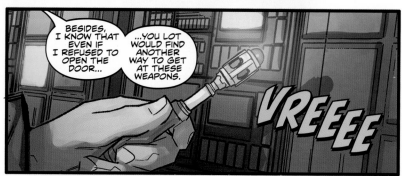

BESIDES, I KNOW THAT EVEN IF I REFUSED TO OPEN THE DOOR...

...YOU LOT WOULD FIND ANOTHER WAY TO GET AT THESE WEAPONS.

VREEEE

CLIK

SHFFF

CLIK

SHFFF

CLIK

SHFFF

SHALL WE?

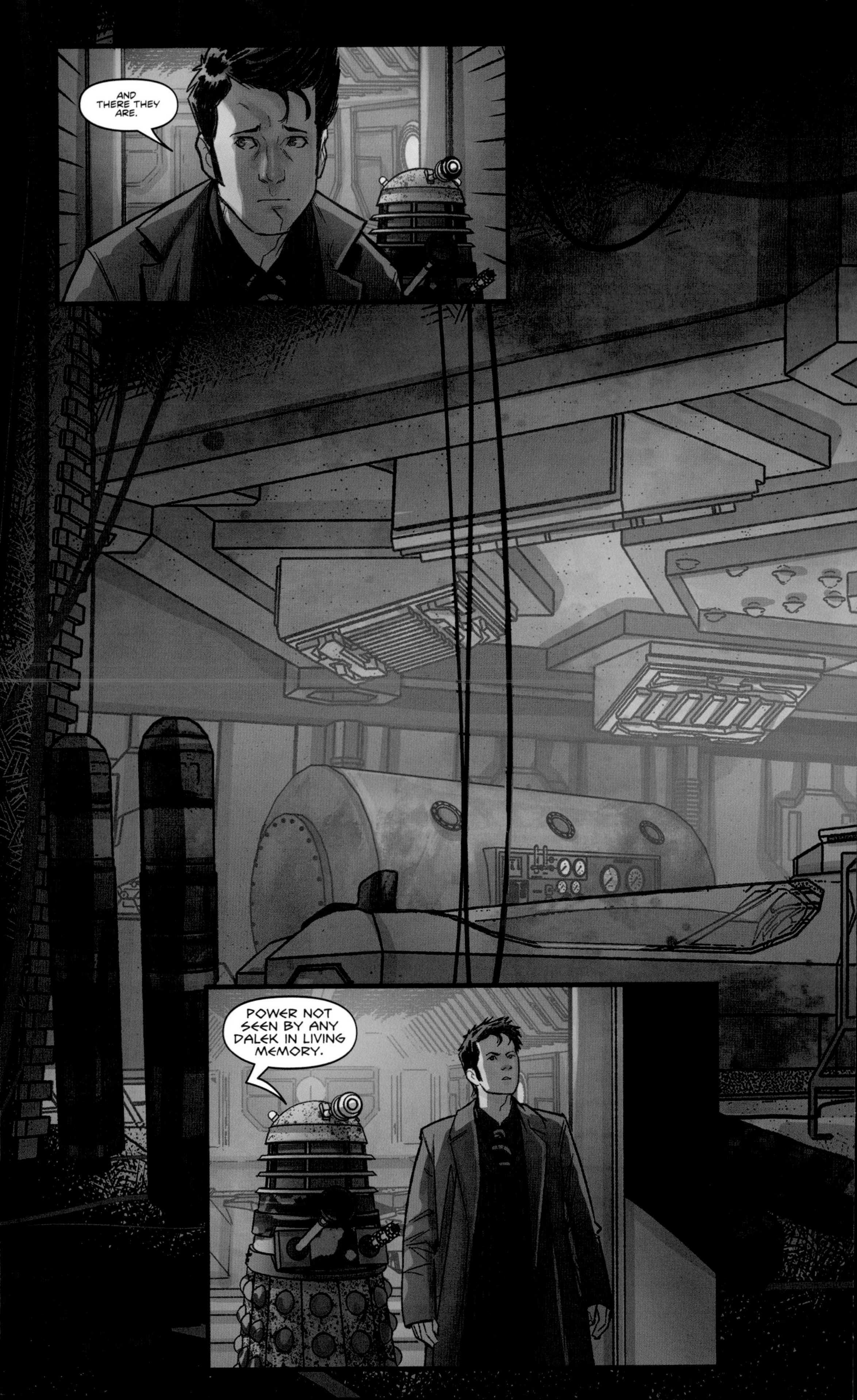
AND THERE THEY ARE.
POWER NOT SEEN BY ANY DALEK IN LIVING MEMORY.

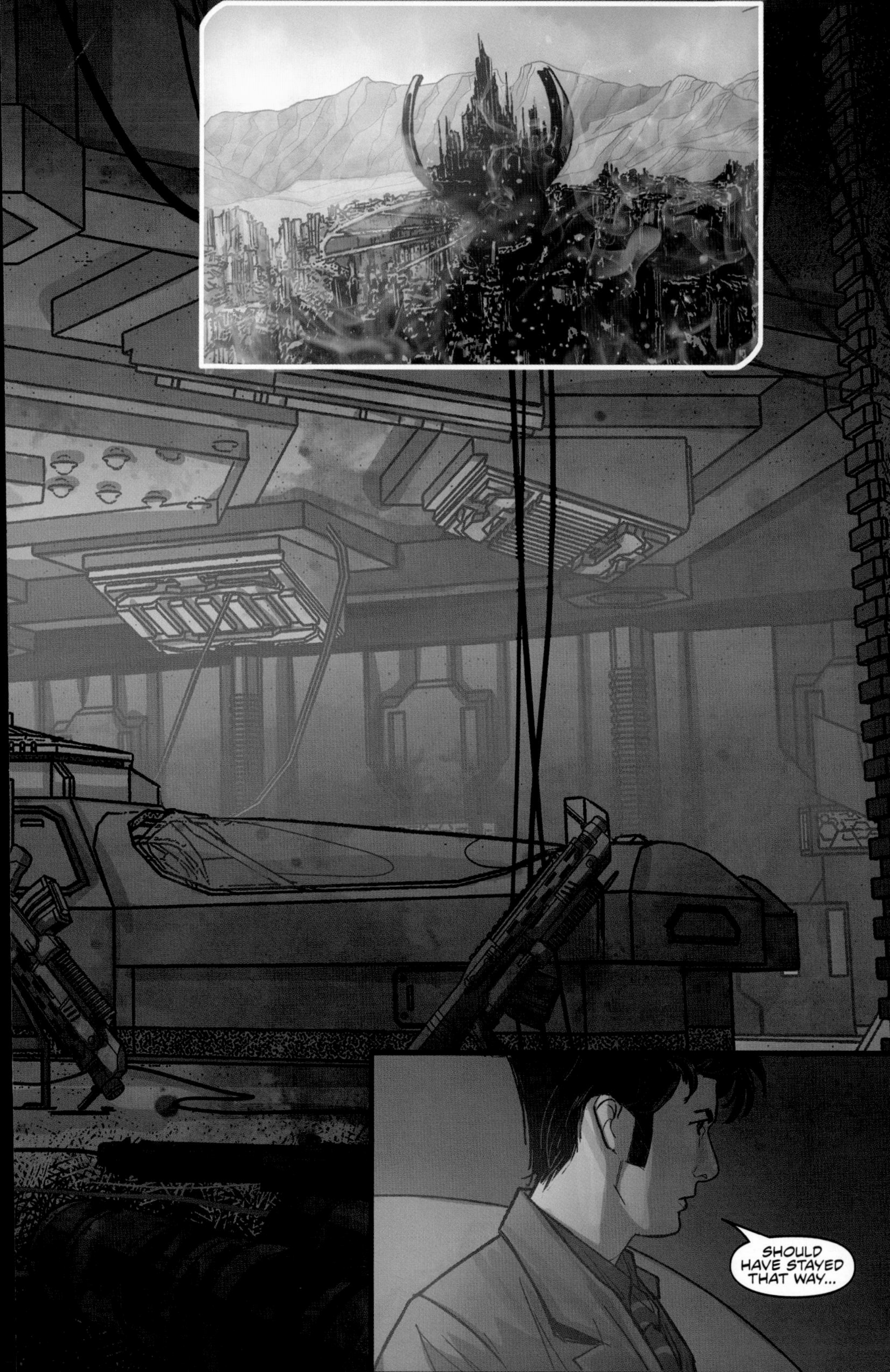
SHOULD HAVE STAYED THAT WAY...

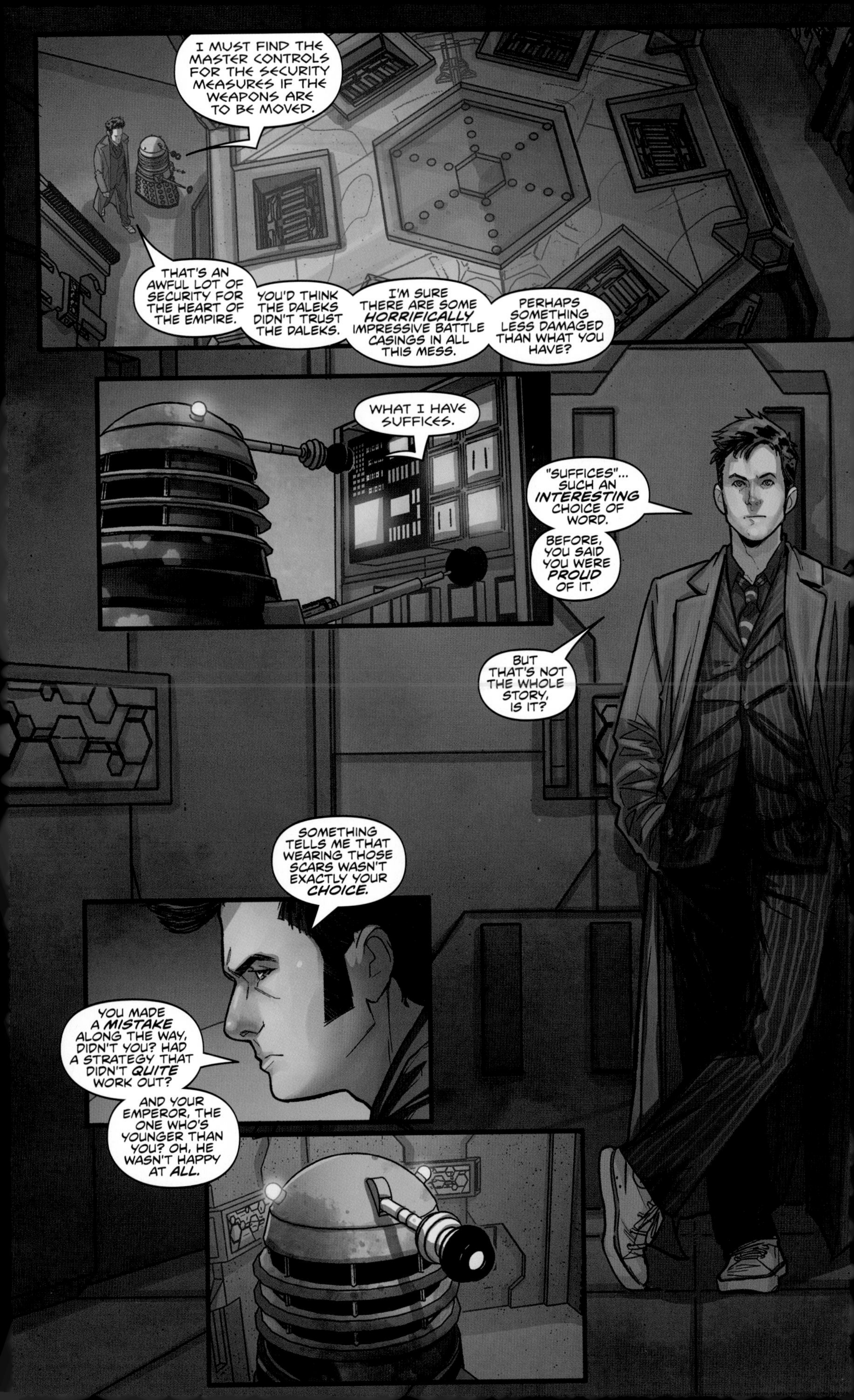
I MUST FIND THE MASTER CONTROLS FOR THE SECURITY MEASURES IF THE WEAPONS ARE TO BE MOVED.
THAT'S AN AWFUL LOT OF SECURITY FOR THE HEART OF THE EMPIRE.
YOU'D THINK THE DALEKS DIDN'T TRUST THE DALEKS.
I'M SURE THERE ARE SOME HORRIFICALLY IMPRESSIVE BATTLE CASINGS IN ALL THIS MESS.
PERHAPS SOMETHING LESS DAMAGED THAN WHAT YOU HAVE?
WHAT I HAVE SUFFICES.
"SUFFICES"... SUCH AN INTERESTING CHOICE OF WORD.
BEFORE, YOU SAID YOU WERE PROUD OF IT.
BUT THAT'S NOT THE WHOLE STORY, IS IT?
SOMETHING TELLS ME THAT WEARING THOSE SCARS WASN'T EXACTLY YOUR CHOICE.
YOU MADE A MISTAKE ALONG THE WAY, DIDN'T YOU? HAD A STRATEGY THAT DIDN'T QUITE WORK OUT?
AND YOUR EMPEROR, THE ONE WHO'S YOUNGER THAN YOU? OH, HE WASN'T HAPPY AT ALL.

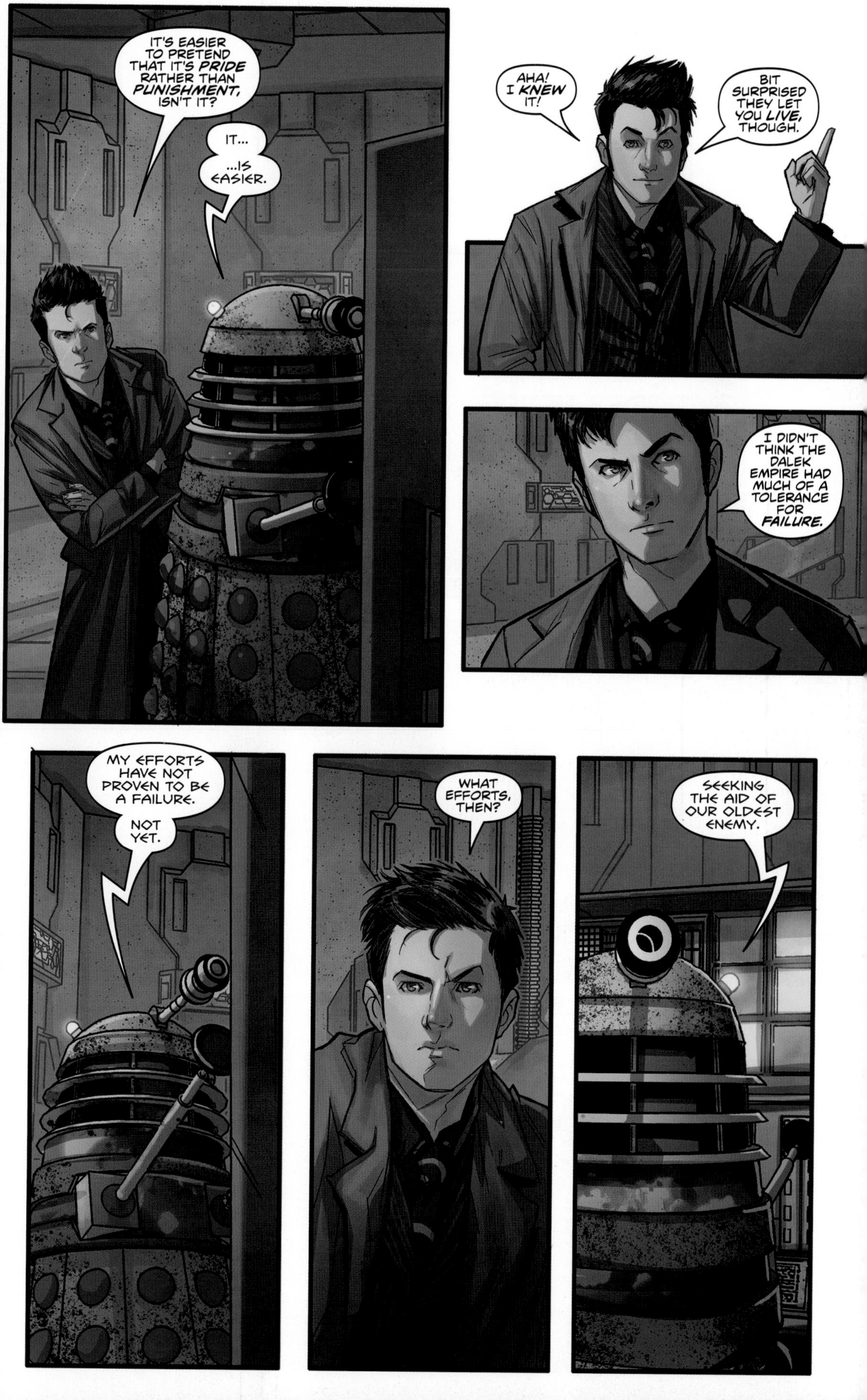
IT'S EASIER TO PRETEND THAT IT'S PRIDE RATHER THAN PUNISHMENT, ISN'T IT?
IT...
...IS EASIER.
AHA! I KNEW IT!
BIT SURPRISED THEY LET YOU LIVE, THOUGH.
I DIDN'T THINK THE DALEK EMPIRE HAD MUCH OF A TOLERANCE FOR FAILURE.
MY EFFORTS HAVE NOT PROVEN TO BE A FAILURE.
NOT YET.
WHAT EFFORTS, THEN?
SEEKING THE AID OF OUR OLDEST ENEMY.

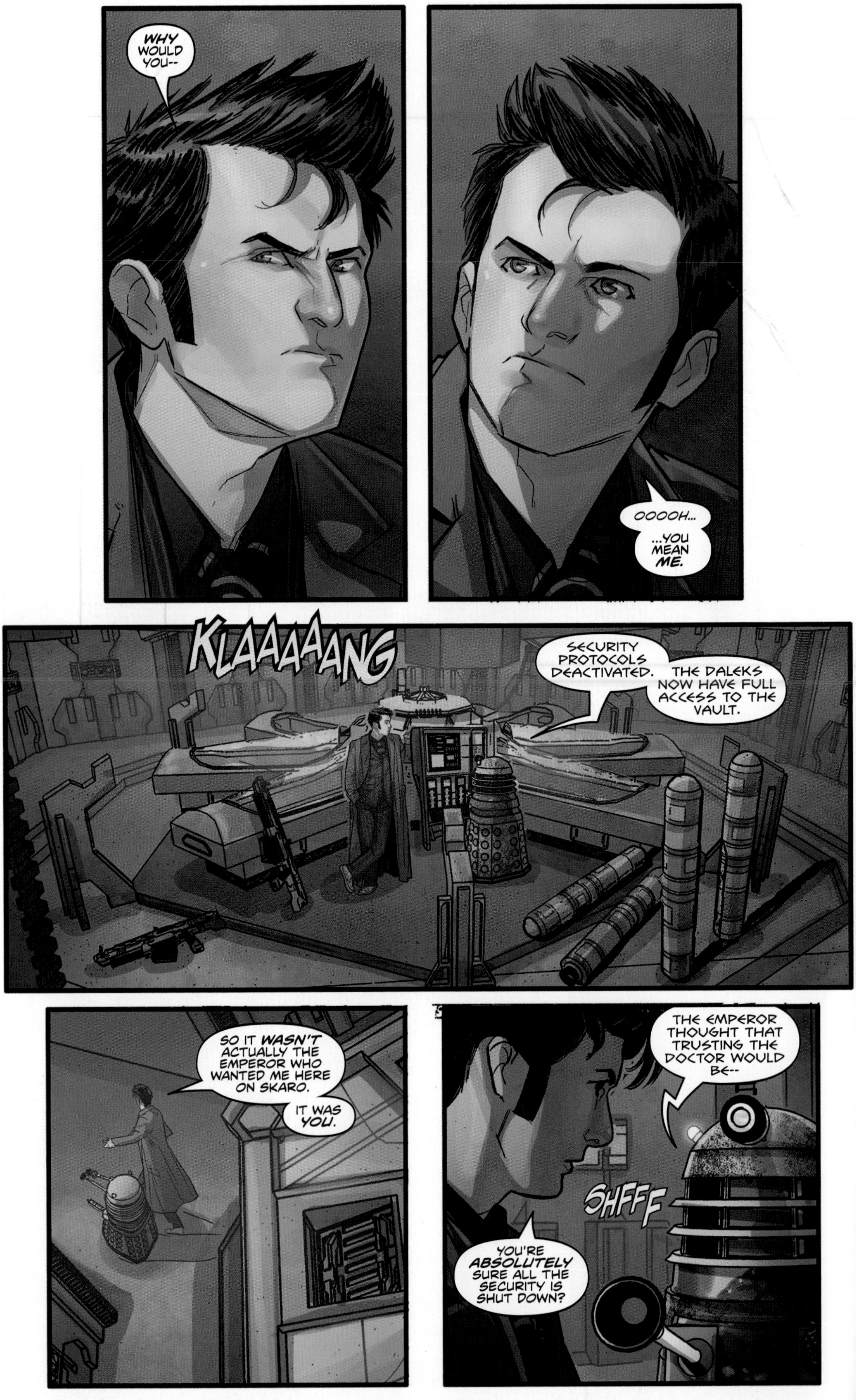
WHY WOULD YOU--
OOOOH... ...YOU MEAN ME.
KLAAAAANG
SECURITY PROTOCOLS DEACTIVATED. THE DALEKS NOW HAVE FULL ACCESS TO THE VAULT.
SO IT WASN'T ACTUALLY THE EMPEROR WHO WANTED ME HERE ON SKARO.
IT WAS YOU.
THE EMPEROR THOUGHT THAT TRUSTING THE DOCTOR WOULD BE--
SHFFF
YOU'RE ABSOLUTELY SURE ALL THE SECURITY IS SHUT DOWN?

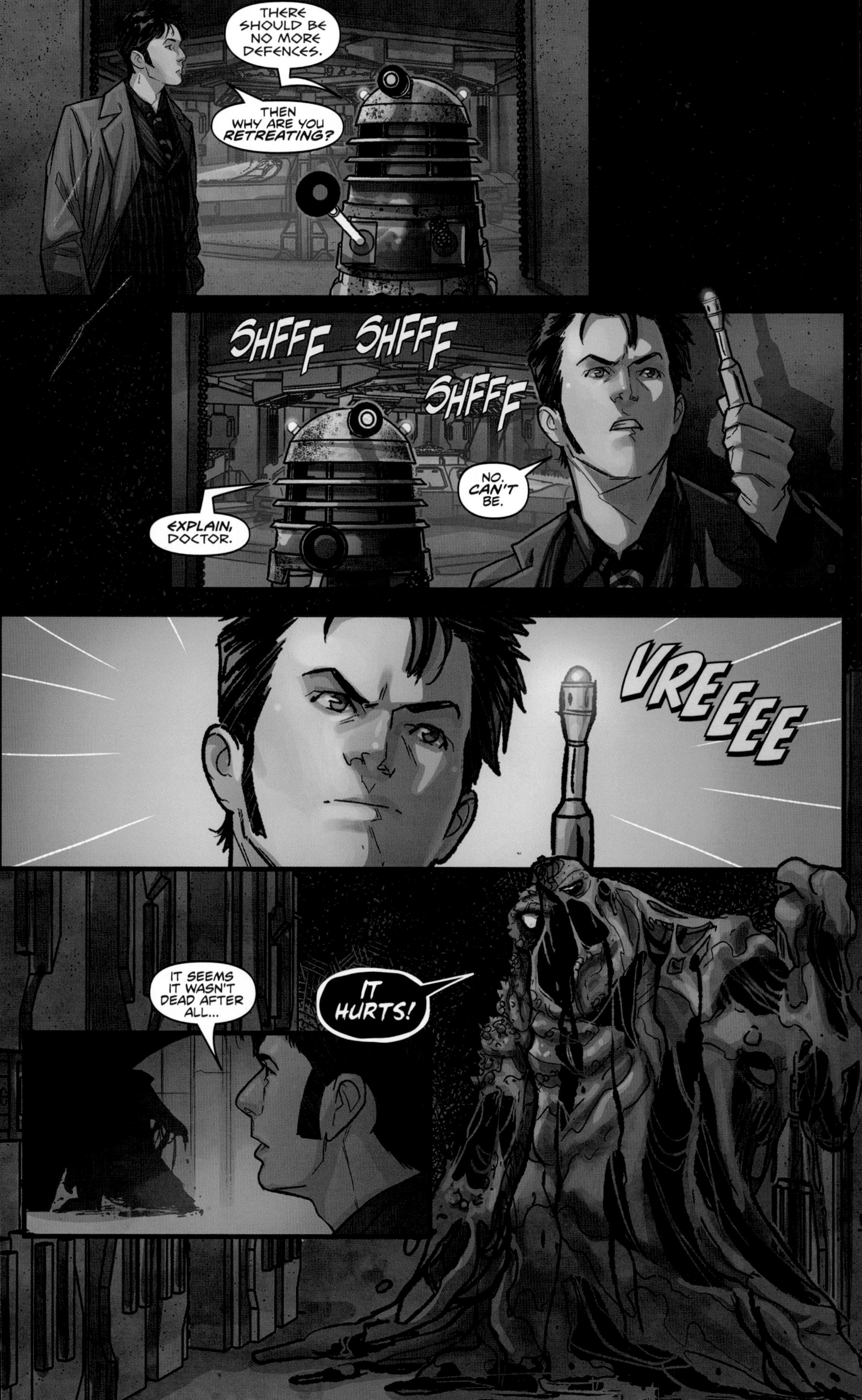
THERE SHOULD BE NO MORE DEFENCES.
THEN WHY ARE YOU RETREATING?
SHFFF SHFFF
SHFFF
EXPLAIN, DOCTOR.
NO. CAN'T BE.
VREEEE
IT SEEMS IT WASN'T DEAD AFTER ALL...
IT HURTS!

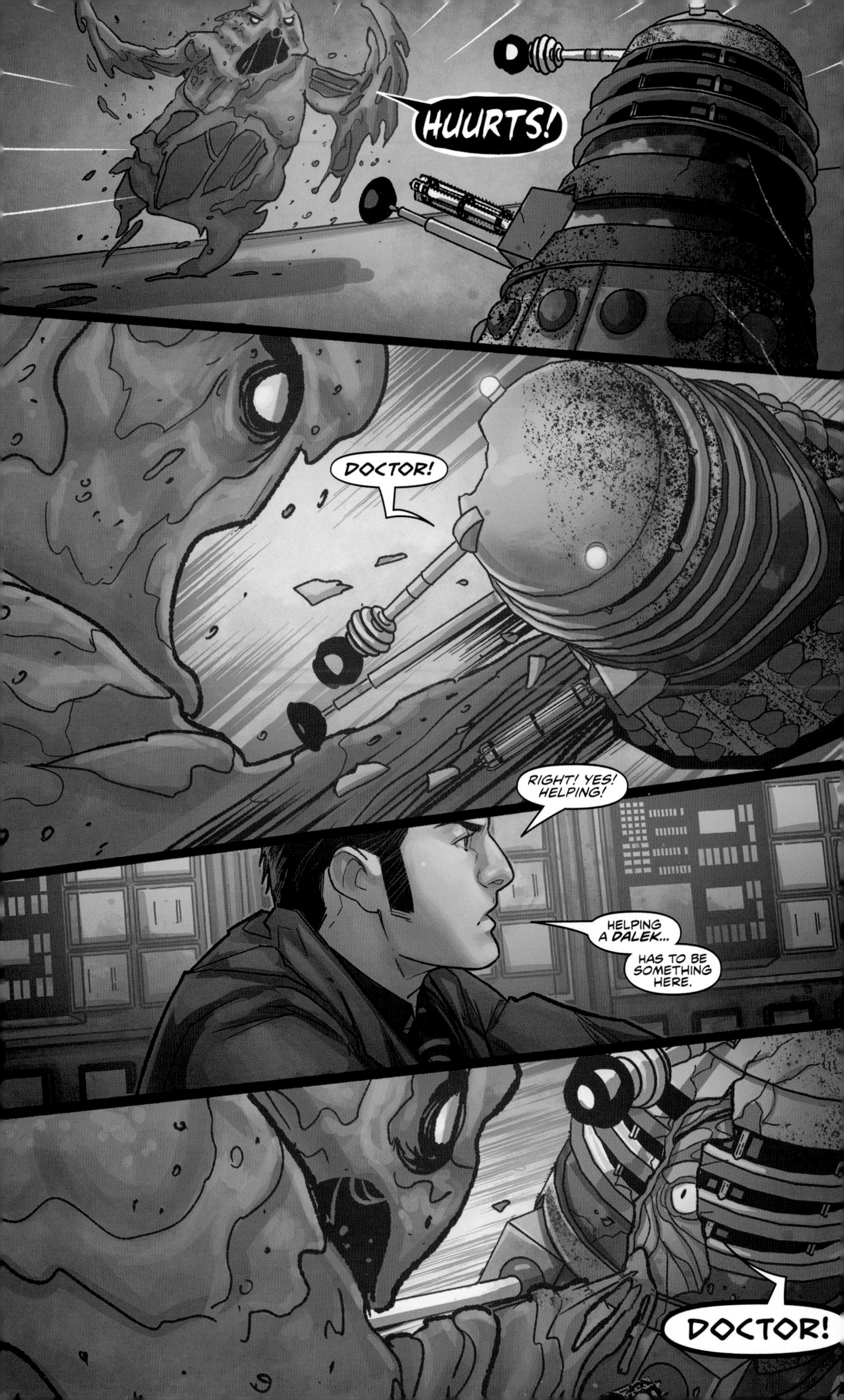
HUURTS!
DOCTOR!
RIGHT! YES! HELPING!
HELPING A DALEK...
HAS TO BE SOMETHING HERE.
DOCTOR!

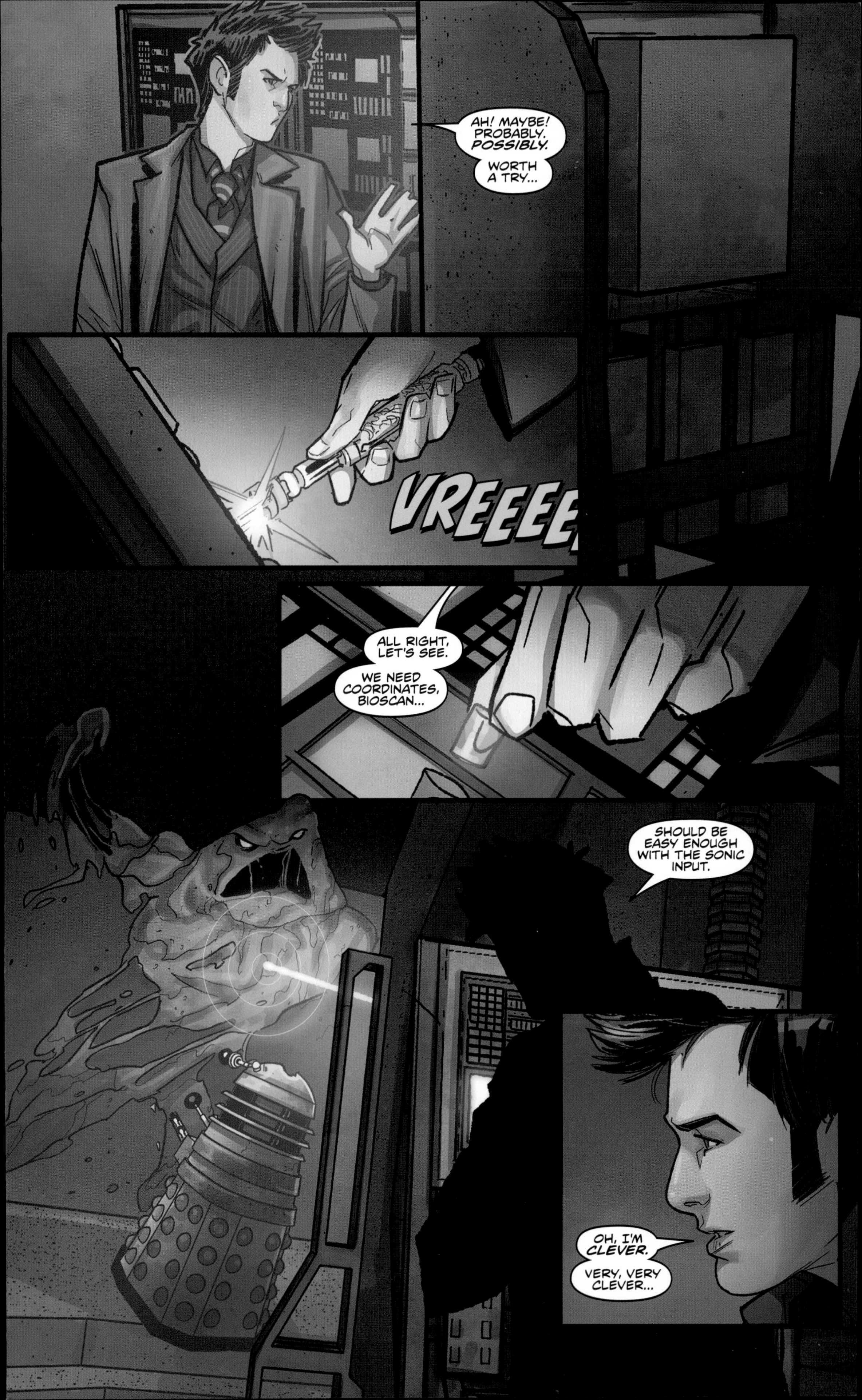
AH! MAYBE! PROBABLY. *POSSIBLY.*
WORTH A TRY...
VREEEEE
ALL RIGHT, LET'S SEE.
WE NEED COORDINATES, BIOSCAN...
SHOULD BE EASY ENOUGH WITH THE SONIC INPUT.
OH, I'M *CLEVER.*
VERY, VERY CLEVER...

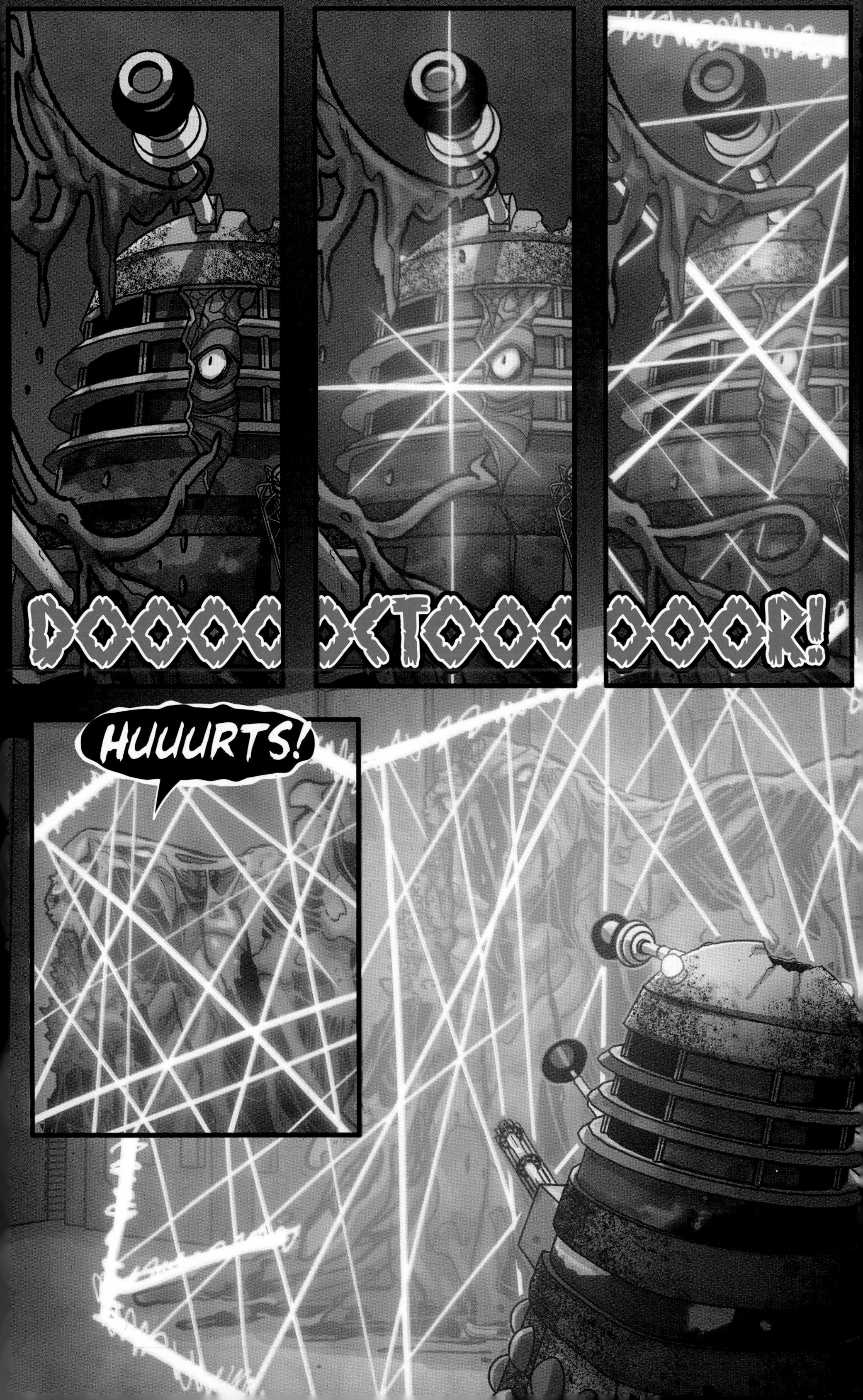
DOOOOOCTOOOOOOOR!
HUUURTS!

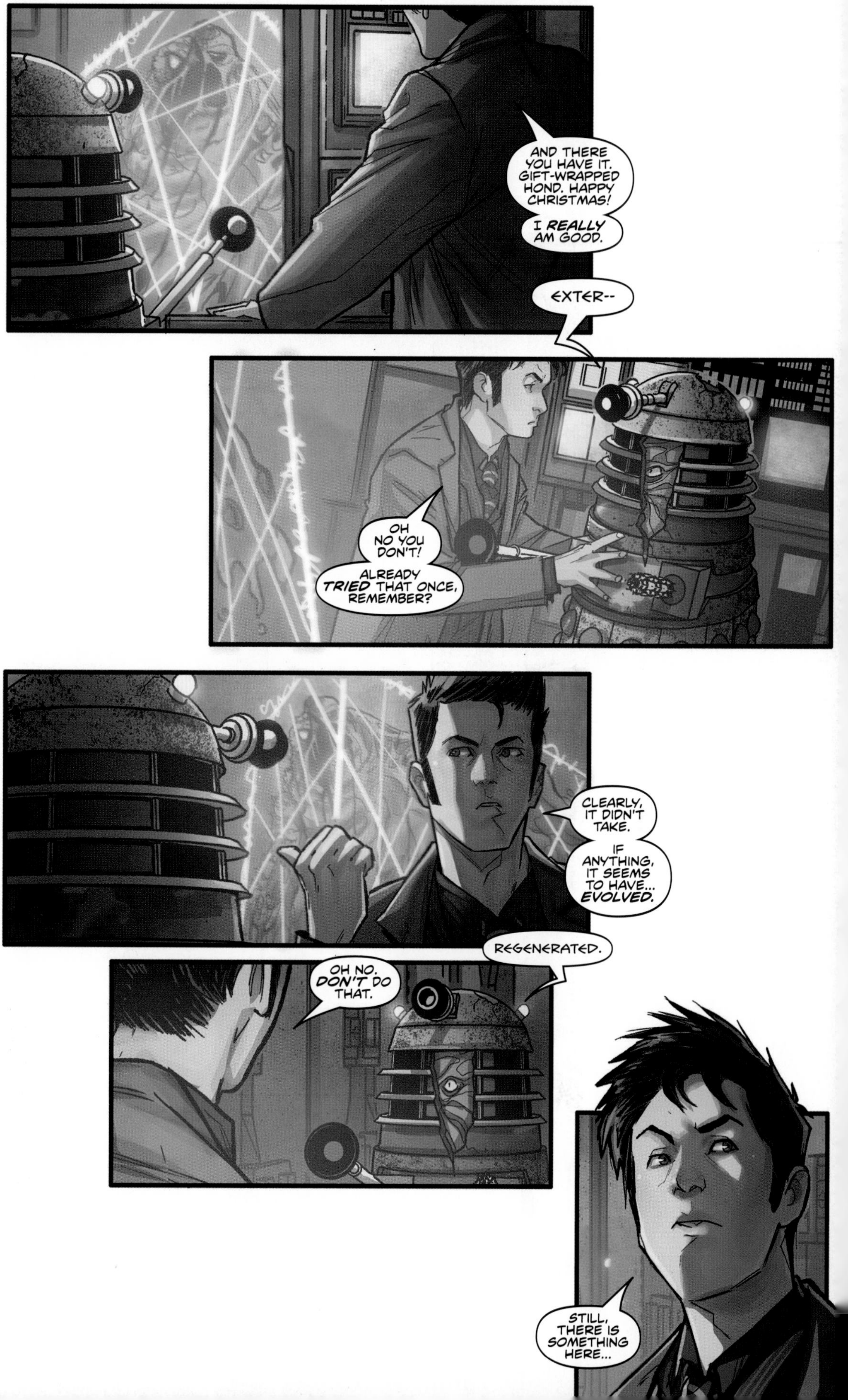
AND THERE YOU HAVE IT. GIFT-WRAPPED HOND. HAPPY CHRISTMAS!
I REALLY AM GOOD.
EXTER--
OH NO YOU DON'T!
ALREADY TRIED THAT ONCE, REMEMBER?
CLEARLY, IT DIDN'T TAKE.
IF ANYTHING, IT SEEMS TO HAVE... EVOLVED.
REGENERATED.
OH NO. DON'T DO THAT.
STILL, THERE IS SOMETHING HERE...

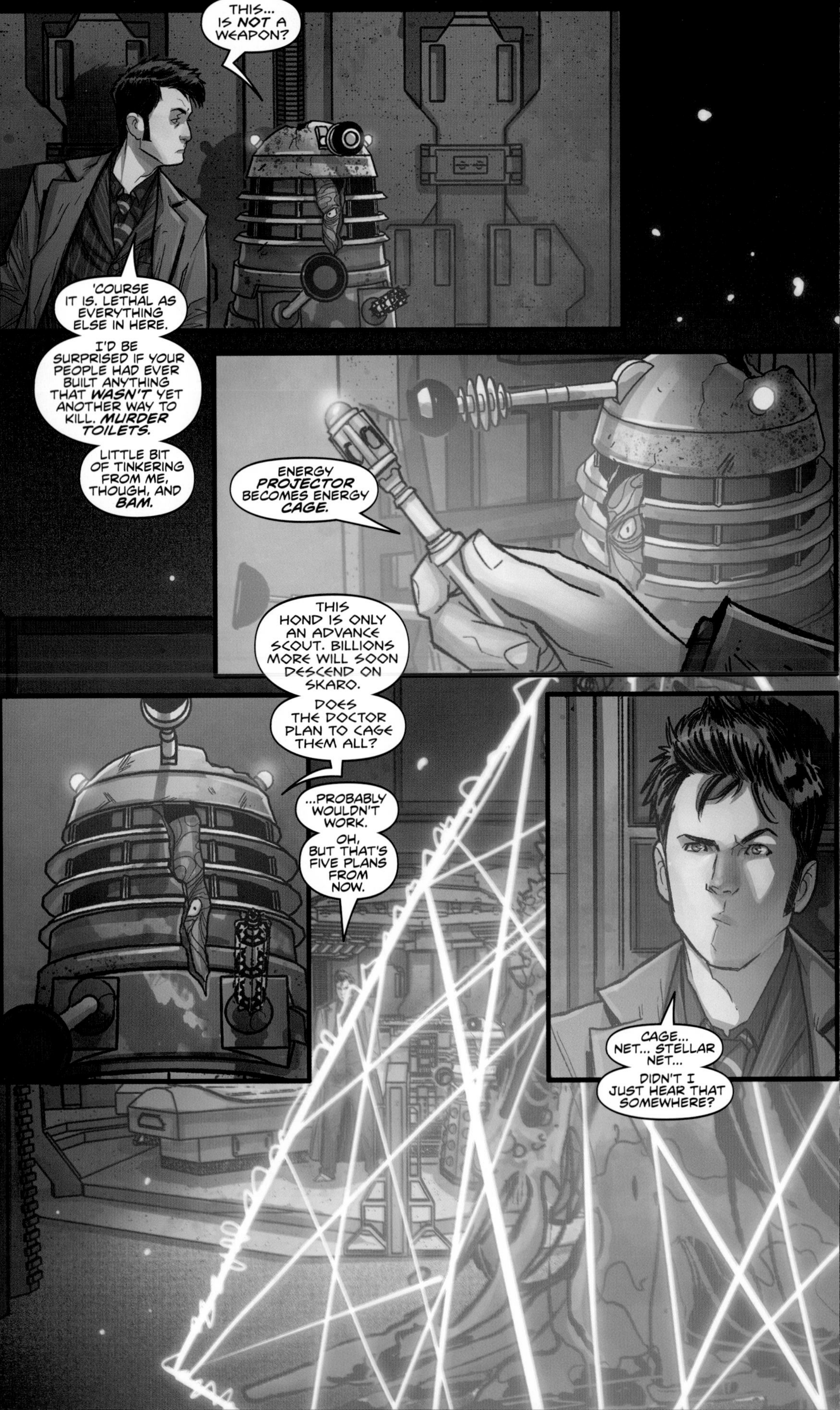
THIS... IS NOT A WEAPON?
'COURSE IT IS. LETHAL AS EVERYTHING ELSE IN HERE.
I'D BE SURPRISED IF YOUR PEOPLE HAD EVER BUILT ANYTHING THAT WASN'T YET ANOTHER WAY TO KILL. MURDER TOILETS.
LITTLE BIT OF TINKERING FROM ME, THOUGH, AND BAM.
ENERGY PROJECTOR BECOMES ENERGY CAGE.
THIS HOND IS ONLY AN ADVANCE SCOUT. BILLIONS MORE WILL SOON DESCEND ON SKARO.
DOES THE DOCTOR PLAN TO CAGE THEM ALL?
...PROBABLY WOULDN'T WORK.
OH, BUT THAT'S FIVE PLANS FROM NOW.
CAGE... NET... STELLAR NET...
DIDN'T I JUST HEAR THAT SOMEWHERE?

YOU HAVE DONE A GREAT SERVICE TO THE DALEK EMPIRE TODAY, DOCTOR.

OH, *WHY* DO YOU HAVE TO SAY THINGS LIKE THAT?

JUST MAKES ME REGRET THE WHOLE THING.

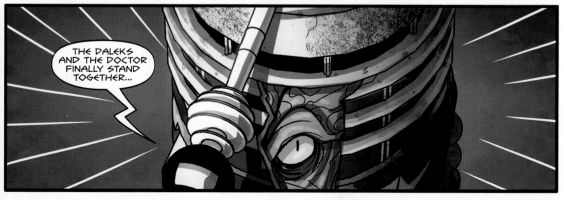

THE DALEKS AND THE DOCTOR FINALLY STAND TOGETHER...

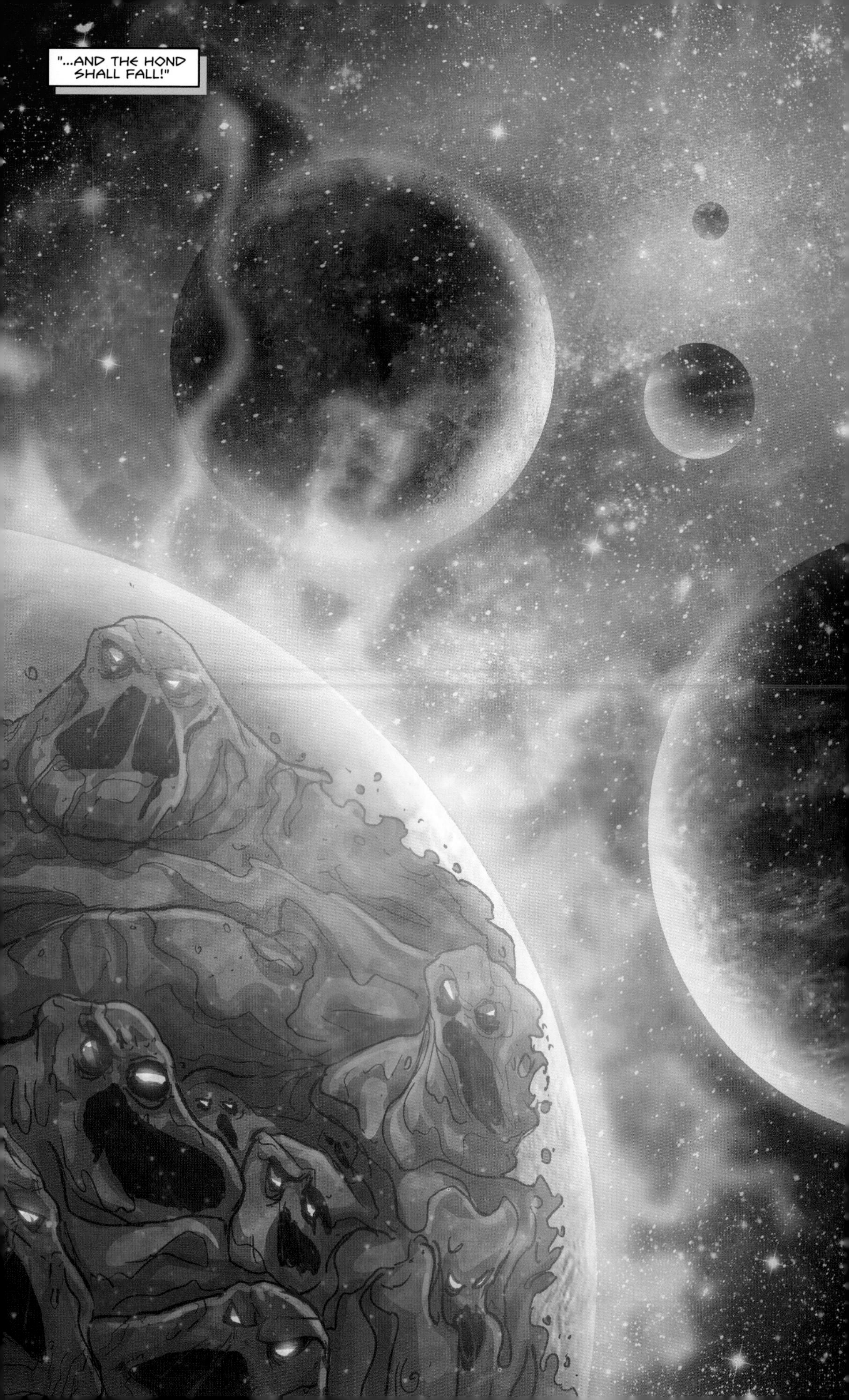
"...AND THE HOND SHALL FALL!"

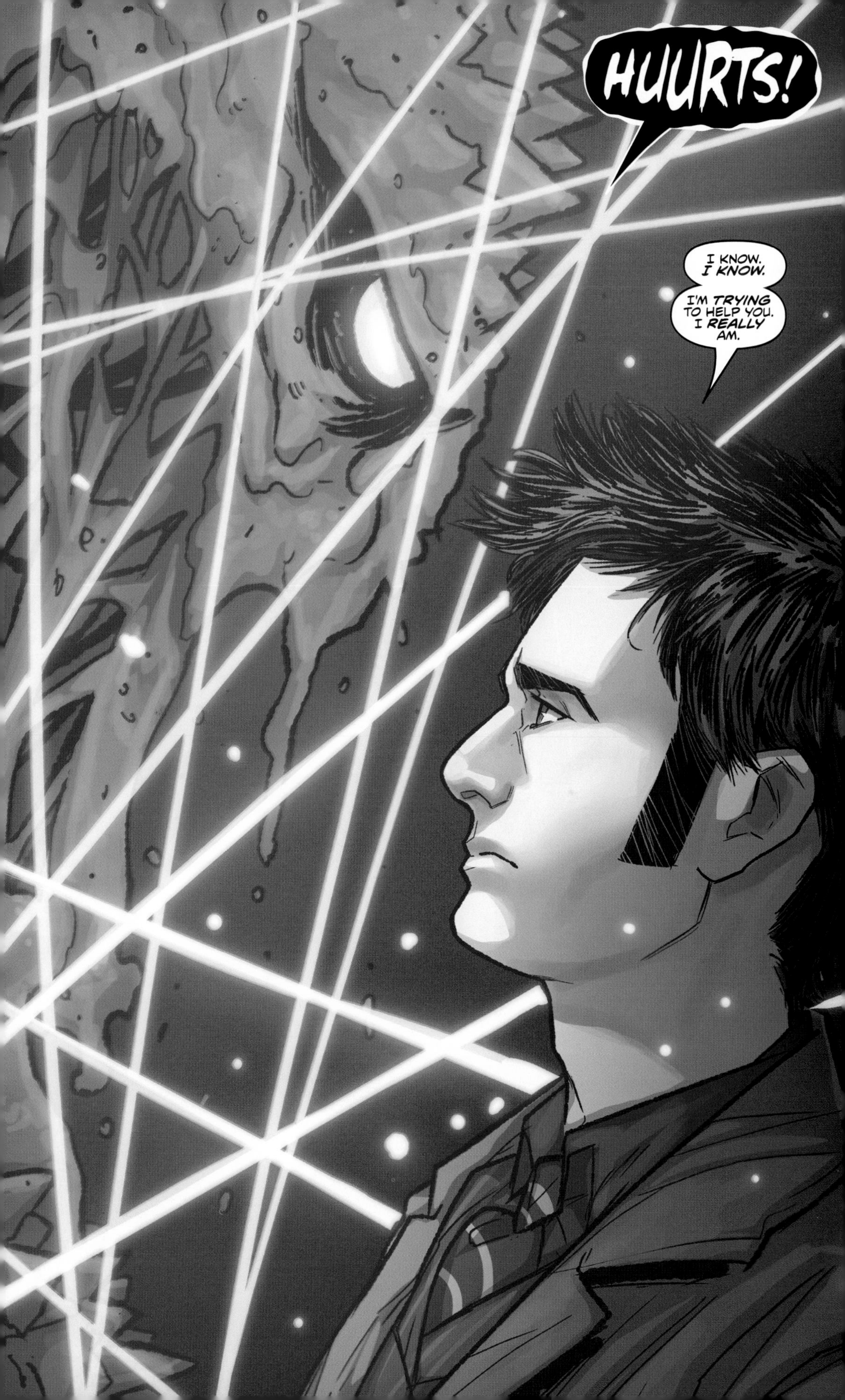
HUURTS!
I KNOW. I KNOW.
I'M TRYING TO HELP YOU. I REALLY AM.

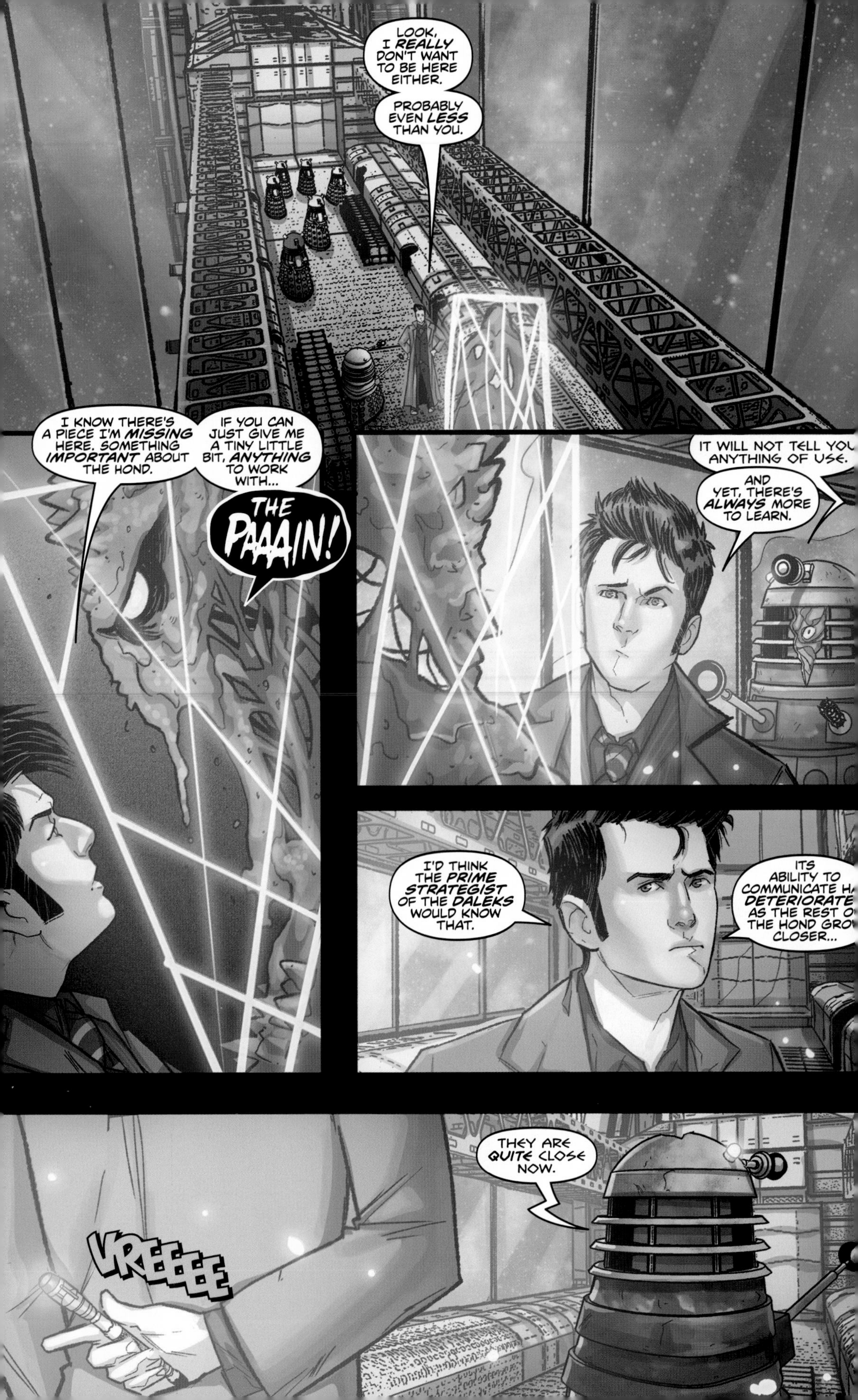
LOOK, I REALLY DON'T WANT TO BE HERE EITHER.
PROBABLY EVEN LESS THAN YOU.
I KNOW THERE'S A PIECE I'M MISSING HERE. SOMETHING IMPORTANT ABOUT THE HOND.
IF YOU CAN JUST GIVE ME A TINY LITTLE BIT, ANYTHING TO WORK WITH...
THE PAAAIN!
IT WILL NOT TELL YOU ANYTHING OF USE.
AND YET, THERE'S ALWAYS MORE TO LEARN.
I'D THINK THE PRIME STRATEGIST OF THE DALEKS WOULD KNOW THAT.
ITS ABILITY TO COMMUNICATE HA DETERIORATE AS THE REST O THE HOND GRO CLOSER...
THEY ARE QUITE CLOSE NOW.
VREEEEE

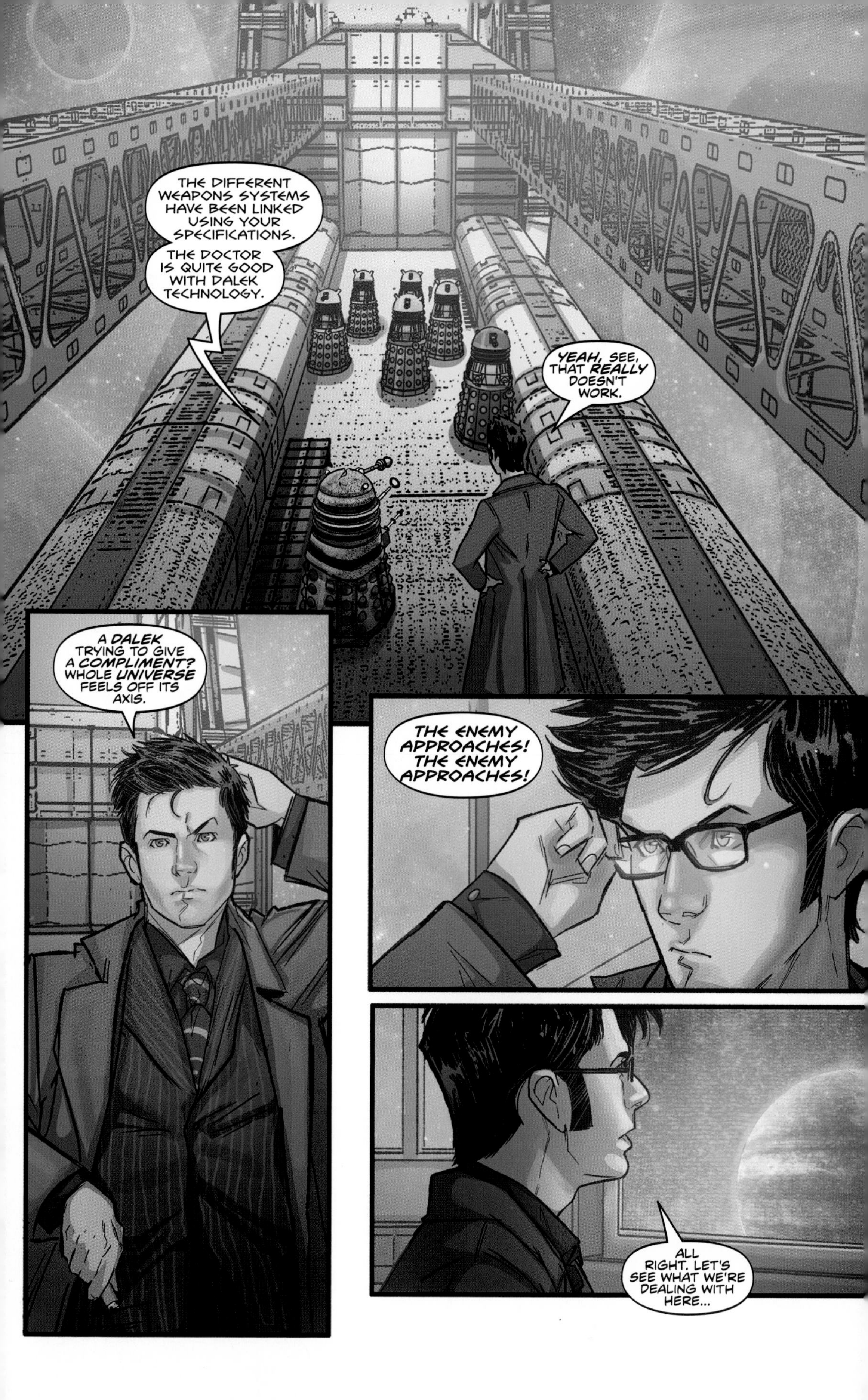
THE DIFFERENT WEAPONS SYSTEMS HAVE BEEN LINKED USING YOUR SPECIFICATIONS.
THE DOCTOR IS QUITE GOOD WITH DALEK TECHNOLOGY.
YEAH, SEE, THAT REALLY DOESN'T WORK.
A DALEK TRYING TO GIVE A COMPLIMENT? WHOLE UNIVERSE FEELS OFF ITS AXIS.
THE ENEMY APPROACHES! THE ENEMY APPROACHES!
ALL RIGHT. LET'S SEE WHAT WE'RE DEALING WITH HERE...

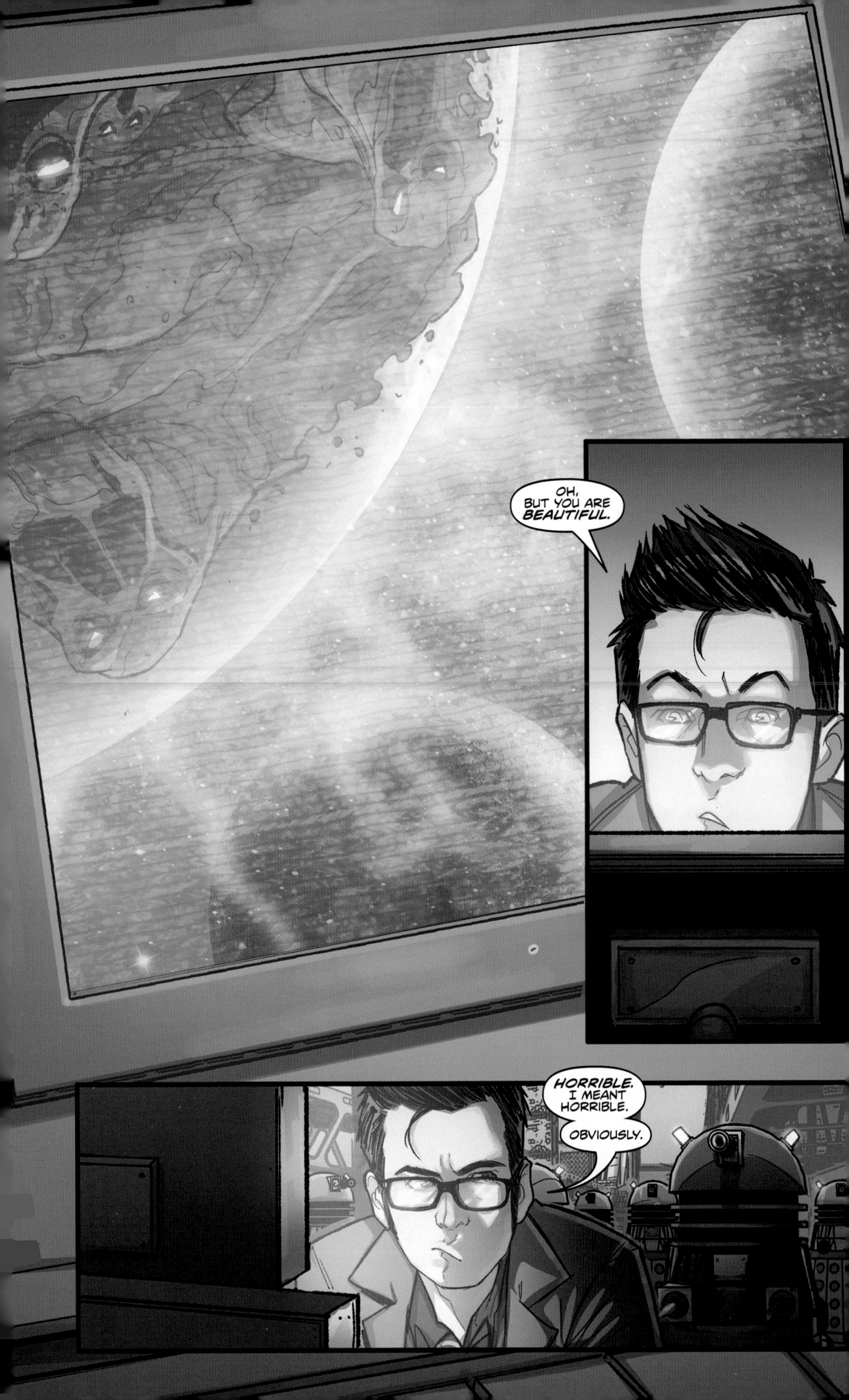
OH, BUT YOU ARE BEAUTIFUL.
HORRIBLE. I MEANT HORRIBLE.
OBVIOUSLY.

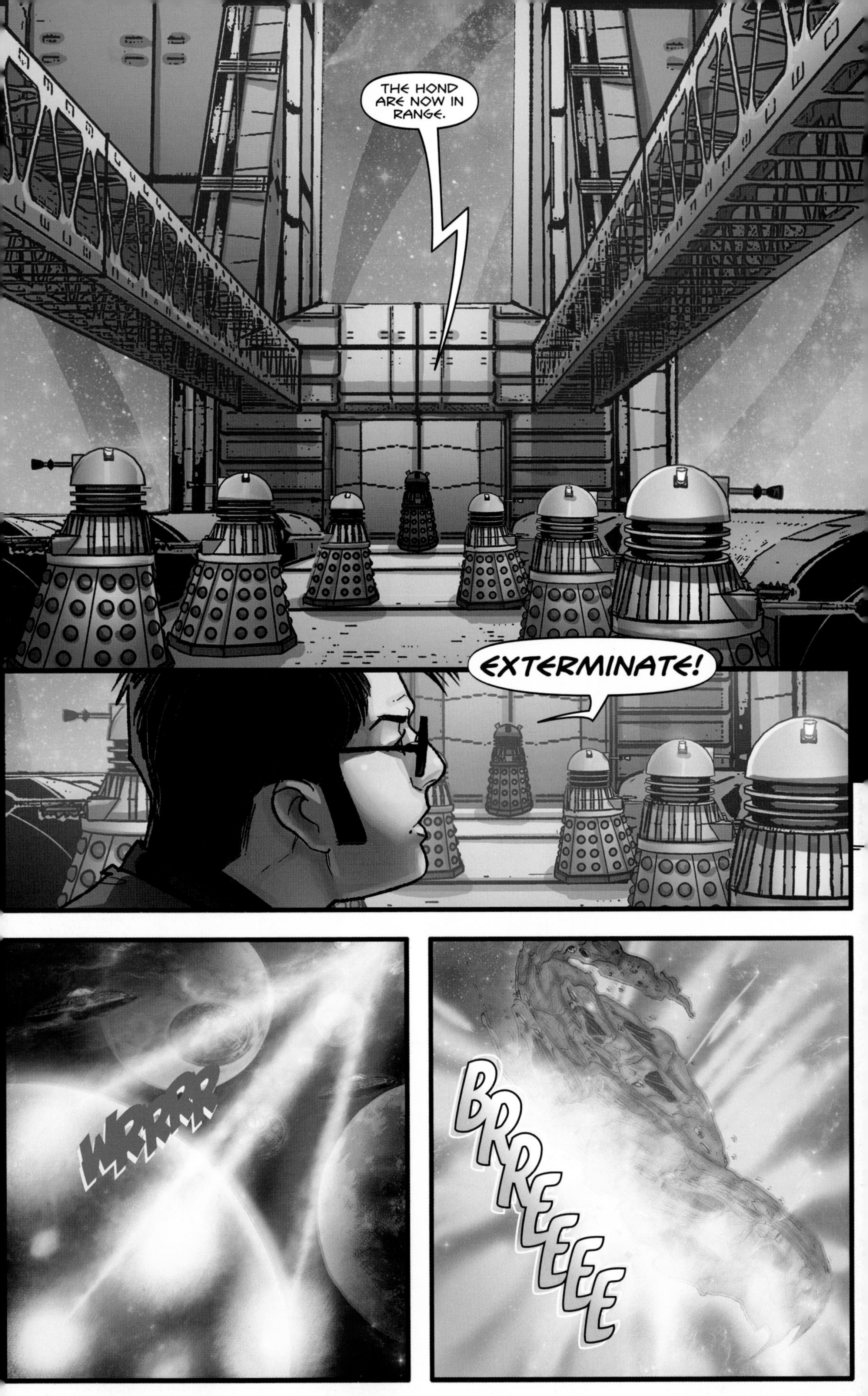
THE HOND ARE NOW IN RANGE.
EXTERMINATE!
WRRRR
BRREEEEE

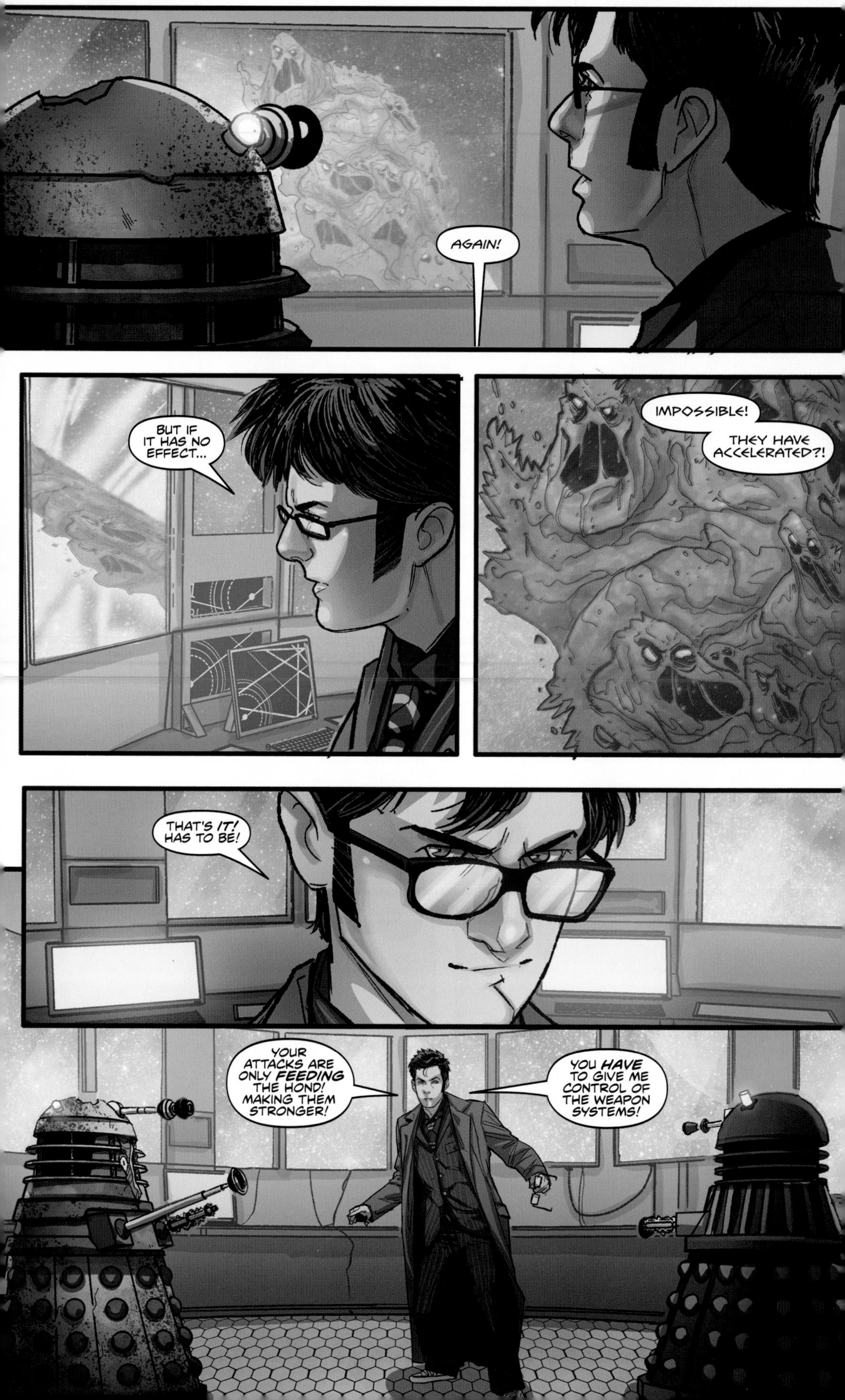
AGAIN!
BUT IF IT HAS NO EFFECT...
IMPOSSIBLE!
THEY HAVE ACCELERATED?!
THAT'S IT! HAS TO BE!
YOUR ATTACKS ARE ONLY FEEDING THE HOND! MAKING THEM STRONGER!
YOU HAVE TO GIVE ME CONTROL OF THE WEAPON SYSTEMS!

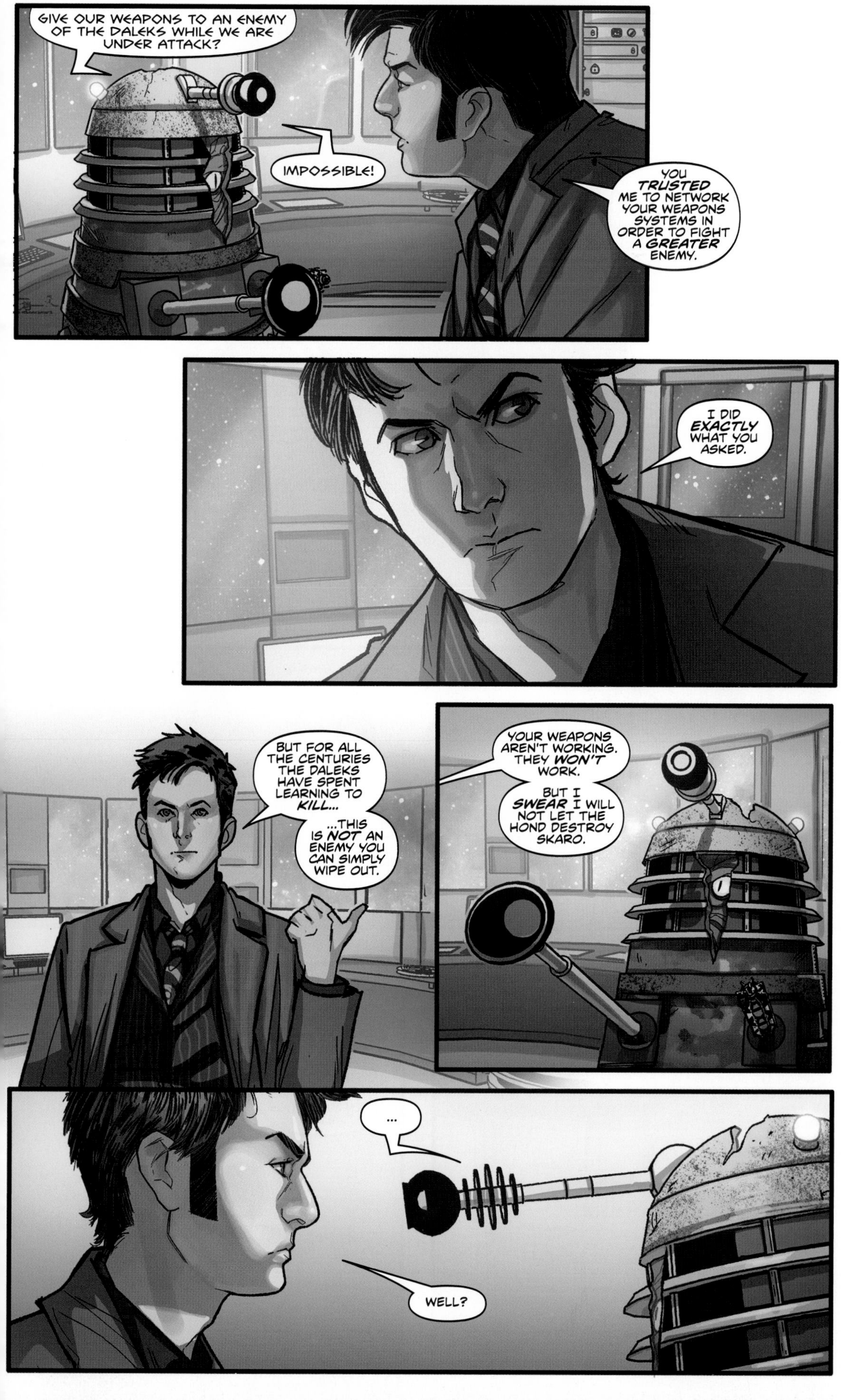
GIVE OUR WEAPONS TO AN ENEMY OF THE DALEKS WHILE WE ARE UNDER ATTACK?
IMPOSSIBLE!
YOU TRUSTED ME TO NETWORK YOUR WEAPONS SYSTEMS IN ORDER TO FIGHT A GREATER ENEMY.
I DID EXACTLY WHAT YOU ASKED.
BUT FOR ALL THE CENTURIES THE DALEKS HAVE SPENT LEARNING TO KILL...
...THIS IS NOT AN ENEMY YOU CAN SIMPLY WIPE OUT.
YOUR WEAPONS AREN'T WORKING. THEY WON'T WORK.
BUT I SWEAR I WILL NOT LET THE HOND DESTROY SKARO.
...
WELL?

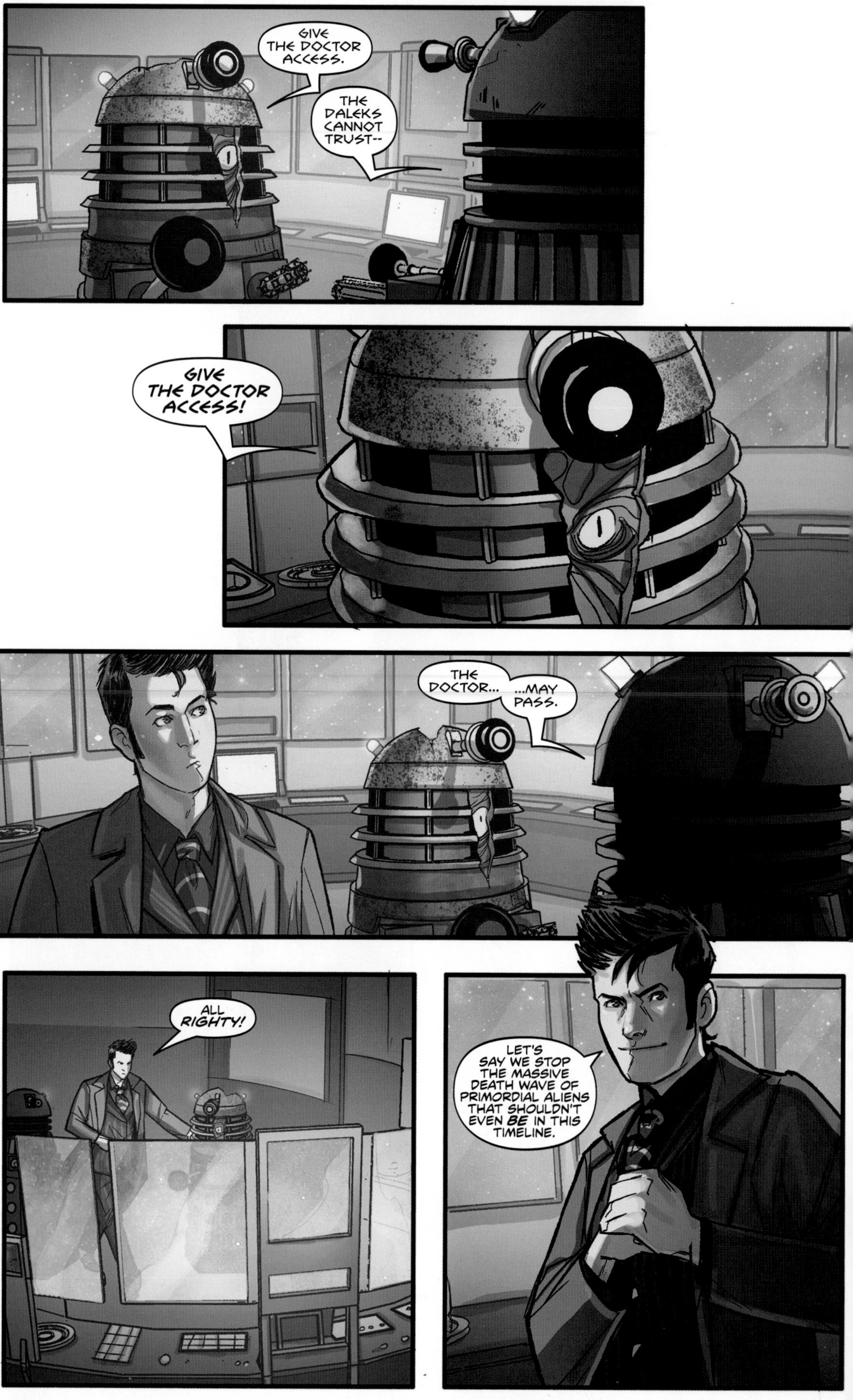
GIVE THE DOCTOR ACCESS.
THE DALEKS CANNOT TRUST--
GIVE THE DOCTOR ACCESS!
THE DOCTOR...
...MAY PASS.
ALL RIGHTY!
LET'S SAY WE STOP THE MASSIVE DEATH WAVE OF PRIMORDIAL ALIENS THAT SHOULDN'T EVEN BE IN THIS TIMELINE.

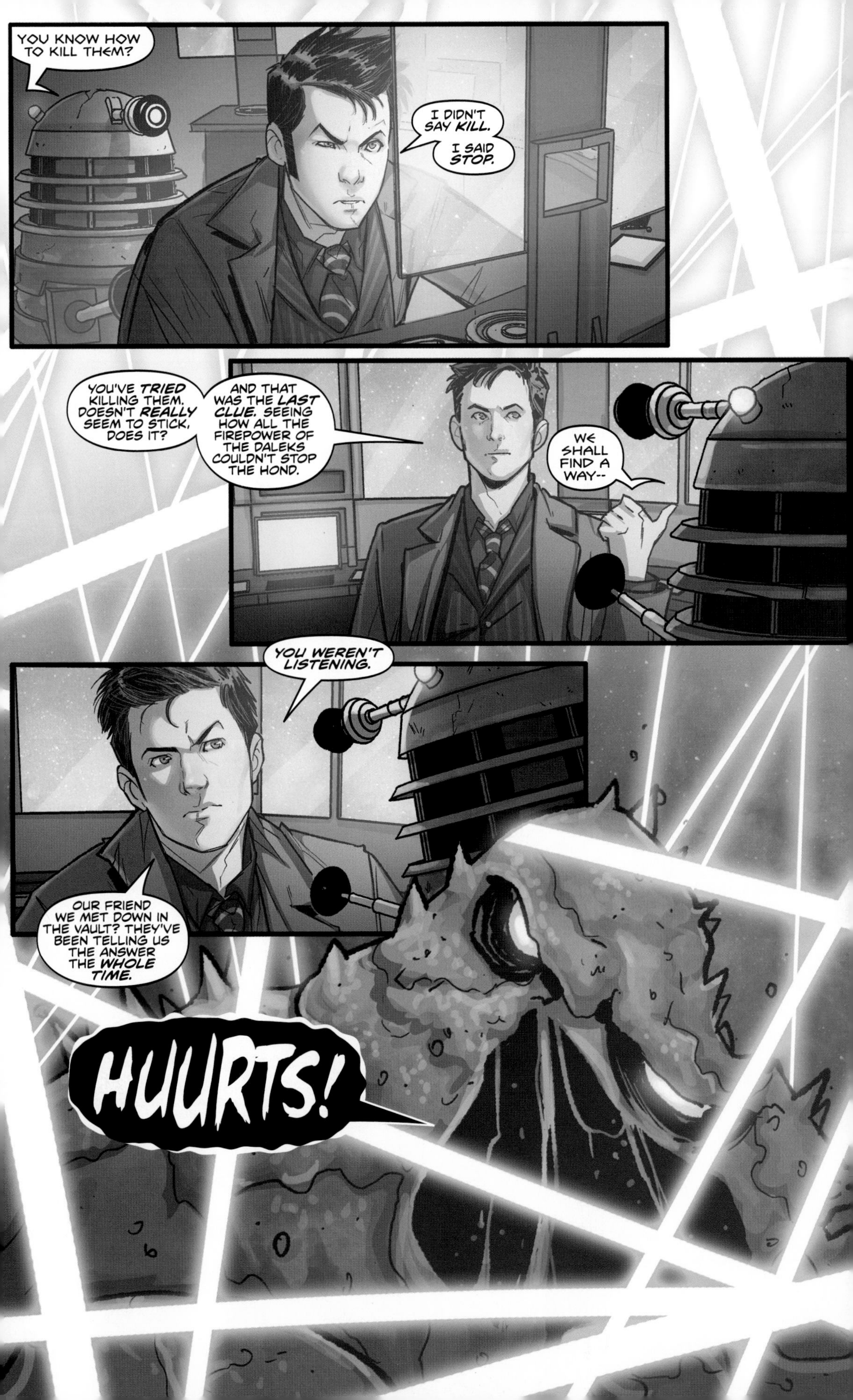
YOU KNOW HOW TO KILL THEM?
I DIDN'T SAY KILL.
I SAID STOP.
YOU'VE TRIED KILLING THEM. DOESN'T REALLY SEEM TO STICK, DOES IT?
AND THAT WAS THE LAST CLUE. SEEING HOW ALL THE FIREPOWER OF THE DALEKS COULDN'T STOP THE HOND.
WE SHALL FIND A WAY--
YOU WEREN'T LISTENING.
OUR FRIEND WE MET DOWN IN THE VAULT? THEY'VE BEEN TELLING US THE ANSWER THE WHOLE TIME.
HUURTS!

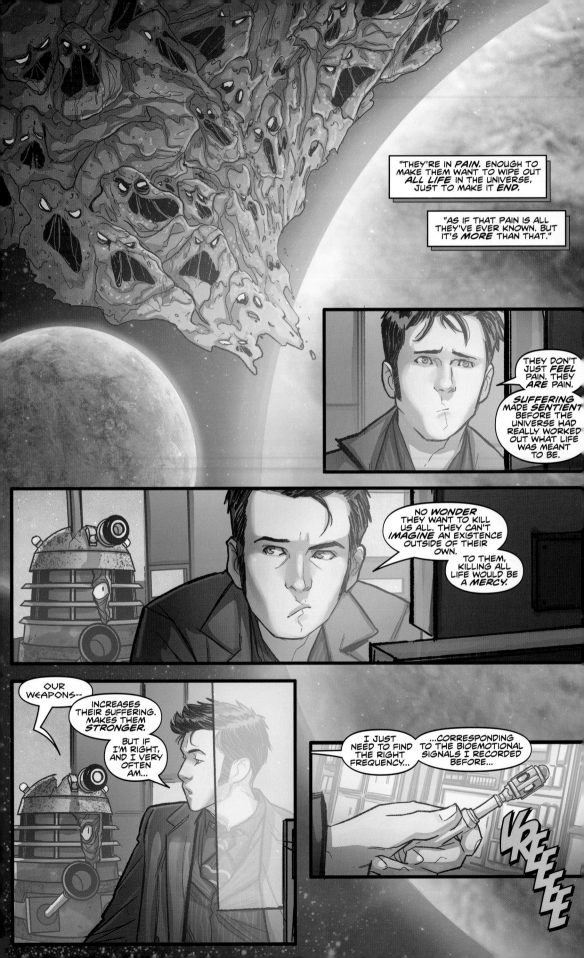

"THEY'RE IN *PAIN*. ENOUGH TO MAKE THEM WANT TO WIPE OUT *ALL LIFE* IN THE UNIVERSE, JUST TO MAKE IT *END*.

"AS IF THAT PAIN IS ALL THEY'VE EVER KNOWN. BUT IT'S *MORE* THAN THAT."

THEY DON'T JUST *FEEL* PAIN. THEY *ARE* PAIN.

*SUFFERING* MADE *SENTIENT* BEFORE THE UNIVERSE HAD REALLY WORKED OUT WHAT LIFE WAS MEANT TO BE.

NO *WONDER* THEY WANT TO KILL US ALL. THEY CAN'T *IMAGINE* AN EXISTENCE OUTSIDE OF THEIR OWN.

TO THEM, KILLING ALL LIFE WOULD BE A *MERCY*.

OUR WEAPONS--

INCREASES THEIR SUFFERING. MAKES THEM *STRONGER*.

BUT IF I'M RIGHT, AND I VERY OFTEN AM...

I JUST NEED TO FIND THE RIGHT FREQUENCY...

...CORRESPONDING TO THE BIOEMOTIONAL SIGNALS I RECORDED BEFORE...

VREEEEE

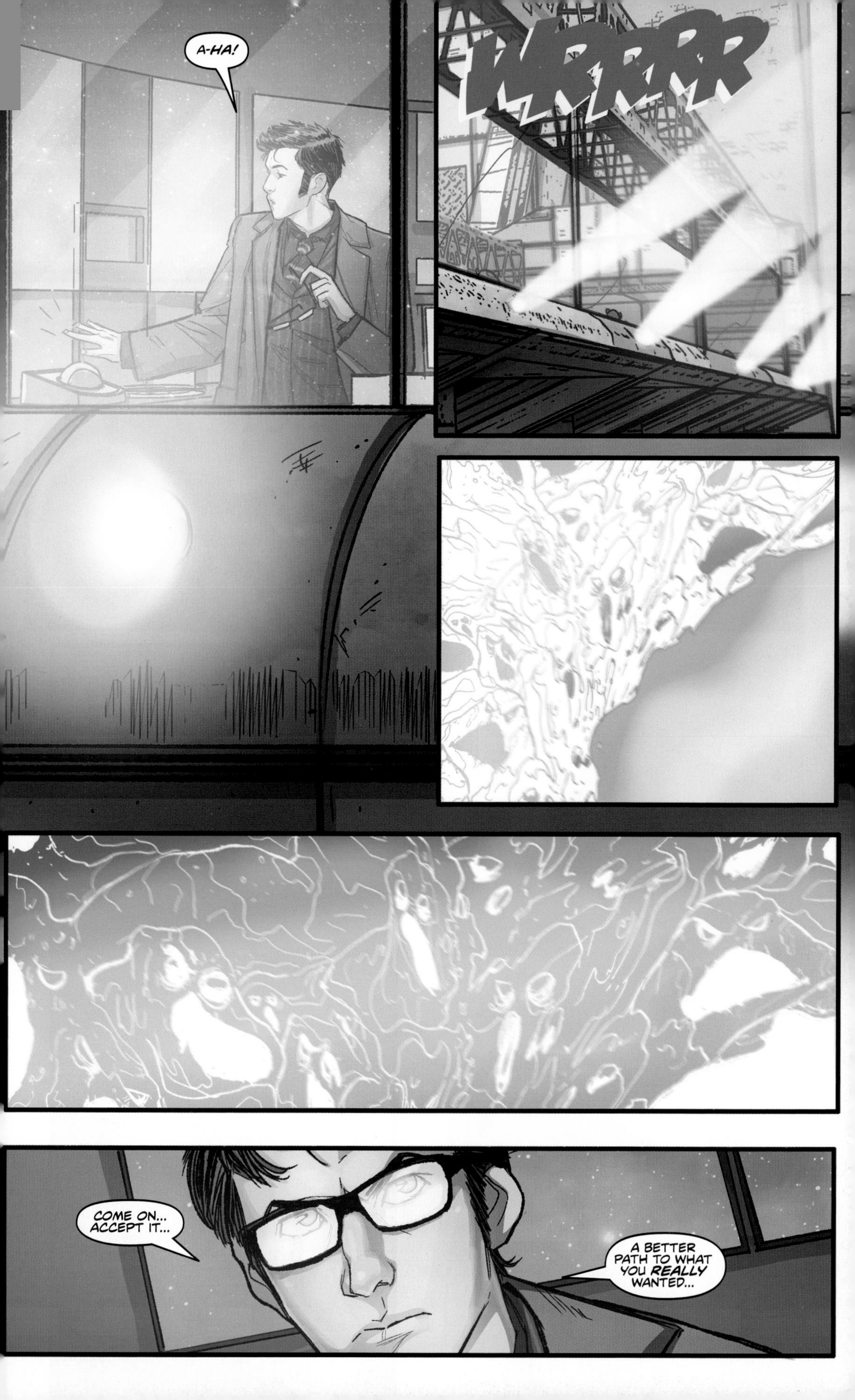
A-HA!
WRRRR
COME ON... ACCEPT IT...
A BETTER PATH TO WHAT YOU REALLY WANTED...

YES!

THE DOCTOR... KILLED THEM?

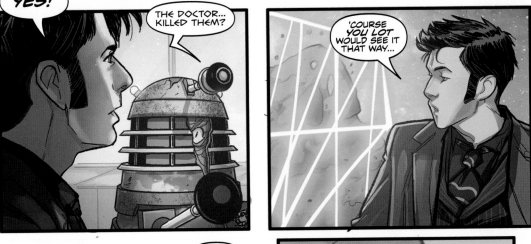

'COURSE *YOU LOT* WOULD SEE IT THAT WAY...

THE PAIN...

GONNNE.

THANNK YOOOUU...

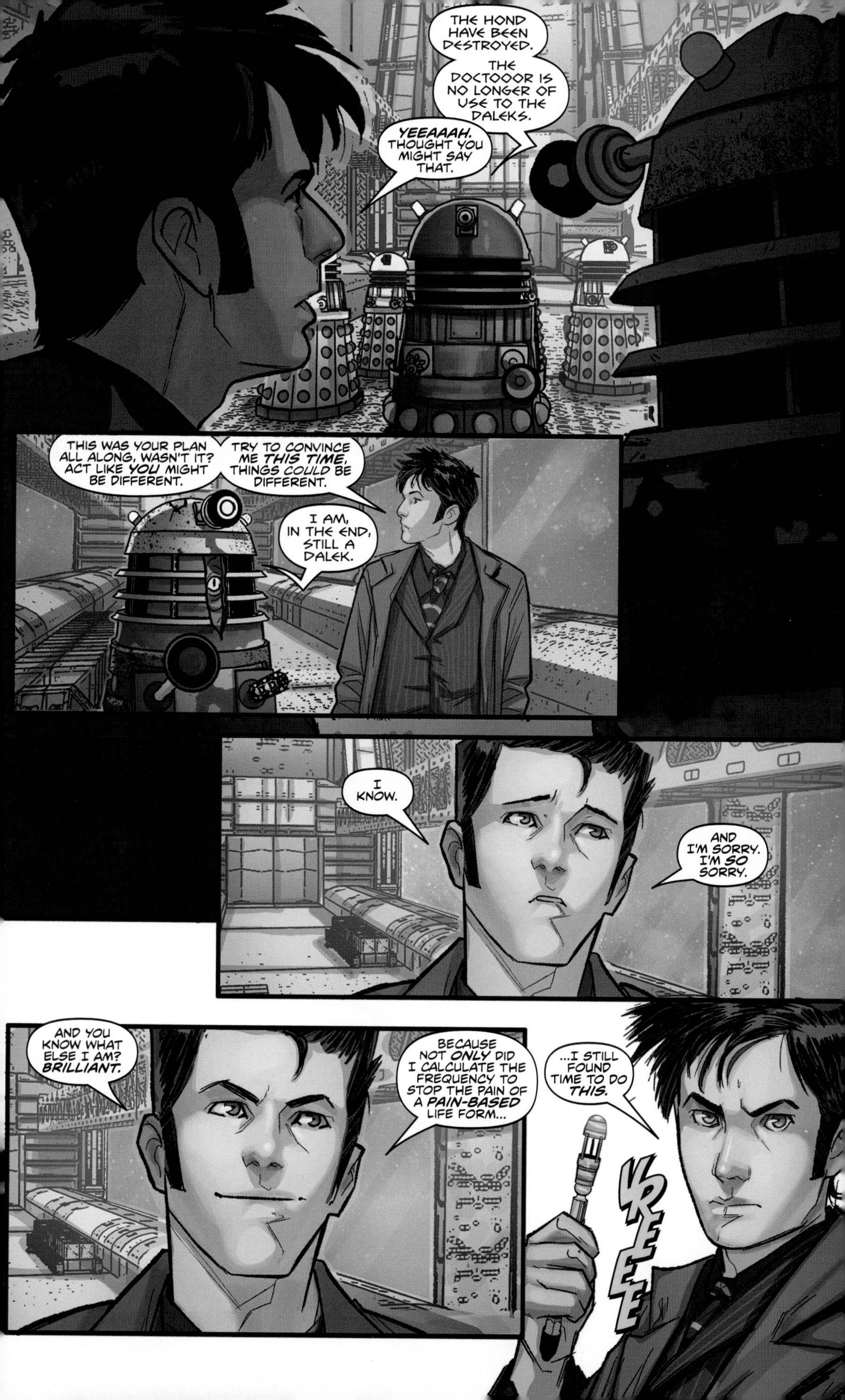
THE HOND HAVE BEEN DESTROYED.
THE DOCTOOOR IS NO LONGER OF USE TO THE DALEKS.
YEEAAAH. THOUGHT YOU MIGHT SAY THAT.
THIS WAS YOUR PLAN ALL ALONG, WASN'T IT? ACT LIKE YOU MIGHT BE DIFFERENT.
TRY TO CONVINCE ME THIS TIME, THINGS COULD BE DIFFERENT.
I AM, IN THE END, STILL A DALEK.
I KNOW.
AND I'M SORRY. I'M SO SORRY.
AND YOU KNOW WHAT ELSE I AM? BRILLIANT.
BECAUSE NOT ONLY DID I CALCULATE THE FREQUENCY TO STOP THE PAIN OF A PAIN-BASED LIFE FORM...
...I STILL FOUND TIME TO DO THIS.
VREEEE

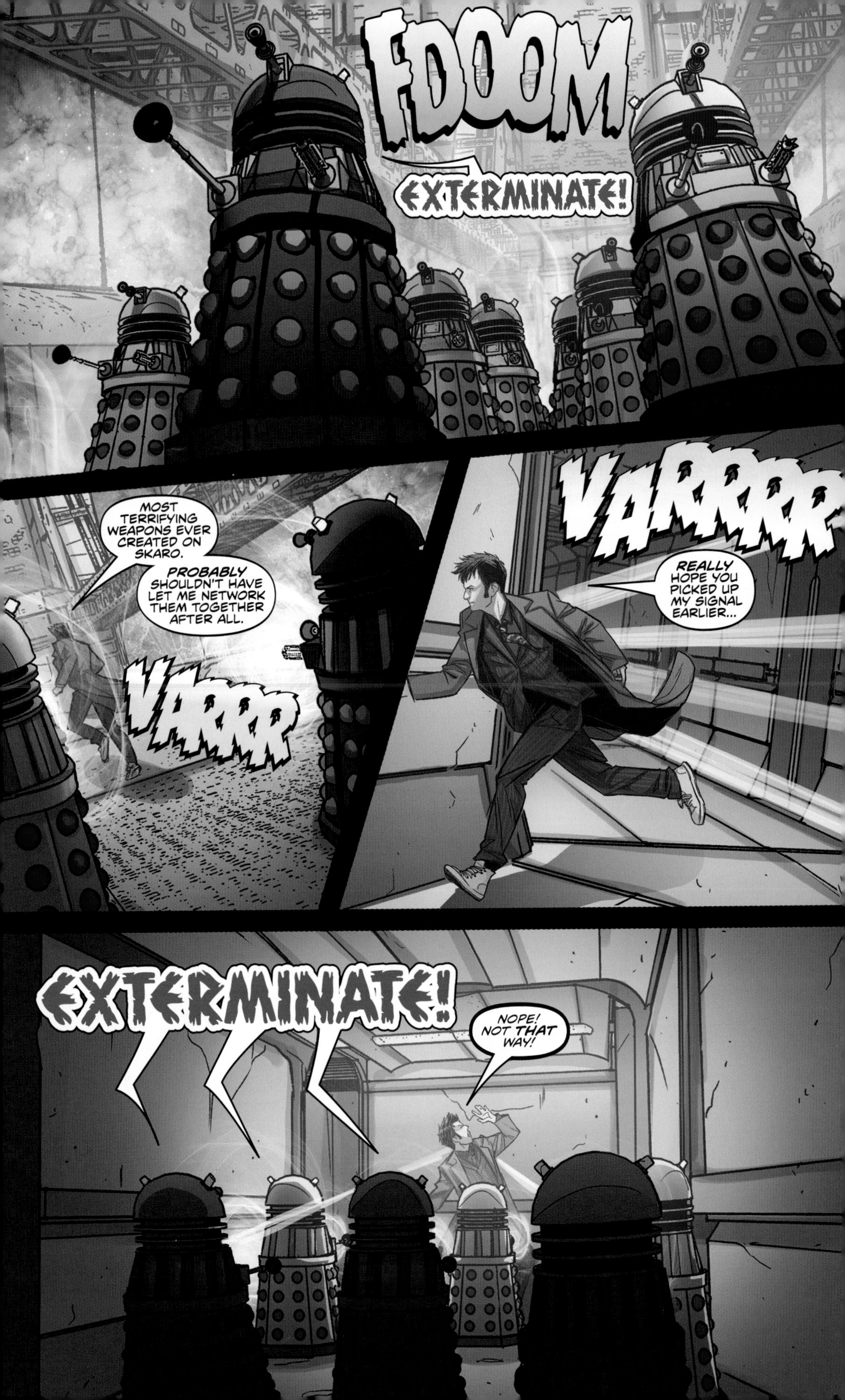
FDOOM
EXTERMINATE!
MOST TERRIFYING WEAPONS EVER CREATED ON SKARO.
PROBABLY SHOULDN'T HAVE LET ME NETWORK THEM TOGETHER AFTER ALL.
VARRP
VARRRP
REALLY HOPE YOU PICKED UP MY SIGNAL EARLIER...
EXTERMINATE!
NOPE! NOT THAT WAY!

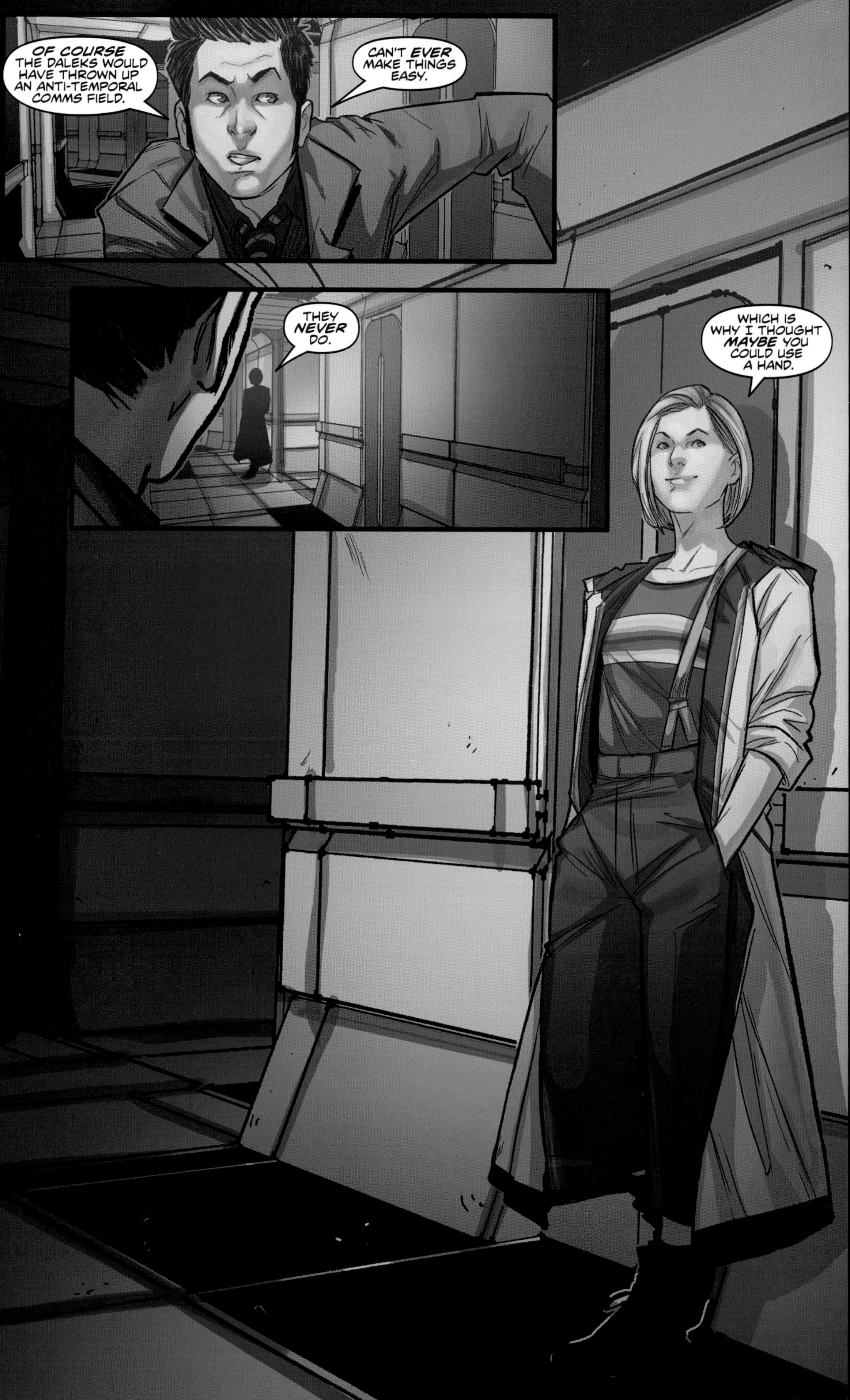
OF COURSE THE DALEKS WOULD HAVE THROWN UP AN ANTI-TEMPORAL COMMS FIELD.
CAN'T EVER MAKE THINGS EASY.
THEY NEVER DO.
WHICH IS WHY I THOUGHT MAYBE YOU COULD USE A HAND.

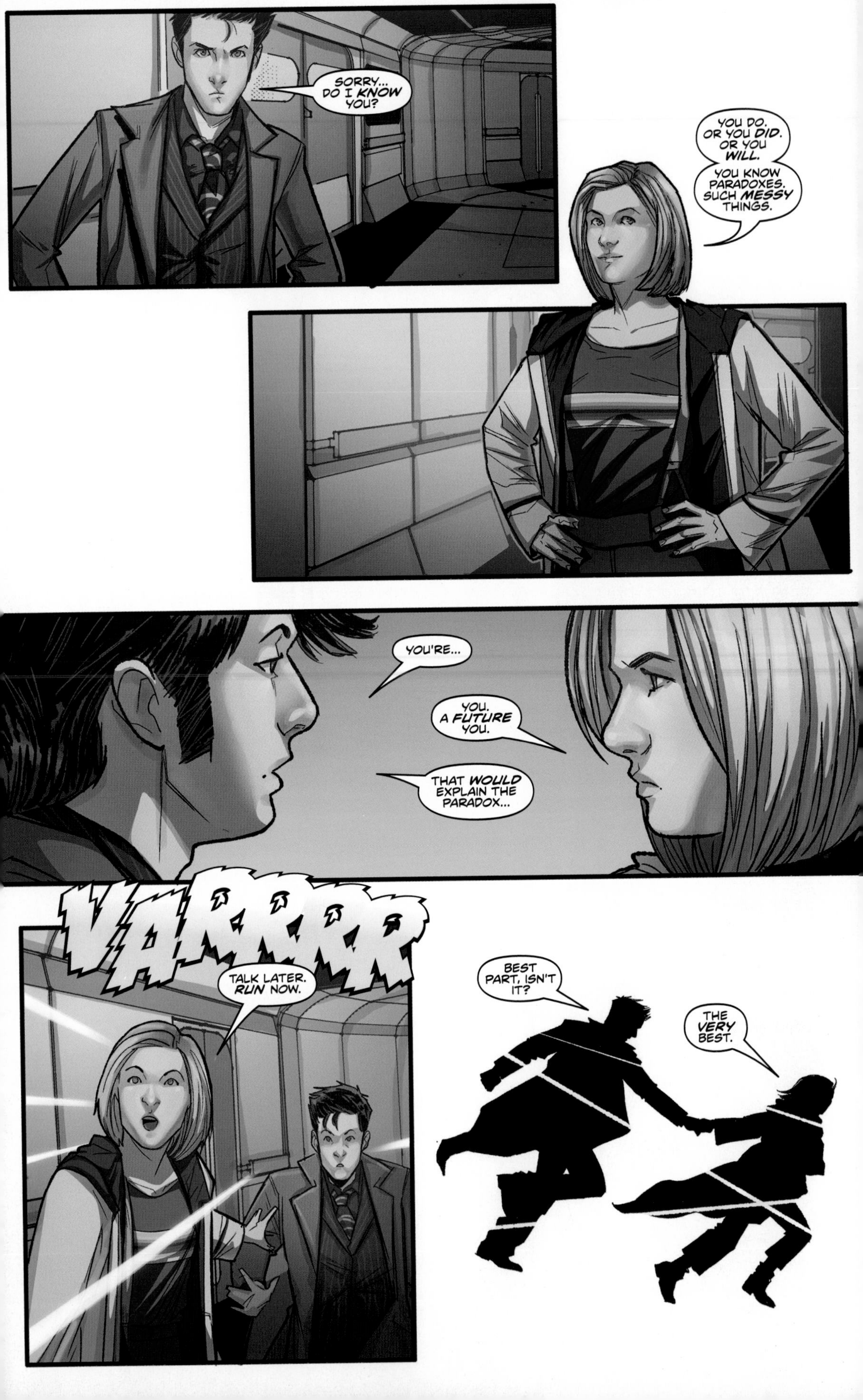
SORRY... DO I KNOW YOU?
YOU DO. OR YOU DID. OR YOU WILL.
YOU KNOW PARADOXES. SUCH MESSY THINGS.
YOU'RE...
YOU. A FUTURE YOU.
THAT WOULD EXPLAIN THE PARADOX...
VARRR
TALK LATER. RUN NOW.
BEST PART, ISN'T IT?
THE VERY BEST.

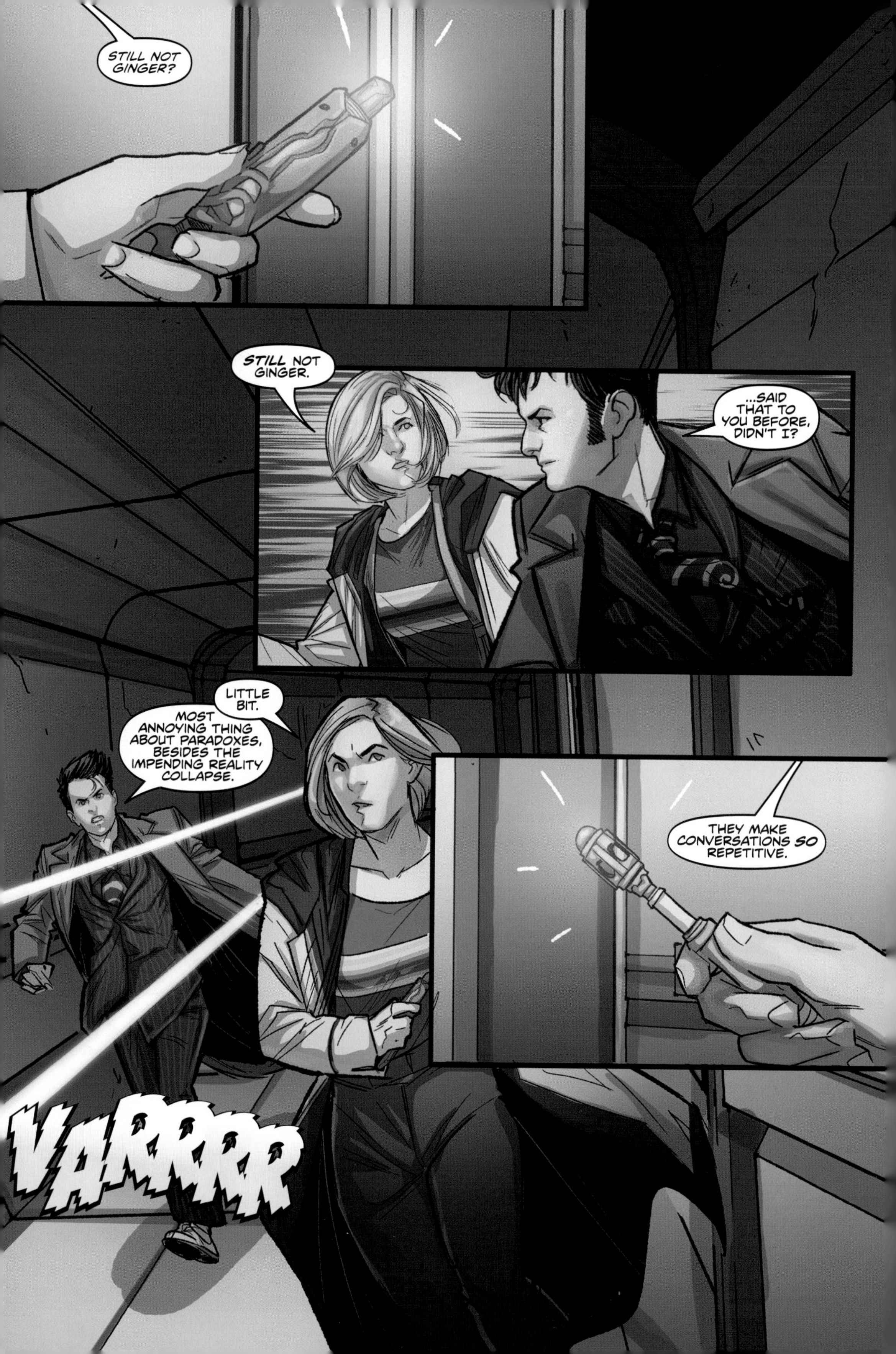
STILL NOT GINGER?
STILL NOT GINGER.
...SAID THAT TO YOU BEFORE, DIDN'T I?
LITTLE BIT.
MOST ANNOYING THING ABOUT PARADOXES, BESIDES THE IMPENDING REALITY COLLAPSE.
THEY MAKE CONVERSATIONS SO REPETITIVE.
VARRRR

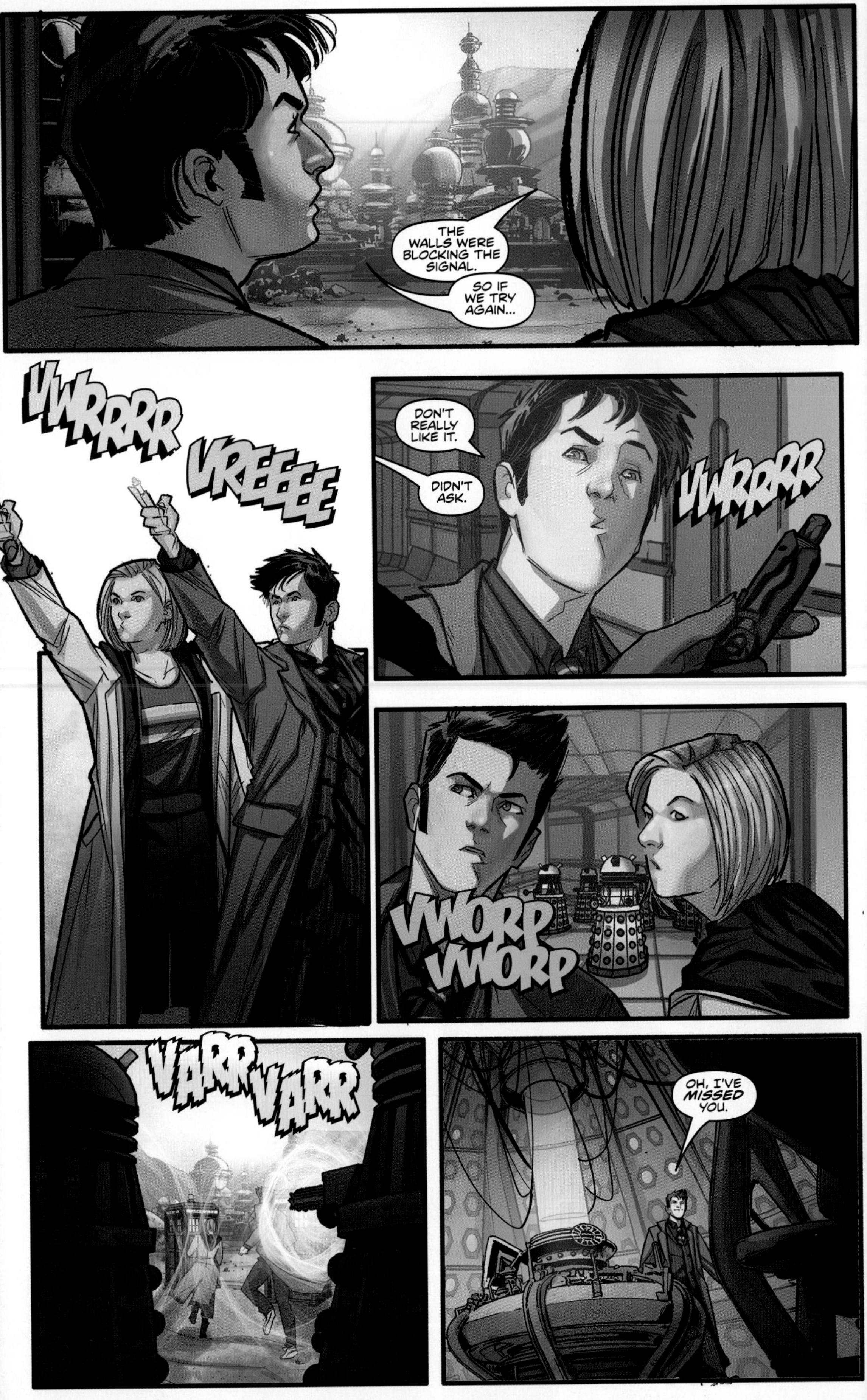
THE WALLS WERE BLOCKING THE SIGNAL.
SO IF WE TRY AGAIN...
VWRRRR
VREEEEE
DON'T REALLY LIKE IT.
DIDN'T ASK.
VWRRRR
VWORP VWORP
VARR VARR
OH, I'VE MISSED YOU.

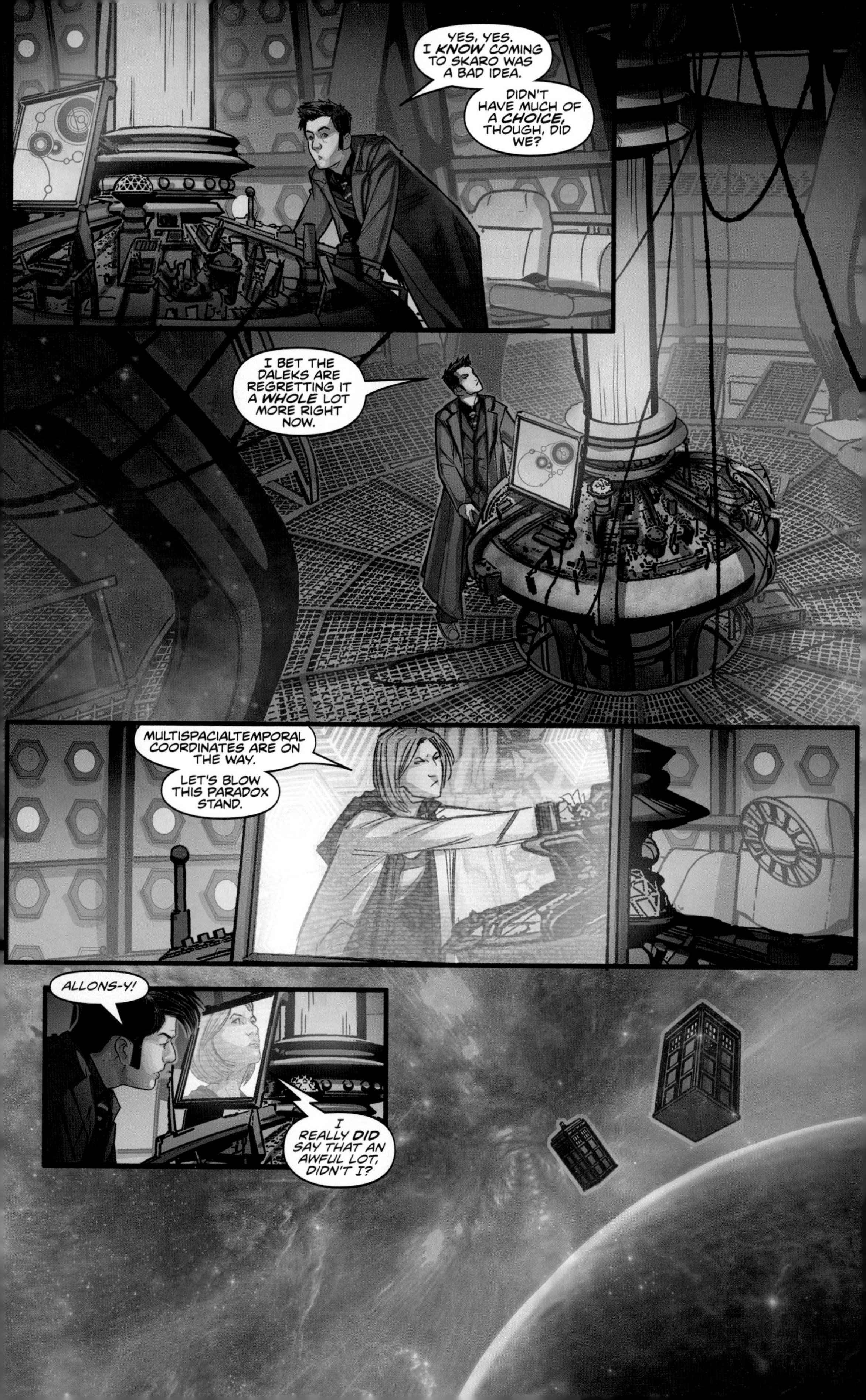
YES, YES. I KNOW COMING TO SKARO WAS A BAD IDEA.
DIDN'T HAVE MUCH OF A CHOICE, THOUGH, DID WE?
I BET THE DALEKS ARE REGRETTING IT A WHOLE LOT MORE RIGHT NOW.
MULTISPACIALTEMPORAL COORDINATES ARE ON THE WAY.
LET'S BLOW THIS PARADOX STAND.
ALLONS-Y!
I REALLY DID SAY THAT AN AWFUL LOT, DIDN'T I?

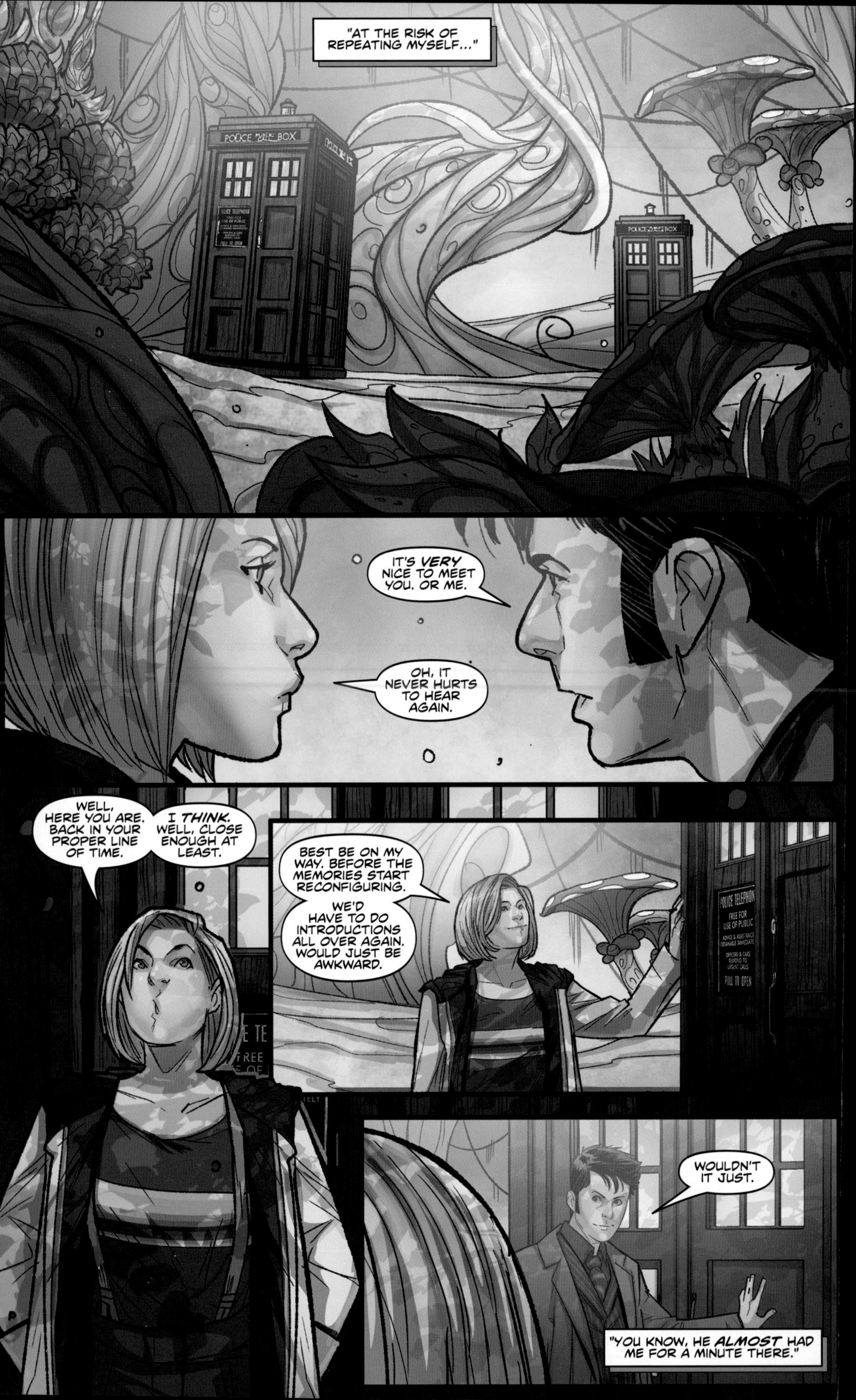

"AT THE RISK OF REPEATING MYSELF..."
POLICE PUBLIC BOX
IT'S VERY NICE TO MEET YOU. OR ME.
OH, IT NEVER HURTS TO HEAR AGAIN.
WELL, HERE YOU ARE. BACK IN YOUR PROPER LINE OF TIME.
I THINK. WELL, CLOSE ENOUGH AT LEAST.
BEST BE ON MY WAY. BEFORE THE MEMORIES START RECONFIGURING.
WE'D HAVE TO DO INTRODUCTIONS ALL OVER AGAIN. WOULD JUST BE AWKWARD.
POLICE TELEPHONE
FREE FOR USE OF PUBLIC
PULL TO OPEN
WOULDN'T IT JUST.
"YOU KNOW, HE ALMOST HAD ME FOR A MINUTE THERE."

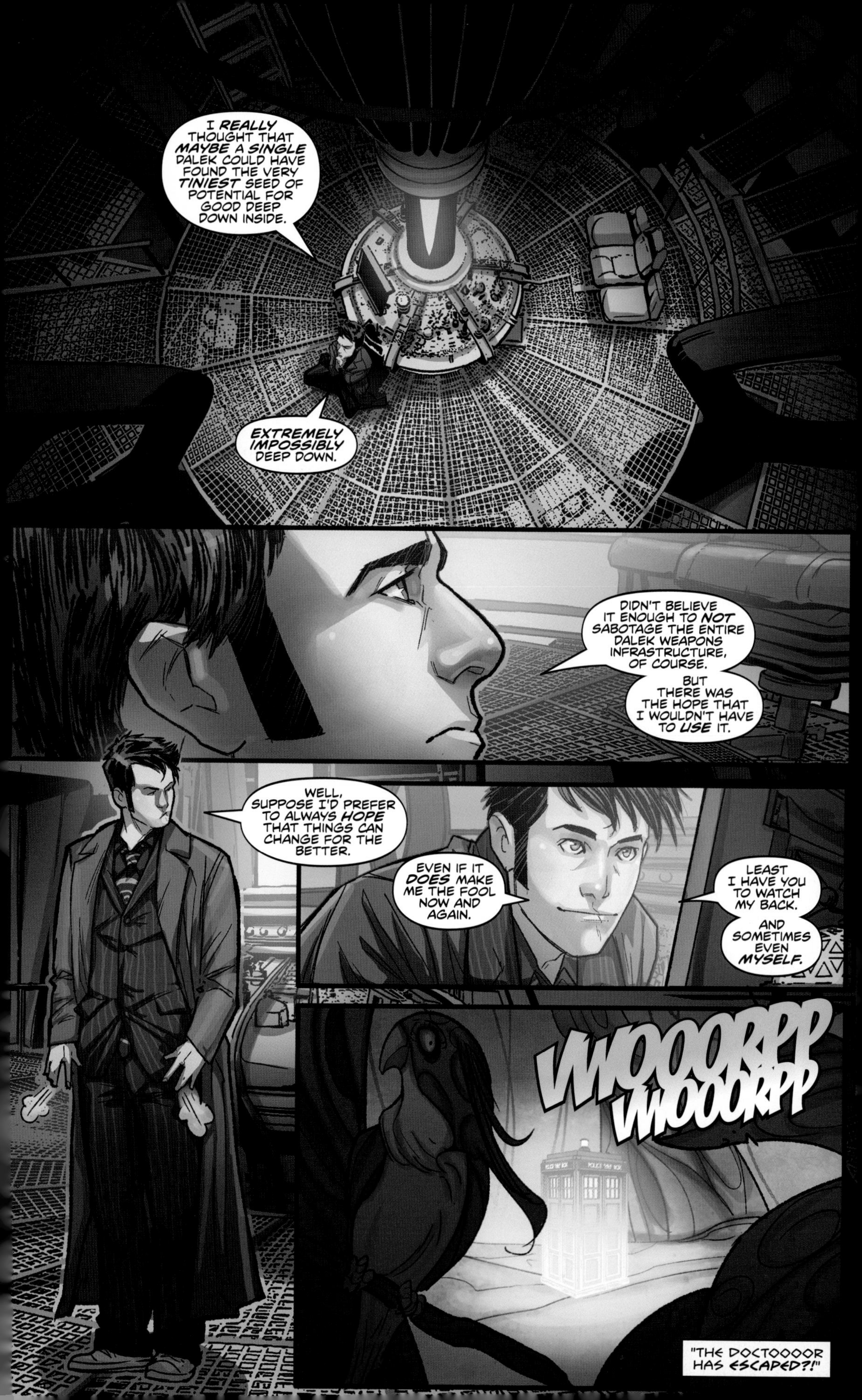

I REALLY THOUGHT THAT MAYBE A SINGLE DALEK COULD HAVE FOUND THE VERY TINIEST SEED OF POTENTIAL FOR GOOD DEEP DOWN INSIDE.
EXTREMELY IMPOSSIBLY DEEP DOWN.
DIDN'T BELIEVE IT ENOUGH TO NOT SABOTAGE THE ENTIRE DALEK WEAPONS INFRASTRUCTURE, OF COURSE.
BUT THERE WAS THE HOPE THAT I WOULDN'T HAVE TO USE IT.
WELL, SUPPOSE I'D PREFER TO ALWAYS HOPE THAT THINGS CAN CHANGE FOR THE BETTER.
EVEN IF IT DOES MAKE ME THE FOOL NOW AND AGAIN.
LEAST I HAVE YOU TO WATCH MY BACK.
AND SOMETIMES EVEN MYSELF.
VWOOORPP
VWOOORPP
"THE DOCTOOOOR HAS ESCAPED?!"

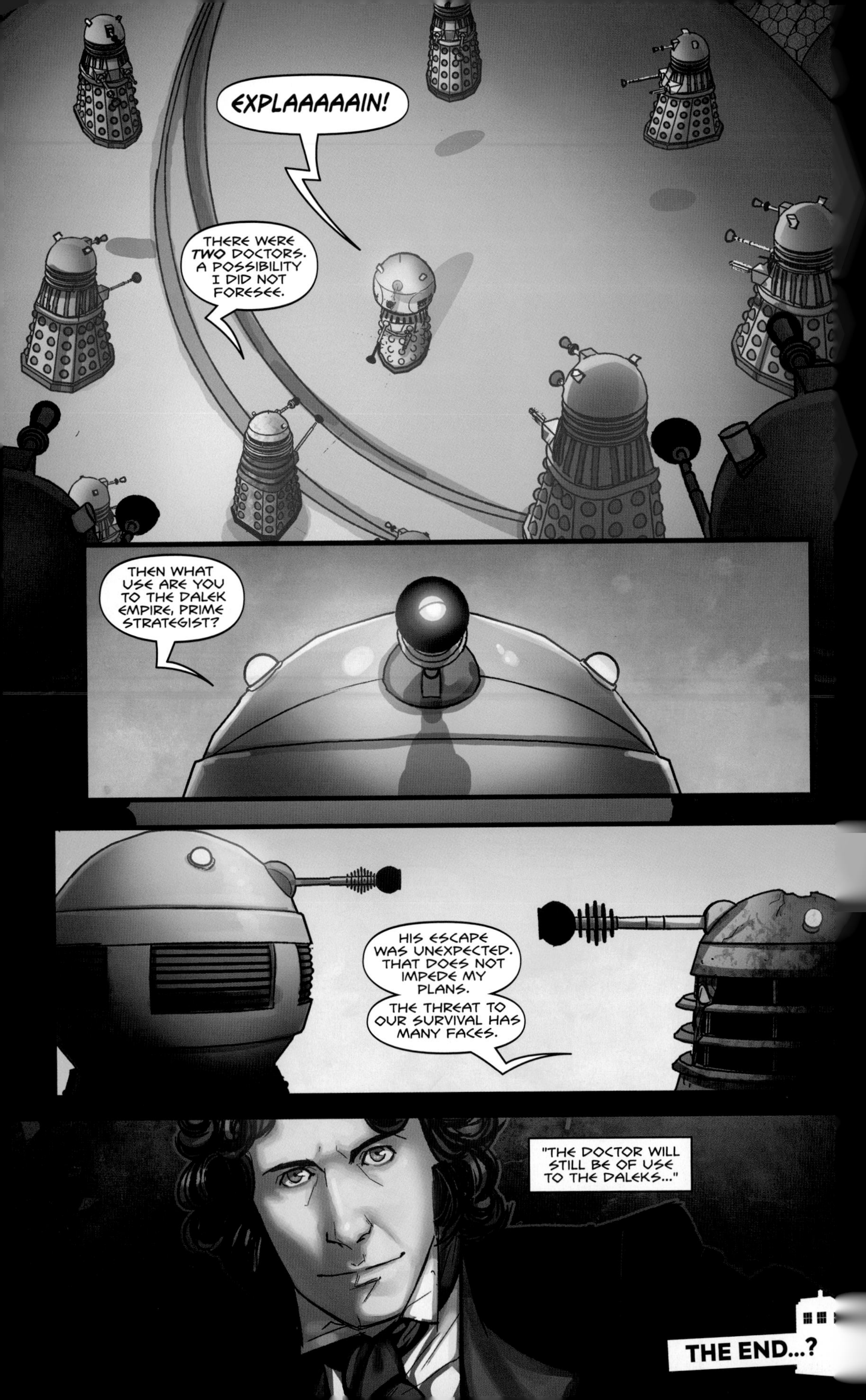
EXPLAAAAAIN!
THERE WERE TWO DOCTORS. A POSSIBILITY I DID NOT FORESEE.
THEN WHAT USE ARE YOU TO THE DALEK EMPIRE, PRIME STRATEGIST?
HIS ESCAPE WAS UNEXPECTED. THAT DOES NOT IMPEDE MY PLANS.
THE THREAT TO OUR SURVIVAL HAS MANY FACES.
"THE DOCTOR WILL STILL BE OF USE TO THE DALEKS..."
THE END...?

BBC

DOCTOR WHO

# TIME LORD VICTORIOUS

## Covers Gallery

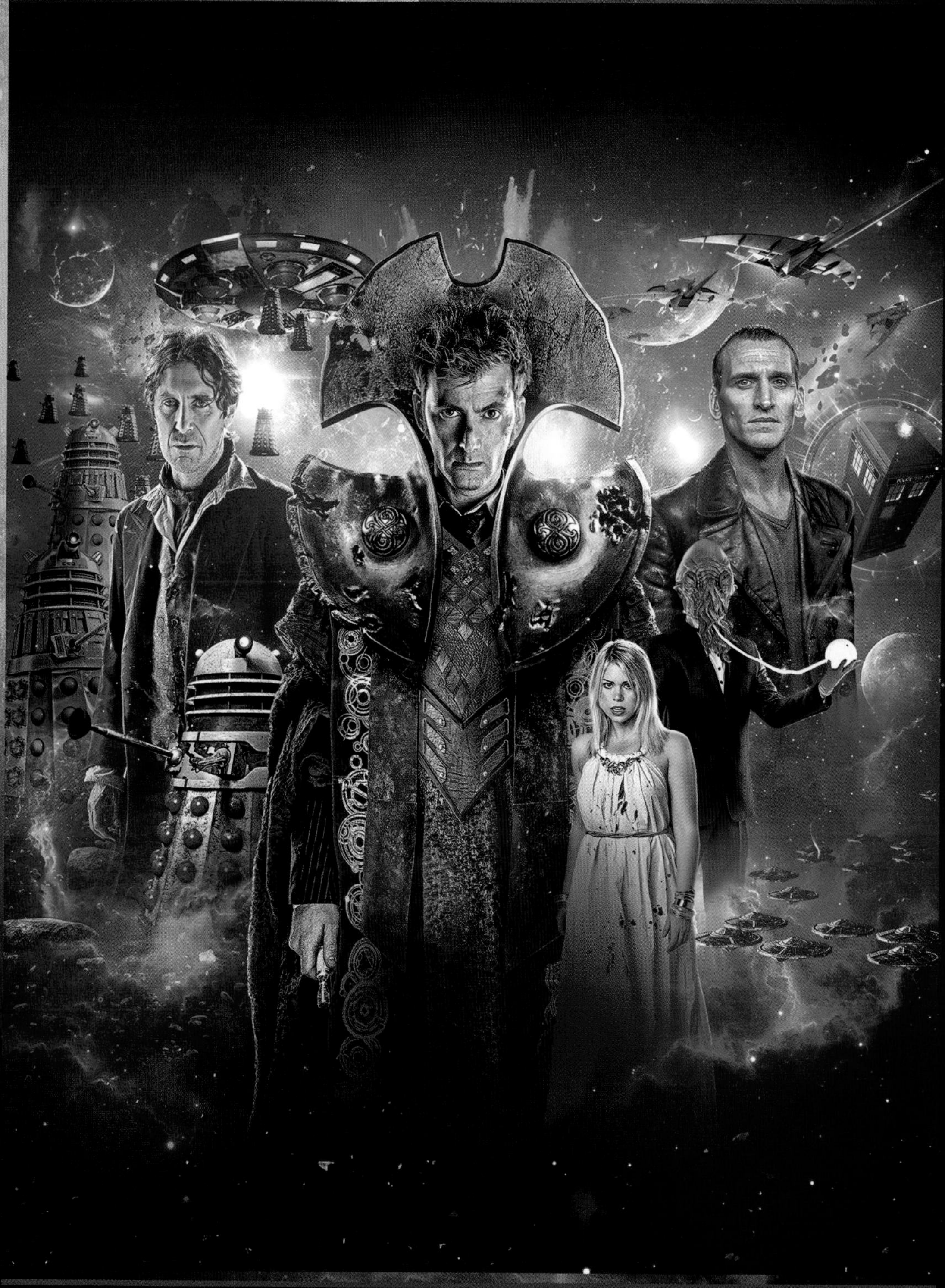

ISSUE #1 COVER A • LEE BINDING

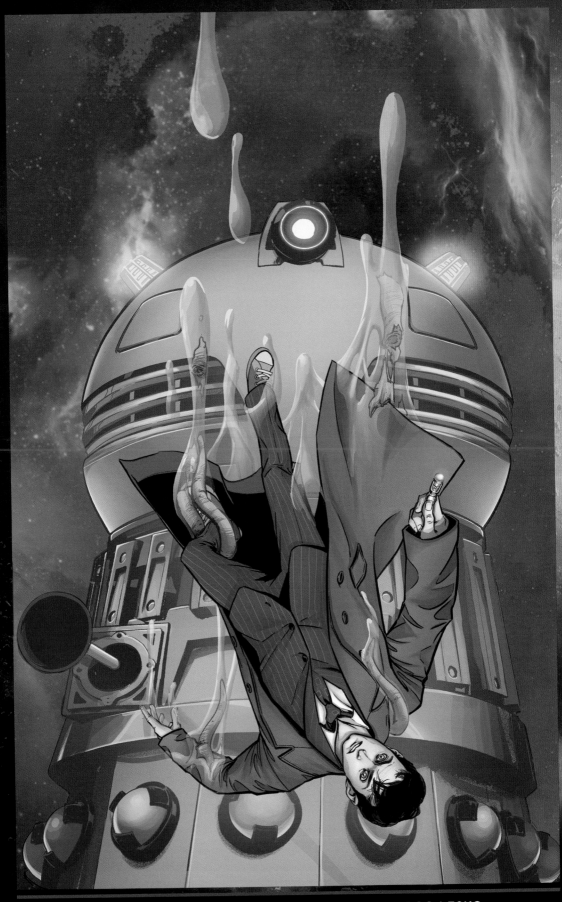

ISSUE #1 COVER B • PRISCILLA PETRAITES & MARCO LESKO

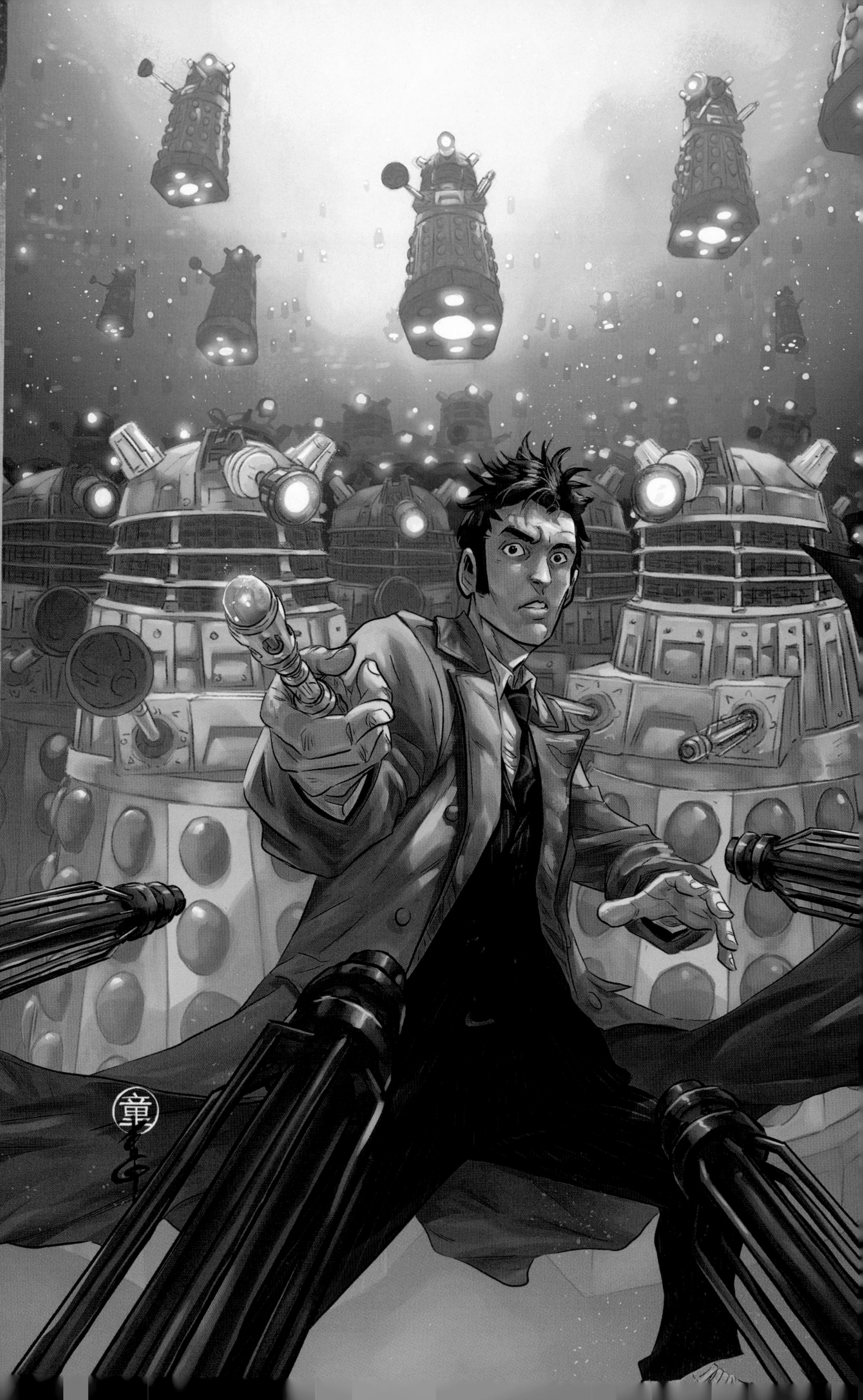

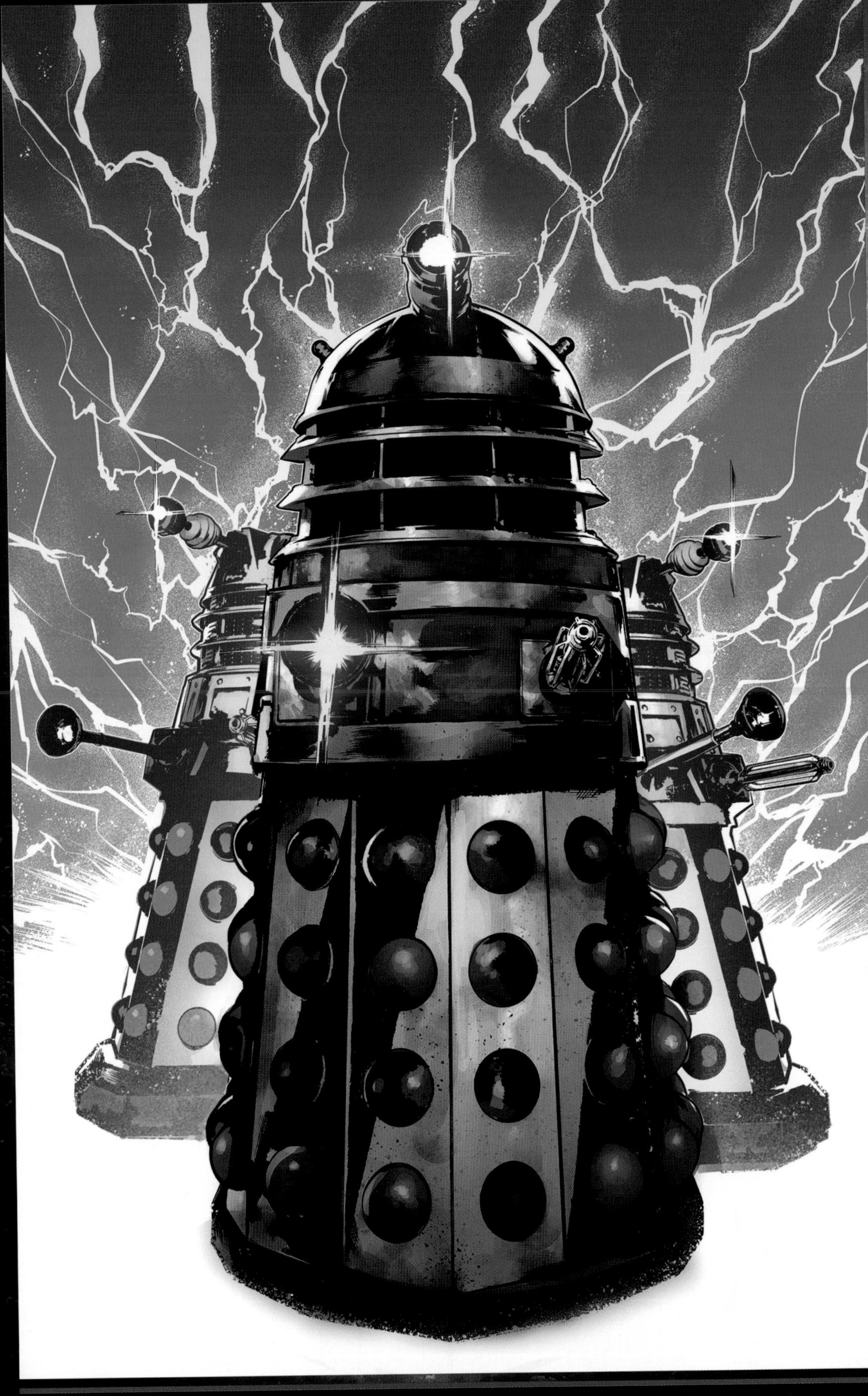

ISSUE #1 COVER D • HENDRY PRASETYA & SUNNY GHO

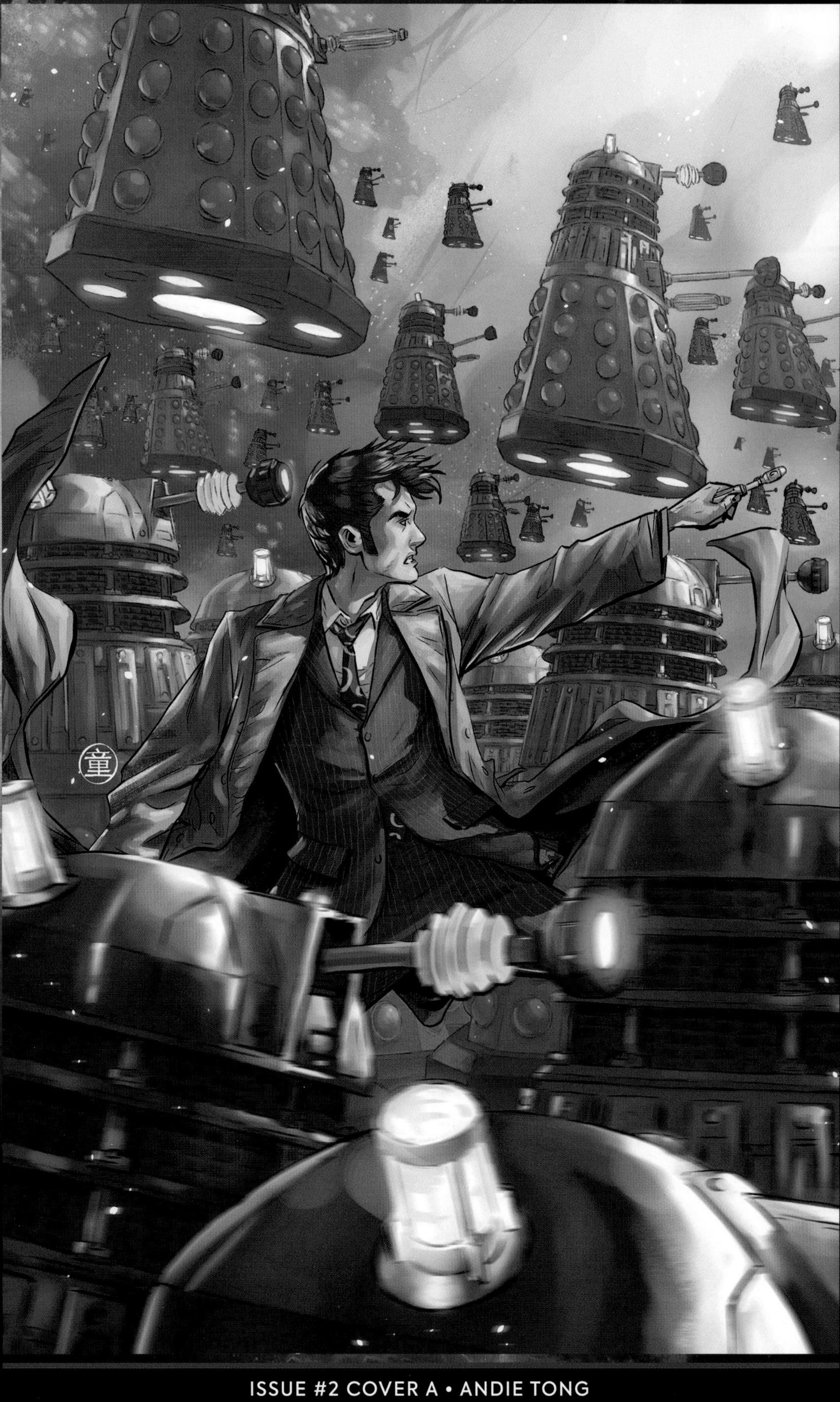

ISSUE #2 COVER A • ANDIE TONG

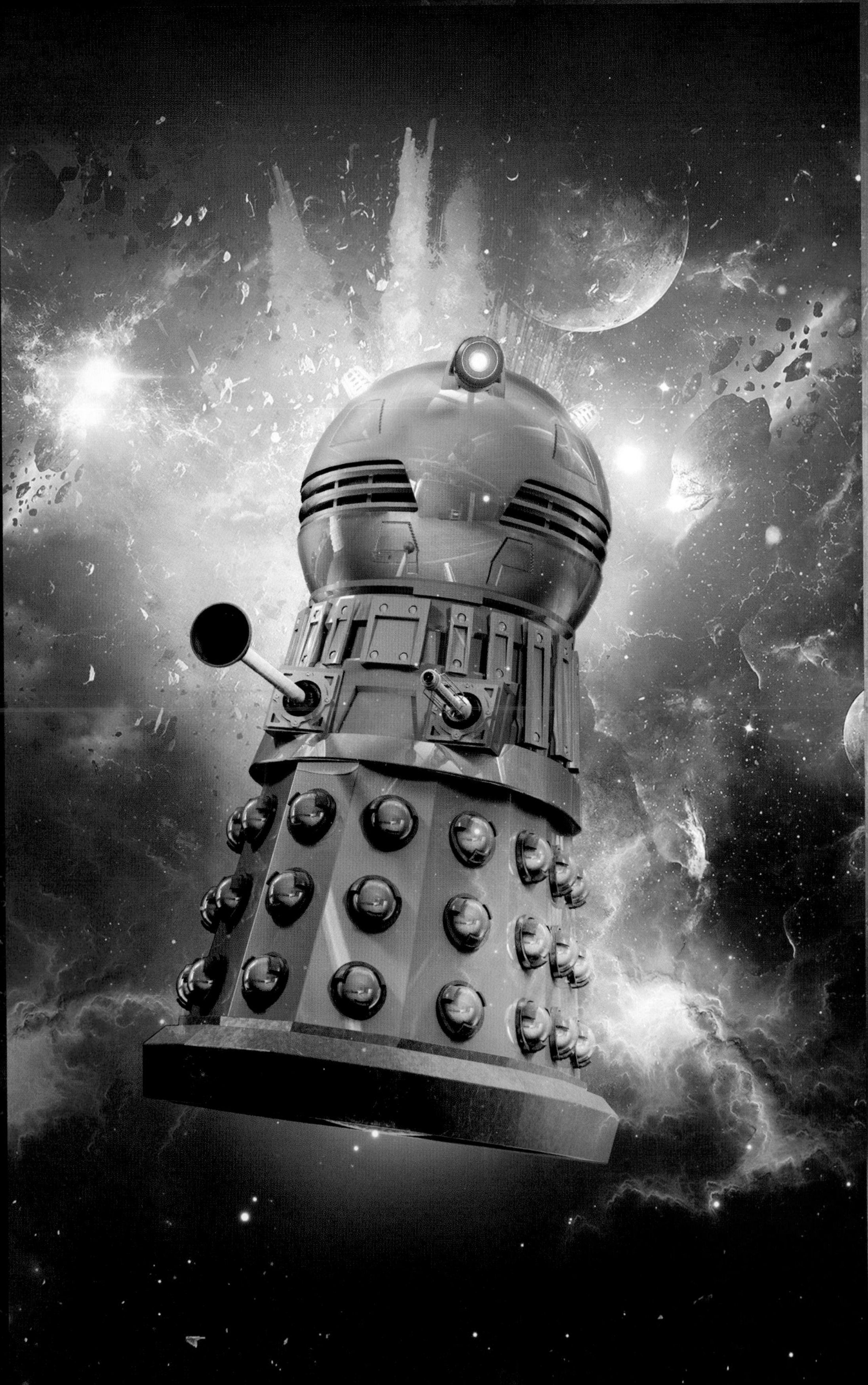

ISSUE #2 COVER B • PHOTO

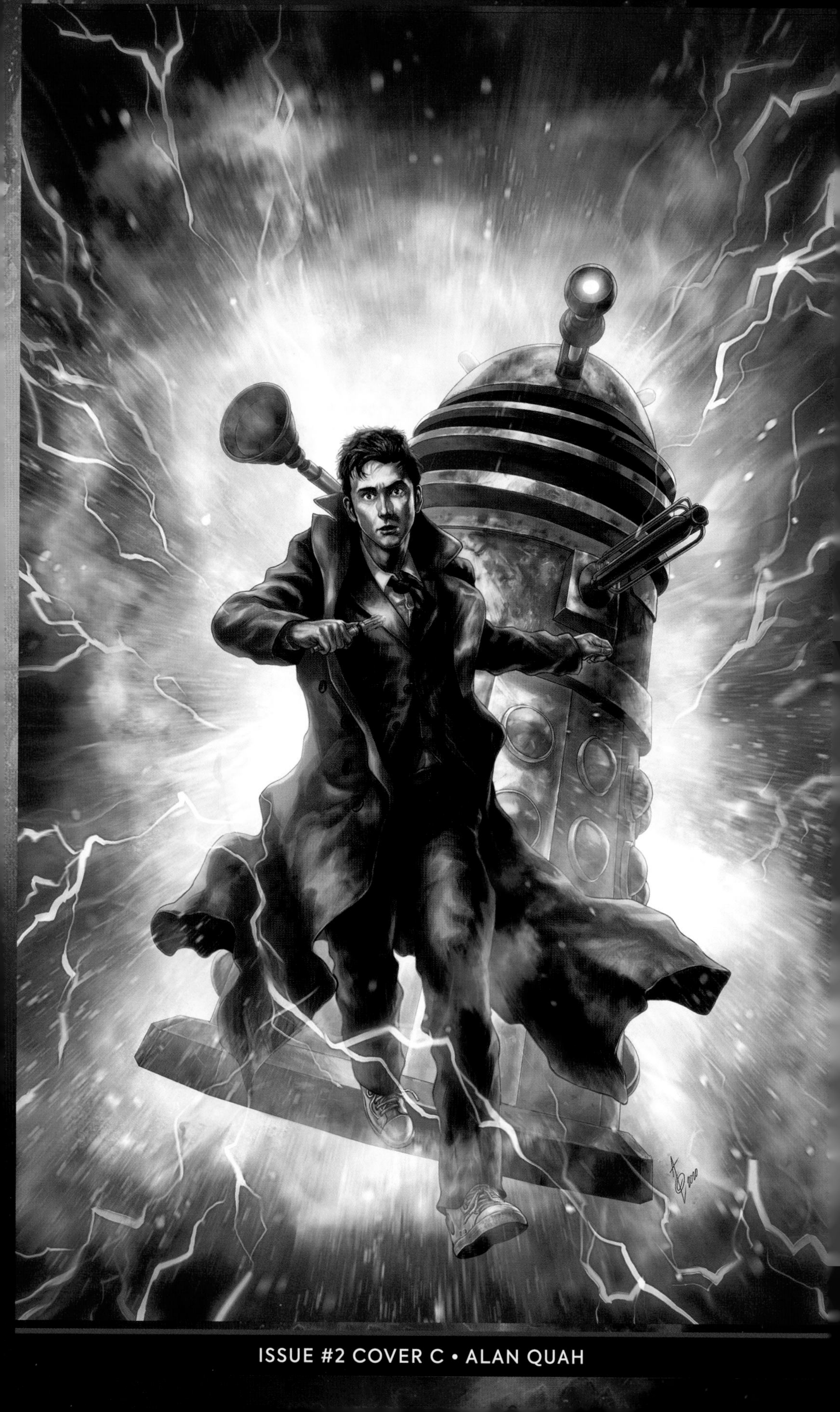

ISSUE #2 COVER C • ALAN QUAH

# Road to Victory
## An interview with James Goss

**Hi James! We're really excited about this incredible *Doctor Who: Time Lord Victorious* crossover series. For those who might not remember, can you give us a bit of background as to what this title signifies?**

*Time Lord Victorious* unites all the Doctor Who licencees to tell a massive, epic story - something goes horribly wrong in the Dark Times at the start of the universe - a problem so big that it draws in various Doctors and the Dalek Empire.

**What is it like exploring this period in the Doctor's story when fans saw a darker side of a character that is loved by so many?**

It's a chance to see what happens when the Tenth Doctor becomes too confident. He's not evil, he's just biting off more than he can chew - and when a Time Lord does that, the universe breaks. He genuinely believes he can achieve anything, but his actions disrupt history on a massive scale. Whenever we've seen the Tenth Doctor go too far (and he does, several times) there's always been a Rose, or a Martha, or a Donna at his side.

This time there's no-one to kick him in the shins... well, until some of his previous incarnations get involved. And even then, it's not black and white - they're just as much the Doctor as he is. What if they start to see his point of view?

**The *Time Lord Victorious* adventure tale is not just something that Titan Comics are doing but is a multi-platform event that BBC Books, Big Finish and many other Doctor Who publishers are also a part of. How excited are you about this epic story featuring the Eighth, Ninth and Tenth Doctor teaming up with familiar faces** and battling foes across audio, novel and comics?

The whole thing is epic but also epically simple. Each licensee tells a self-contained story that forms part of a patchwork quilt. If you just want to read Titan's BRILLIANT comic (where their Tenth Doctor encounters an impossibly resurrected Dalek Empire) then you can - it has a beginning and a middle and an end. But hopefully you'll be inspired to see where the story is picked up in the audio or the books, or take another path entirely - there are lots of different ways to experience *Time Lord Victorious*, and obviously, I'd love people to do all of them, but you don't have to in order to massively enjoy it.

One of the great things about the fandom is that they're excellent at helping each other out and recommending things to each other. It's going to be so much fun watching them flag "well, if you're wondering how X got there, you'll love the comics-".

The other unique thing about *Doctor Who* is that it's a time travel brand, so the audience are used to consuming stories that are then enhanced by later episodes which actually take place earlier. They're a smart, positive fanbase – and this has been designed to be an inclusive, not an exclusive adventure. You don't need a huge amount of built-in knowledge – Doctor Who is a Time Lord and the Daleks are nasty just about covers it.

**While these stories feature multiple different doctors, each with their own quirks and personalities, what do you think is the overarching link that connects this character in their many iterations?**
The fundamental feature of the Doctor is that they're all kind people. Even when the Tenth Doctor goes too far, it's out of kindness. He really, really wants to do something good, and gets so wrapped up in that, that he loses sight of himself for a moment – and then looks around and goes "Wait, how did I end up here?"
It's great that he's being challenged by two former selves who've suffered in different ways – the Eighth Doctor is an optimist who learns the universe doesn't love him back, and the Ninth Doctor is a man rebuilding his life after he's lost everything. Seeing them come together is going to be interesting.

**What is it about this epic storyline that you think will excite fans the most?**
It's designed to be FUN. Each strand

of it puts entertainment first. This is *Doctor Who* you can take home to meet your mum. There are space battles and assassins and vampires and decisions that crack the universe open. The Titan comic alone features the Daleks at their most cunning and most vicious. And every *Doctor Who* fan wants to share how brilliant the show is with a friend – and hopefully *Time Lord Victorious* will allow them to do that endlessly.

# The Art Process
## Creating Doctor Who

LAYOUT AND INKS BY ROBERTA INGRANATA
COLORS BY ENRICA EREN ANGIOLINI

A pivotal moment in Defender of the Daleks - the Doctor sees his mortal enemies for the first time. Little does he know they want his help...

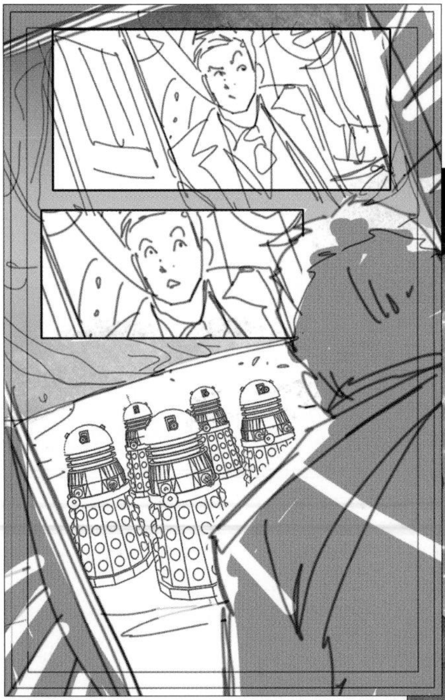

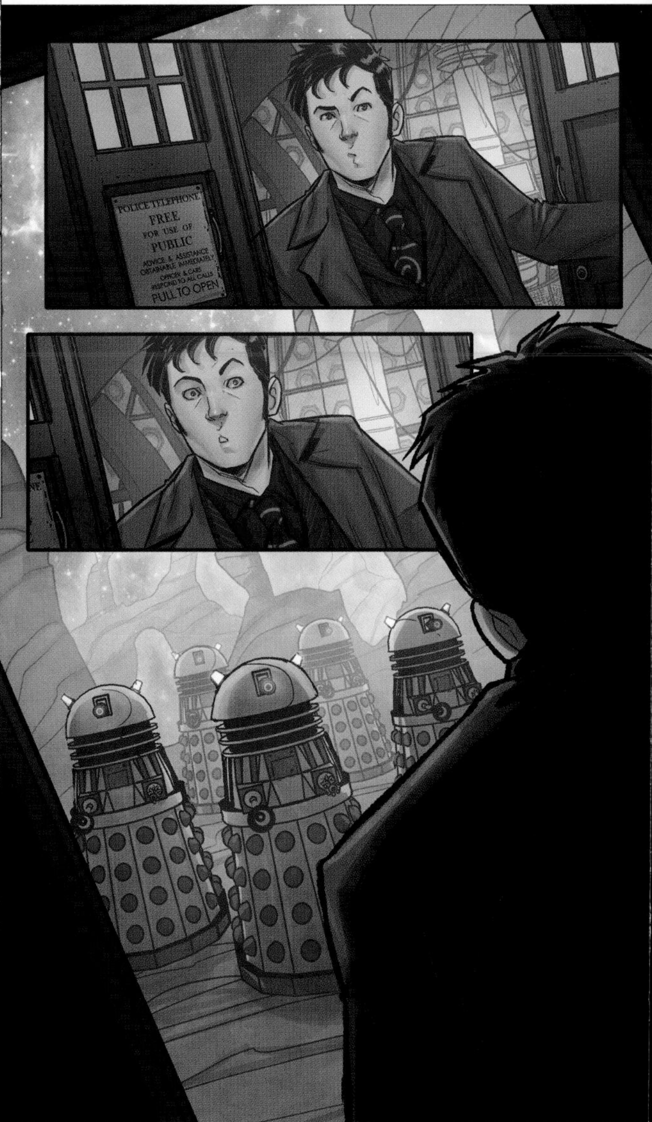
POLICE TELEPHONE
FREE
FOR USE OF
PUBLIC
PULL TO OPEN

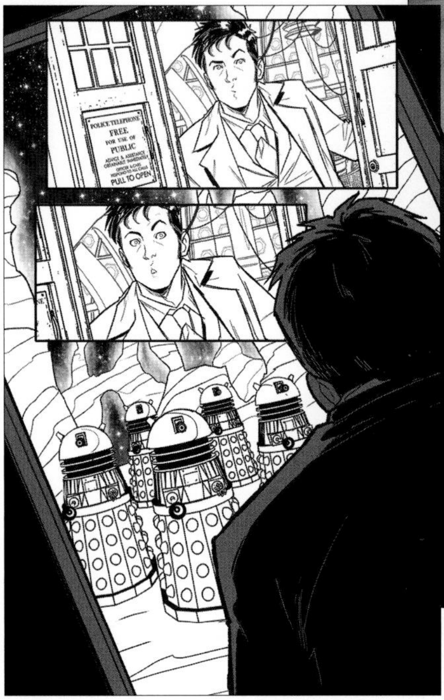
POLICE TELEPHONE
FREE
FOR USE OF
PUBLIC
PULL TO OPEN

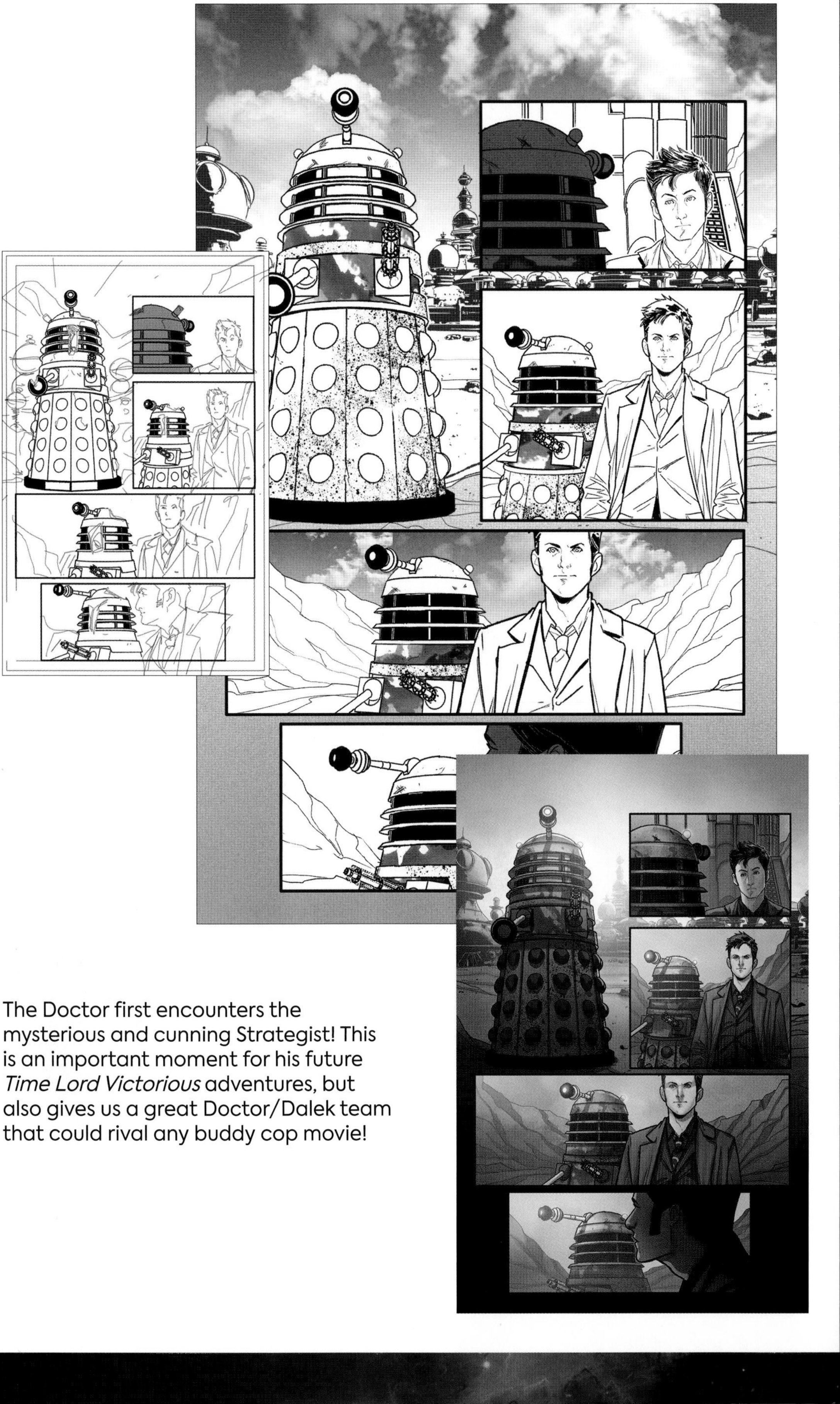

The Doctor first encounters the mysterious and cunning Strategist! This is an important moment for his future *Time Lord Victorious* adventures, but also gives us a great Doctor/Dalek team that could rival any buddy cop movie!

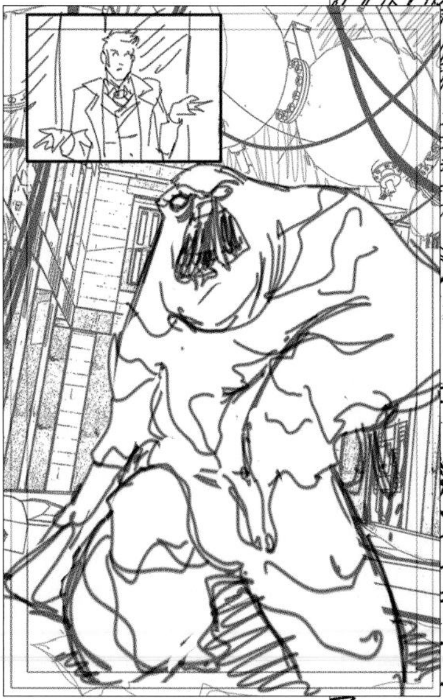

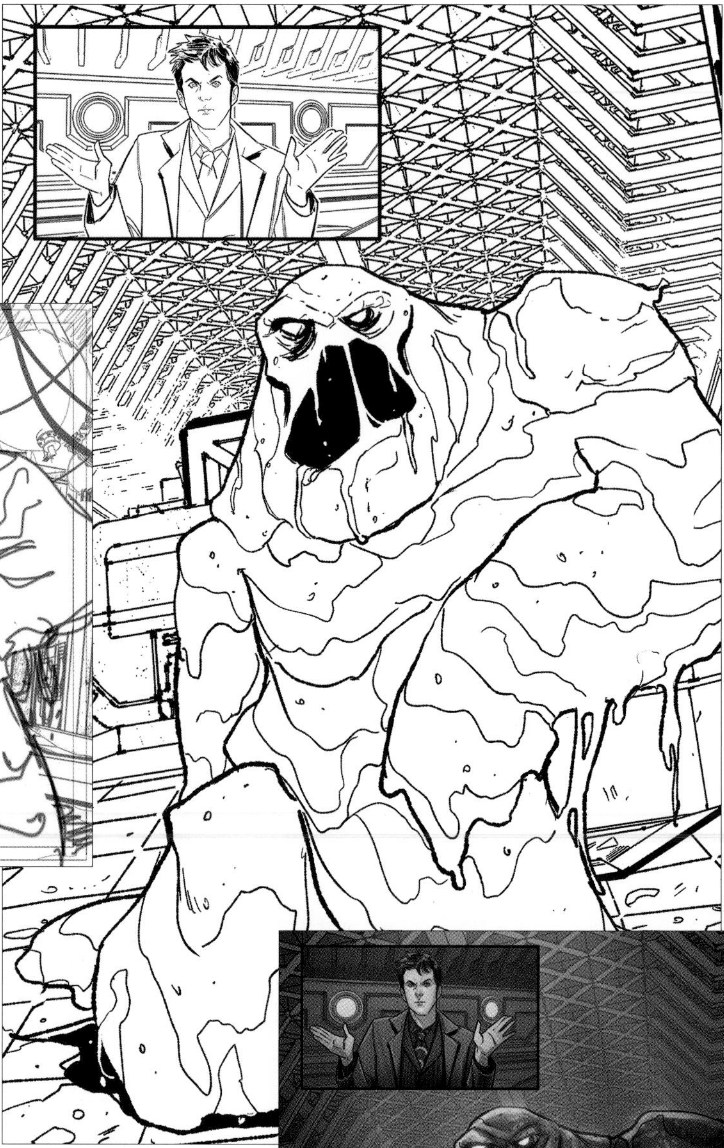

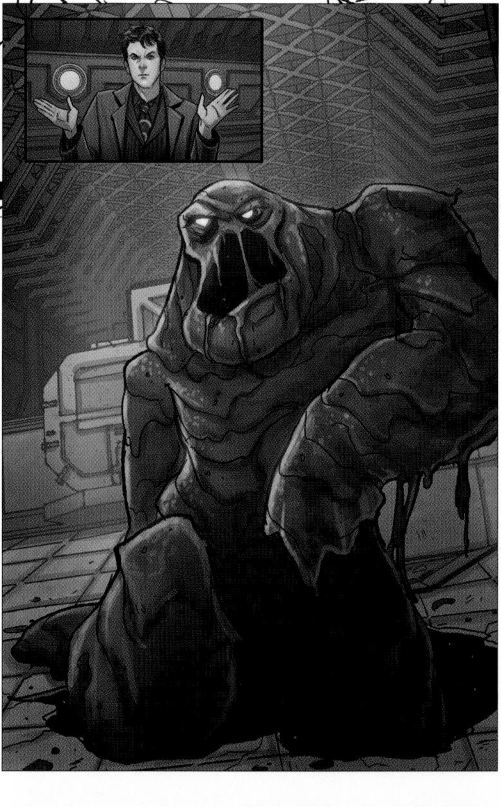

Here we see the menacing reveal of the entity that is: the Hond! Creatures of pain and suffering, death is left in their wake across the universe. This striking panel shows their sheer monstrosity and yet there is an essence of melancholy here, which of course the Doctor understands all too well.

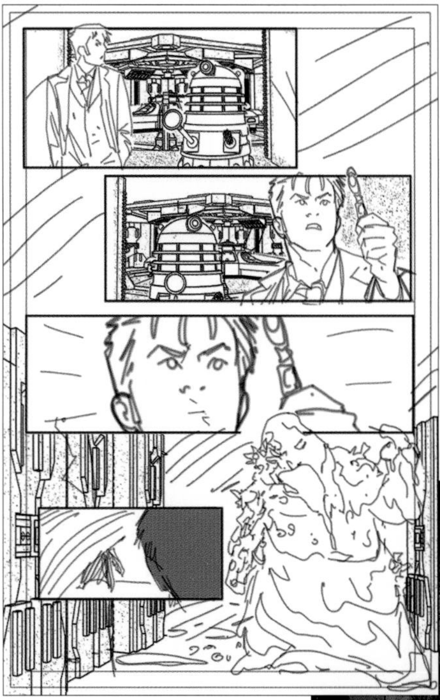

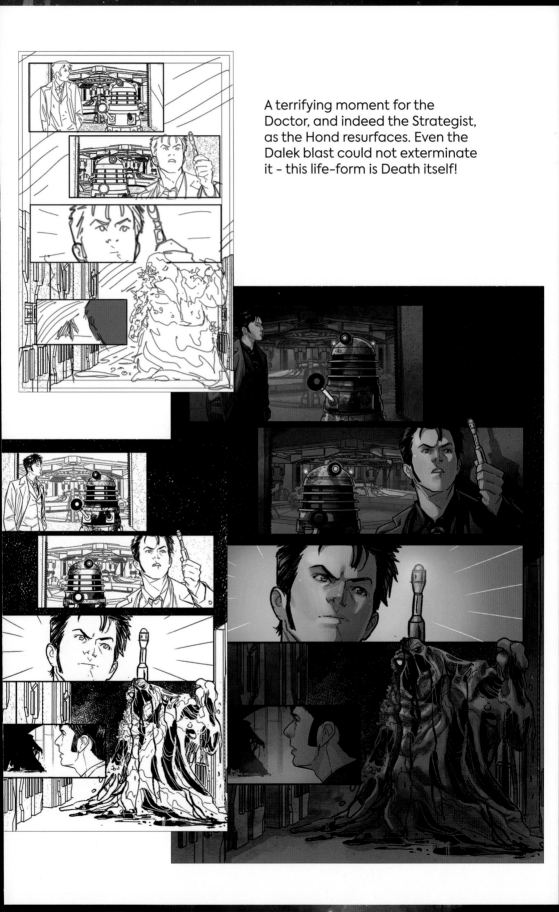

A terrifying moment for the Doctor, and indeed the Strategist, as the Hond resurfaces. Even the Dalek blast could not exterminate it - this life-form is Death itself!

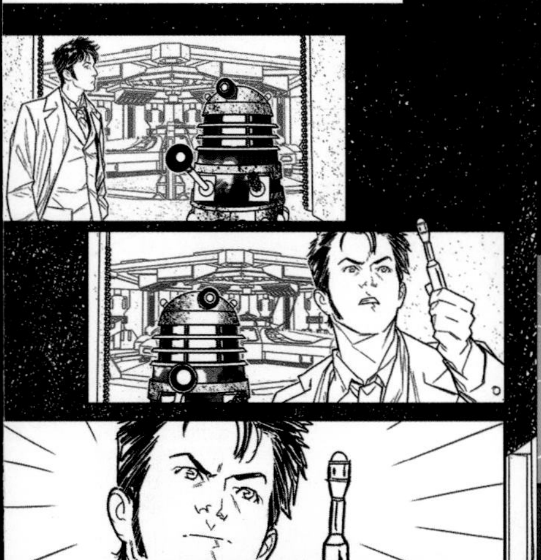

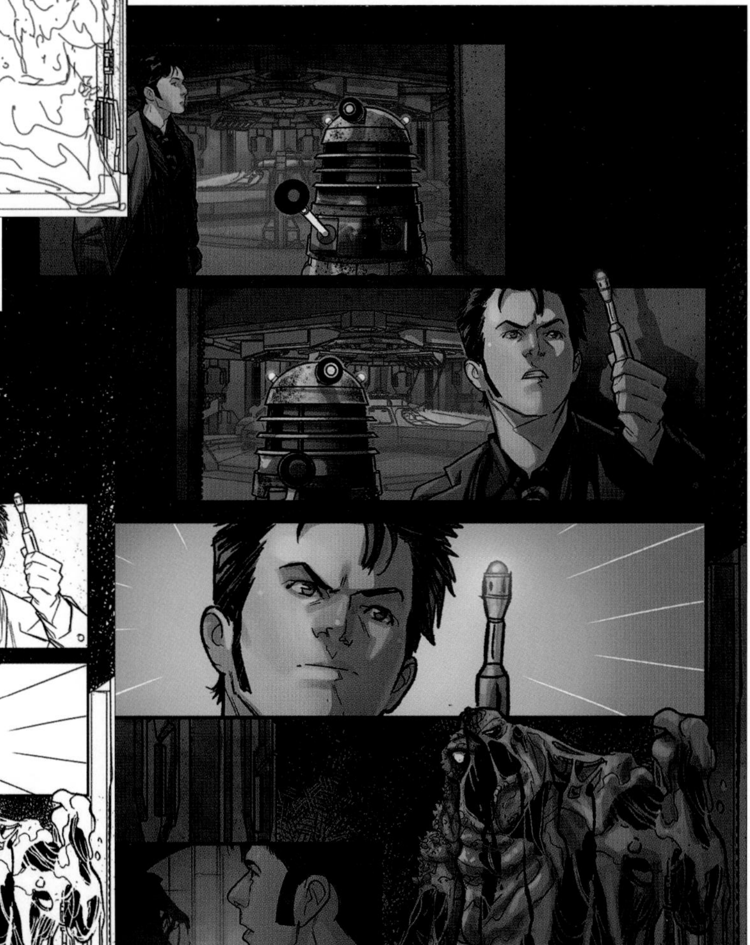

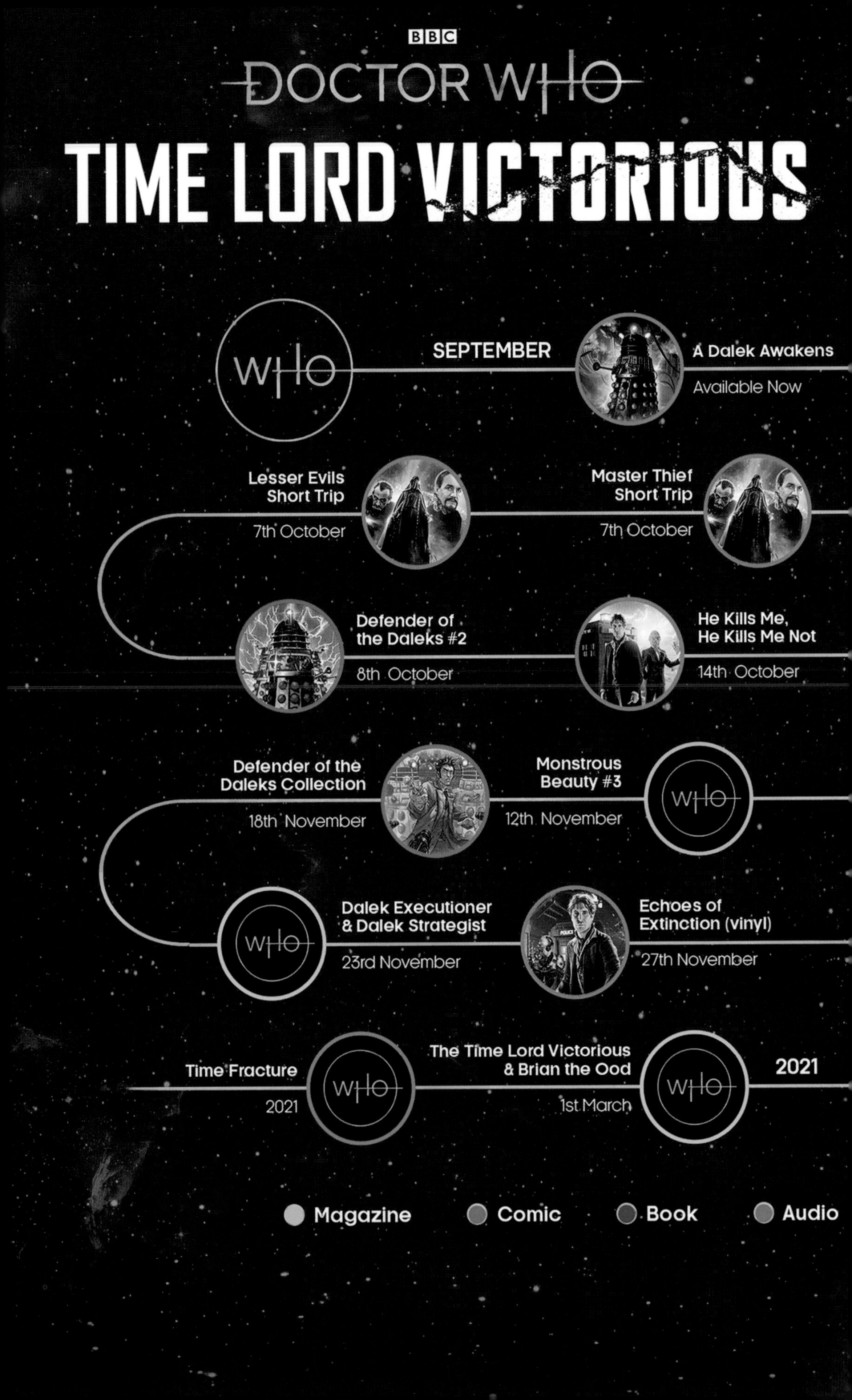
BBC
DOCTOR WHO
TIME LORD VICTORIOUS
SEPTEMBER
A Dalek Awakens
Available Now
Lesser Evils
Short Trip
7th October
Master Thief
Short Trip
7th October
Defender of
the Daleks #2
8th October
He Kills Me,
He Kills Me Not
14th October
Defender of the
Daleks Collection
18th November
Monstrous
Beauty #3
12th November
Dalek Executioner
& Dalek Strategist
23rd November
Echoes of
Extinction (vinyl)
27th November
Time Fracture
2021
The Time Lord Victorious
& Brian the Ood
1st March
2021
Magazine
Comic
Book
Audio

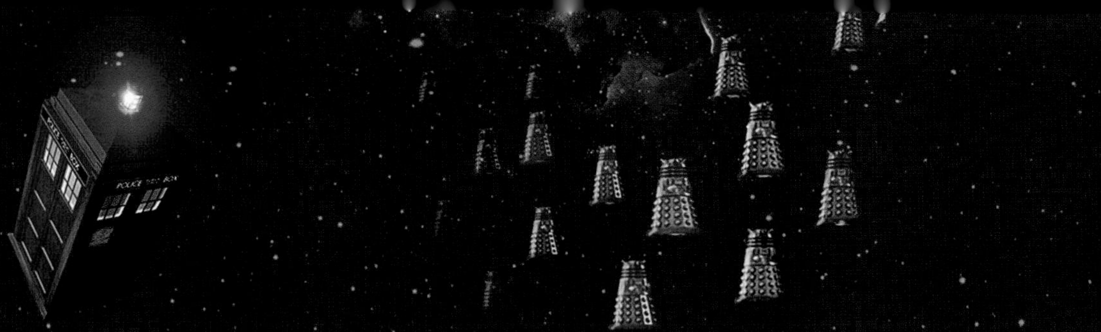

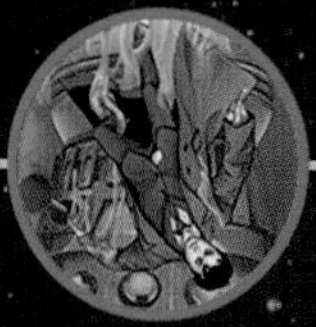

**Defender of the Daleks #1**
2nd September

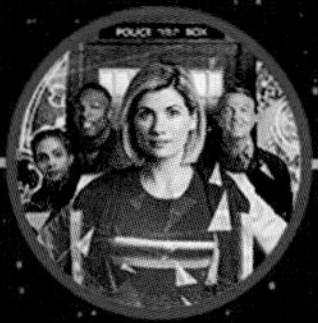

**The Annual 2021**
3rd September

**Monstrous Beauty #1**
17th September

## OCTOBER

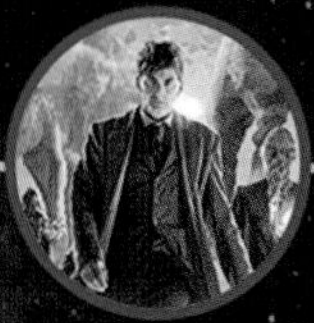

**The Knight, The Fool and the Dead**
1st October

**Monstrous Beauty #2**
15th October

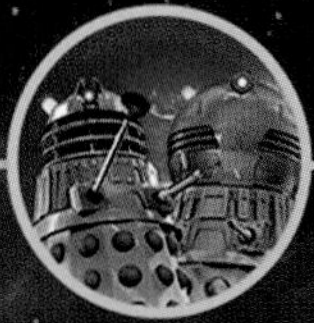

**Dalek Emperor & Dalek Drone**
20th October

## NOVEMBER

**Dalek Commander & Dalek Scientist**
1st November

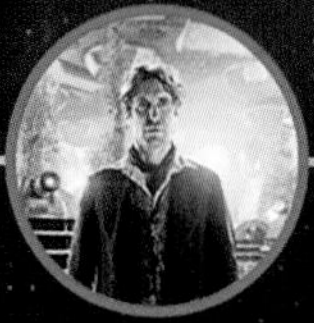

**The Enemy of My Enemy**
11th November

## DECEMBER

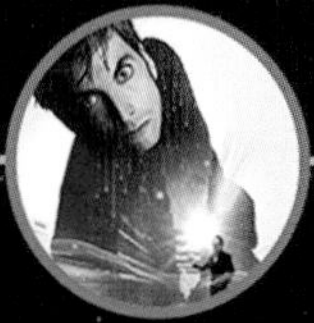

**The Minds of Magnox**
3rd December

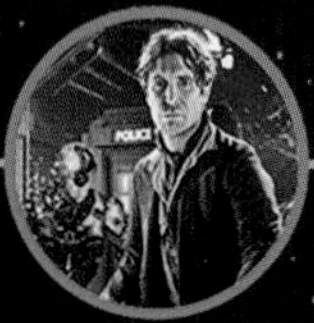

**Echoes of Extinction**
4th December

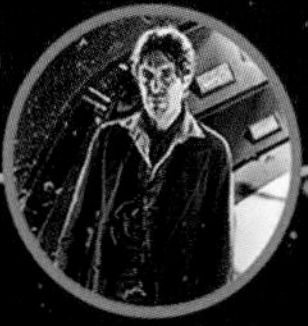

**Mutually Assured Destruction**
9th December

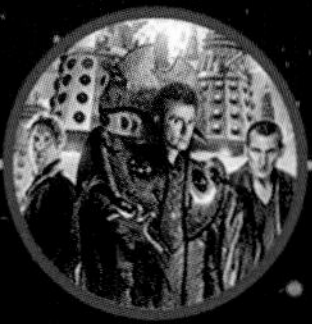

**All Flesh is Grass**
10th December

Merchandise

Live Experience (UK only)

**FOR MORE INFORMATION VISIT**
**TimeLordVictorious.com**

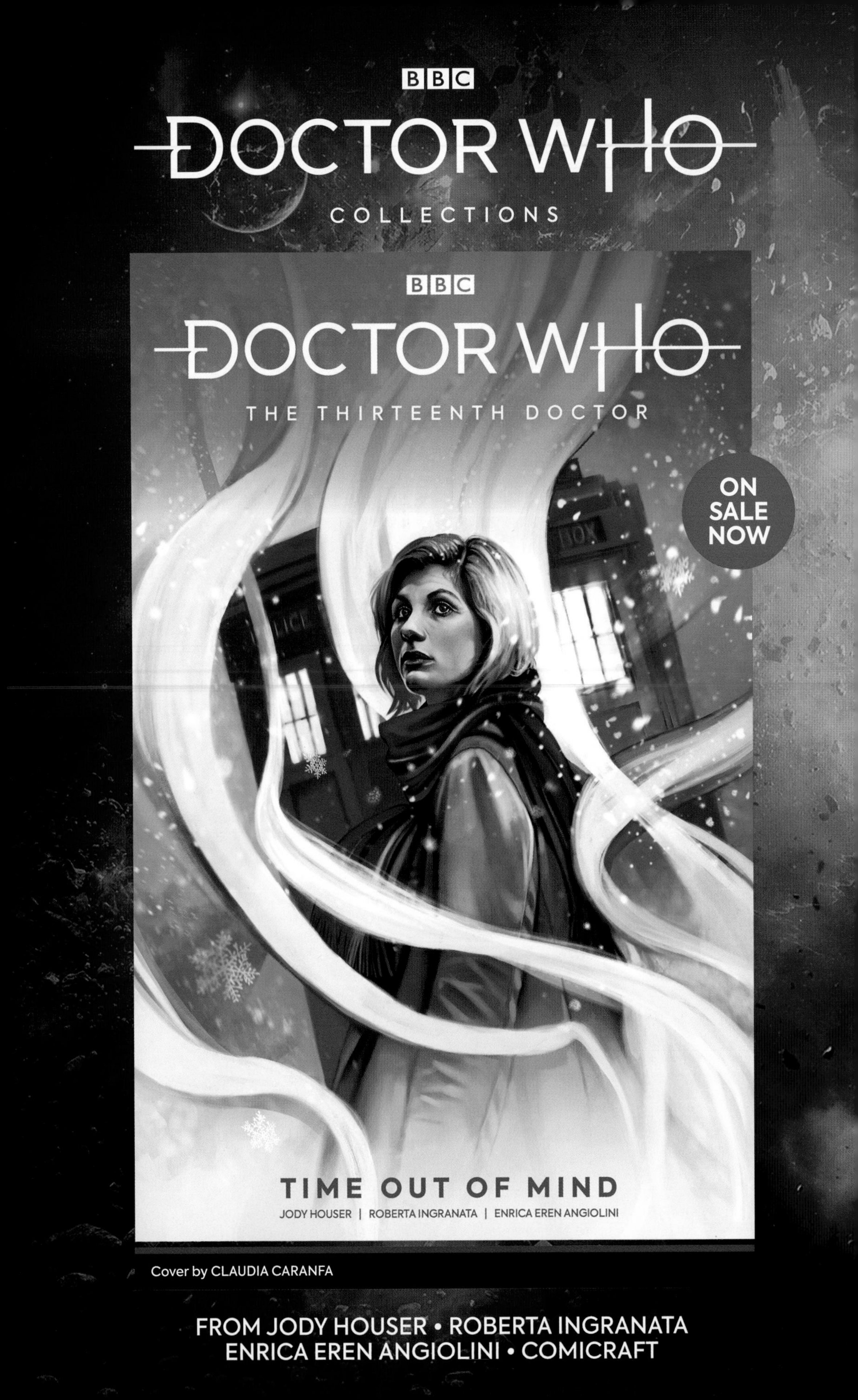
BBC
DOCTOR WHO
COLLECTIONS
BBC
DOCTOR WHO
THE THIRTEENTH DOCTOR
ON SALE NOW
TIME OUT OF MIND
JODY HOUSER | ROBERTA INGRANATA | ENRICA EREN ANGIOLINI
Cover by CLAUDIA CARANFA
FROM JODY HOUSER • ROBERTA INGRANATA
ENRICA EREN ANGIOLINI • COMICRAFT

**BBC**

# DOCTOR WHO

## A TALE OF TWO TIME LORDS

ON SALE NOW

**A LITTLE HELP FROM MY FRIENDS**

JODY HOUSER • ROBERTA INGRANATA
ENRICA EREN ANGIOLINI

Cover by WILL BROOKS

**FROM JODY HOUSER • ROBERTA INGRANATA
ENRICA EREN ANGIOLINI • COMICRAFT**

BBC DOCTOR WHO

# READER'S GUIDE

With so many amazing *Doctor Who* collections already on the shelves, it co
be difficult to know where to start. That's where this handy guide comes in!
And don't be overwhelmed – every collection is designed to be welcoming,
whatever your knowledge of *Doctor Who*.

## THE TWELFTH DOCTOR

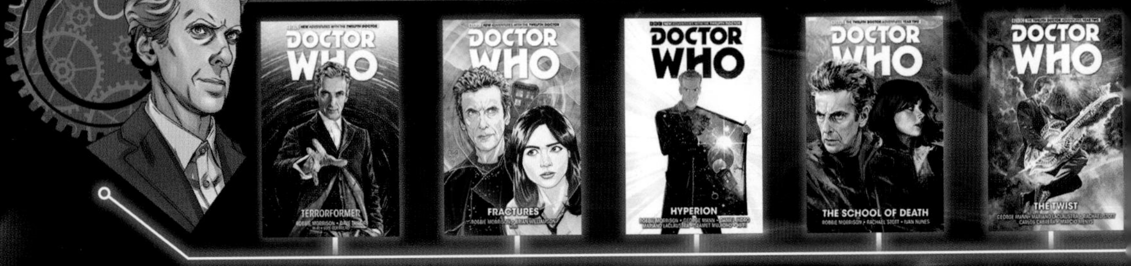

VOL. 1: TERRORFORMER

VOL. 2: FRACTURES

VOL. 3: HYPERION

YEAR TWO BEGINS! VOL. 4: SCHOOL OF DEATH

VOL. 5: THE TWIST

## THE ELEVENTH DOCTOR

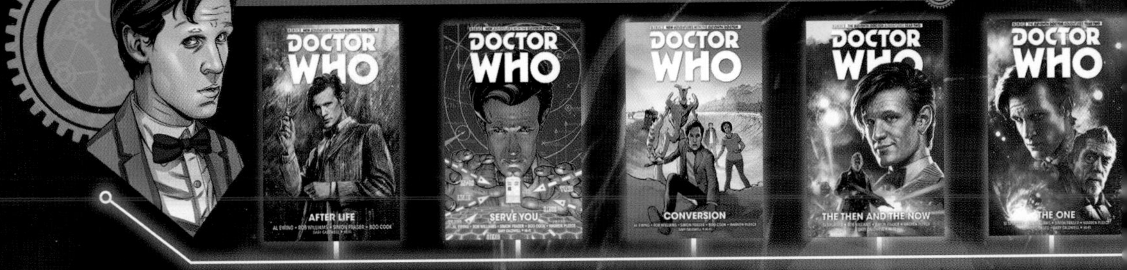

VOL. 1: AFTER LIFE

VOL. 2: SERVE YOU

VOL. 3: CONVERSION

YEAR TWO BEGINS! VOL. 4: THE THEN AND THE NOW

VOL. 5: THE ONE

## THE TENTH DOCTOR

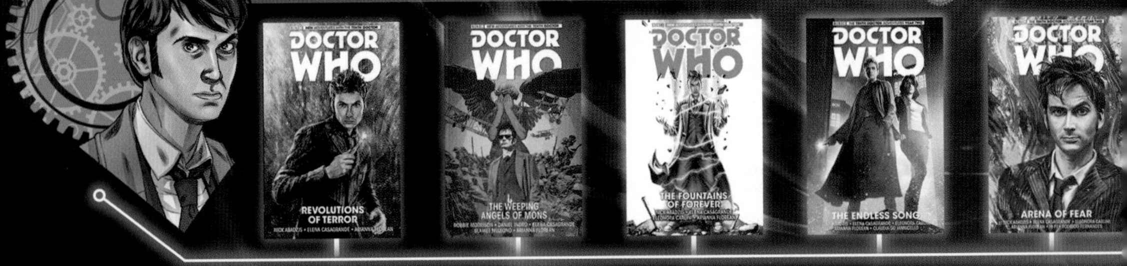

VOL. 1: REVOLUTIONS OF TERROR

VOL. 2: THE WEEPING ANGELS OF MONS

VOL. 3: THE FOUNTAINS OF FOREVER

YEAR TWO BEGINS! VOL. 4: THE ENDLESS SONG

VOL. 5: ARENA OF FEAR

## THE NINTH DOCTOR

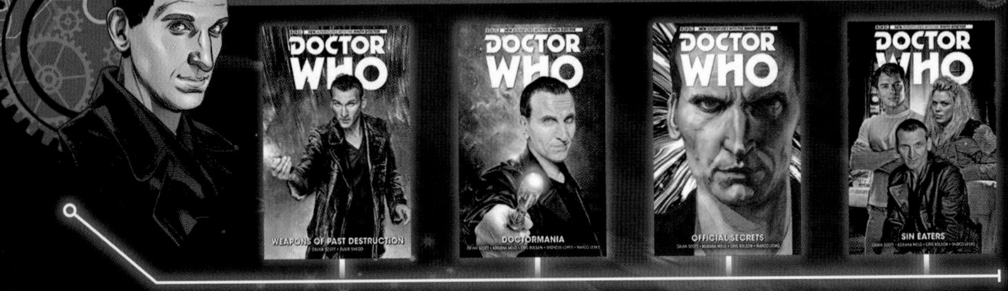

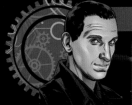

VOL. 1: WEAPONS OF PAST DESTRUCTION

VOL. 2: DOCTORMANIA

VOL. 3: OFFICIAL SECRETS

VOL. 4: SIN EATERS

ch comic series is entirely self-contained and focused on one Doctor, so you can follow one, two, or all your favorite Doctors, as you wish! The series are arranged in TV season-like Years, collected into roughly ee collections per Year. Feel free to start at Volume 1 of any series, or jump straight to the volumes elled in blue! Each book, and every comic, features a catch-up and character guide at the beginning, aking it easy to jump on board – and each comic series has a very different flavor, representative of that ctor's era on screen. If in doubt, set the TARDIS Randomizer and dive in wherever you land!

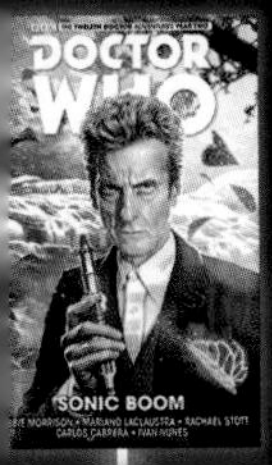


VOL. 6:
SONIC BOOM

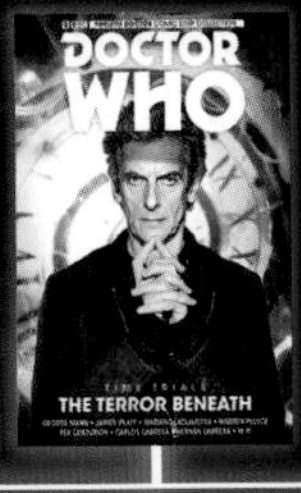


YEAR THREE BEGINS!
TIME TRIALS VOL. 1:
THE TERROR BENEATH

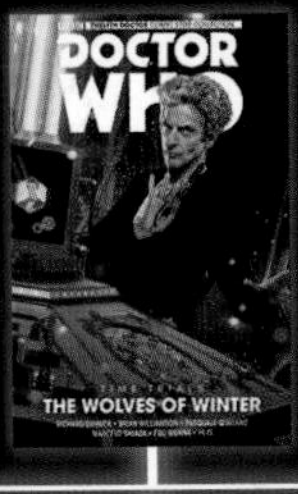


TIME TRIALS VOL. 2:
THE WOLVES
OF WINTER

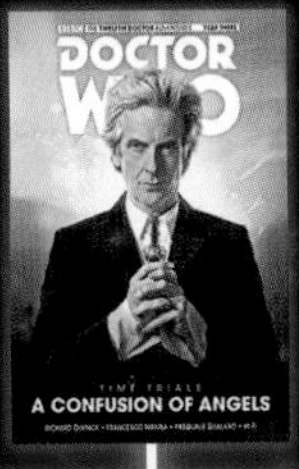


TIME TRIALS VOL. 3:
A CONFUSION OF
ANGELS

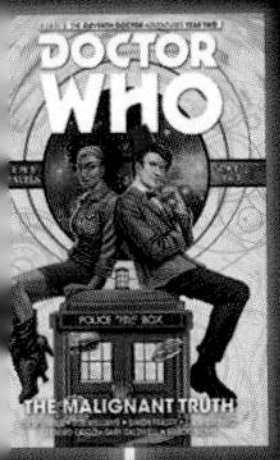


VOL. 6:
E MALIGNANT TRUTH

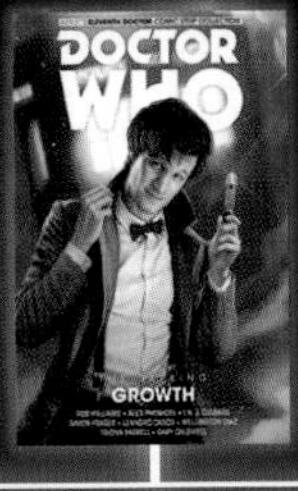


YEAR THREE BEGINS!
THE SAPLING VOL. 1:
GROWTH

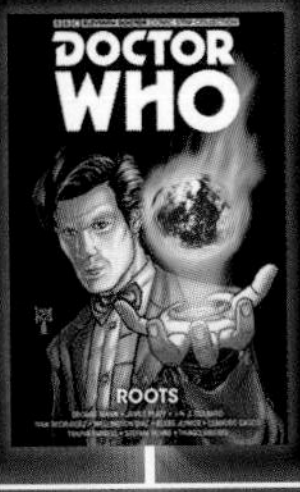


THE SAPLING VOL. 2:
ROOTS

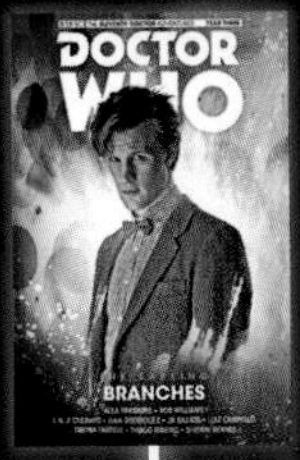


THE SAPLING VOL. 3:
BRANCHES

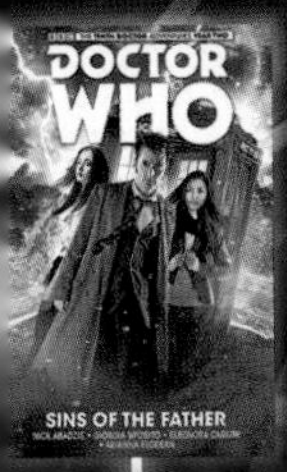


VOL. 6:
INS OF THE FATHER

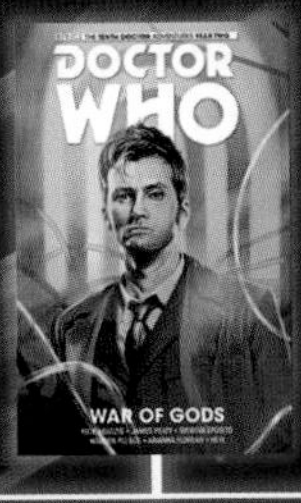


VOL. 7:
WAR OF GODS

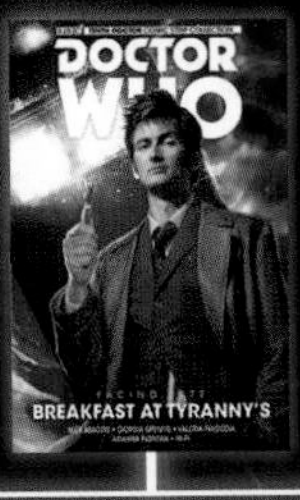


YEAR THREE BEGINS!
FACING FATE VOL. 1:
BREAKFAST AT TYRANNY'S

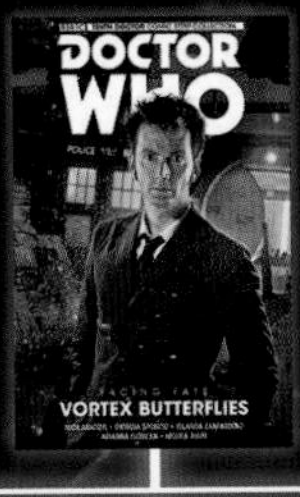


FACING FATE VOL. 2:
VORTEX BUTTERFLIES

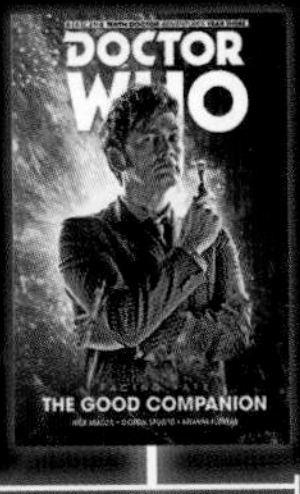


FACING FATE VOL. 3:
THE GOOD COMPANION

## THE THIRTEENTH DOCTOR

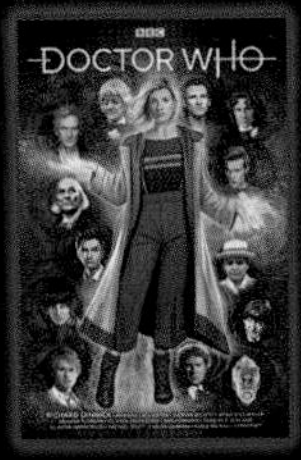


THE MANY
LIVES OF

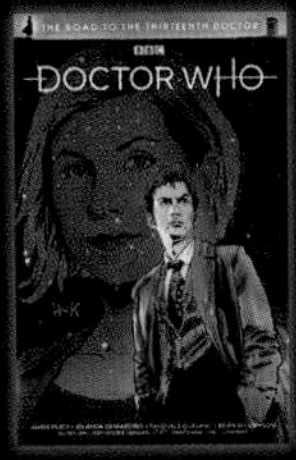


THE ROAD TO THE
THIRTEENTH DOCTOR

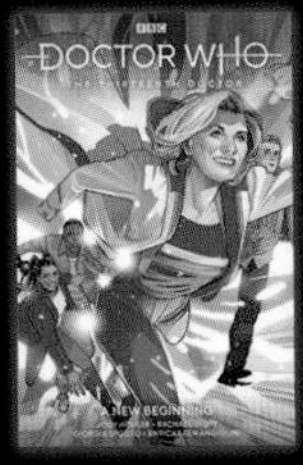


VOL. 1:
A NEW
BEGINNING

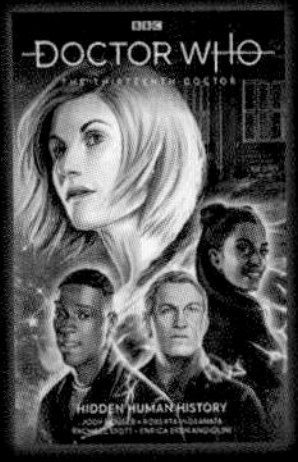


VOL. 2:
HIDDEN HUMAN
HISTORY

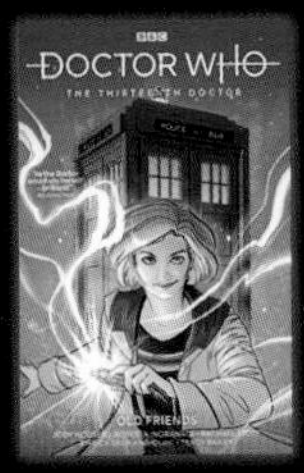


VOL. 3:
OLD FRIENDS

## CLASSIC DOCTORS

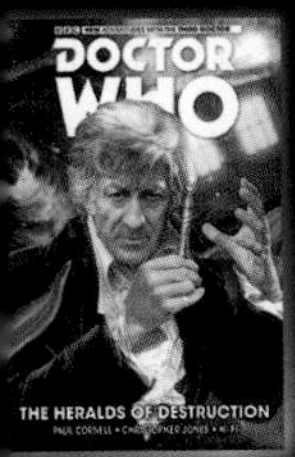


THIRD DOCTOR:
THE HERALDS OF

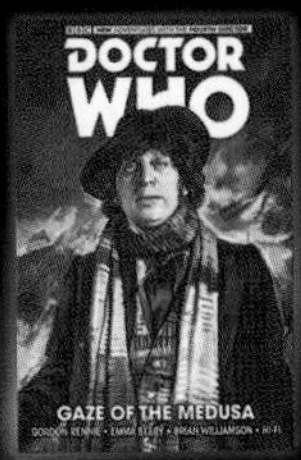


FOURTH DOCTOR:
GAZE OF THE

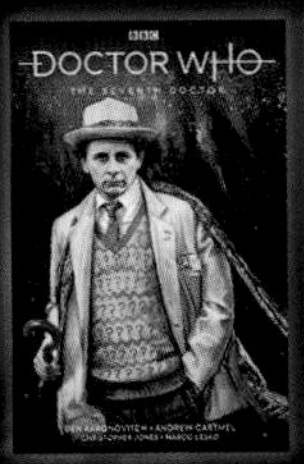


SEVENTH DOCTOR:
OPERATION

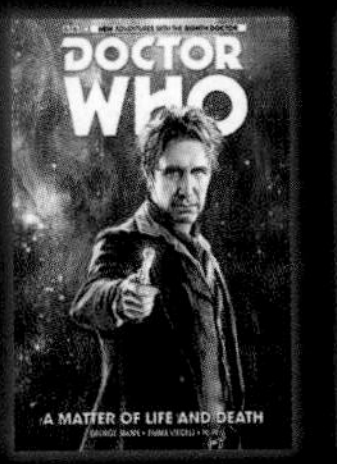


EIGHTH DOCTOR:
A MATTER OF LIFE

## MULTI-DOCTOR EVENTS

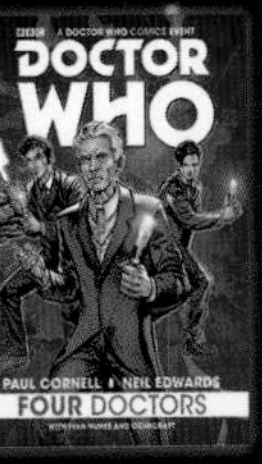


FOUR
DOCTORS

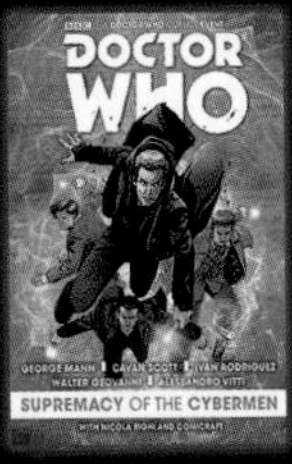


SUPREMACY OF
THE CYBERMEN

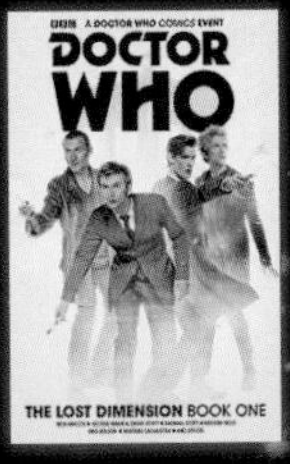


THE LOST
DIMENSION

BBC

# DOCTOR WHO

# TIME LORD VICTORIOUS

## Biographies

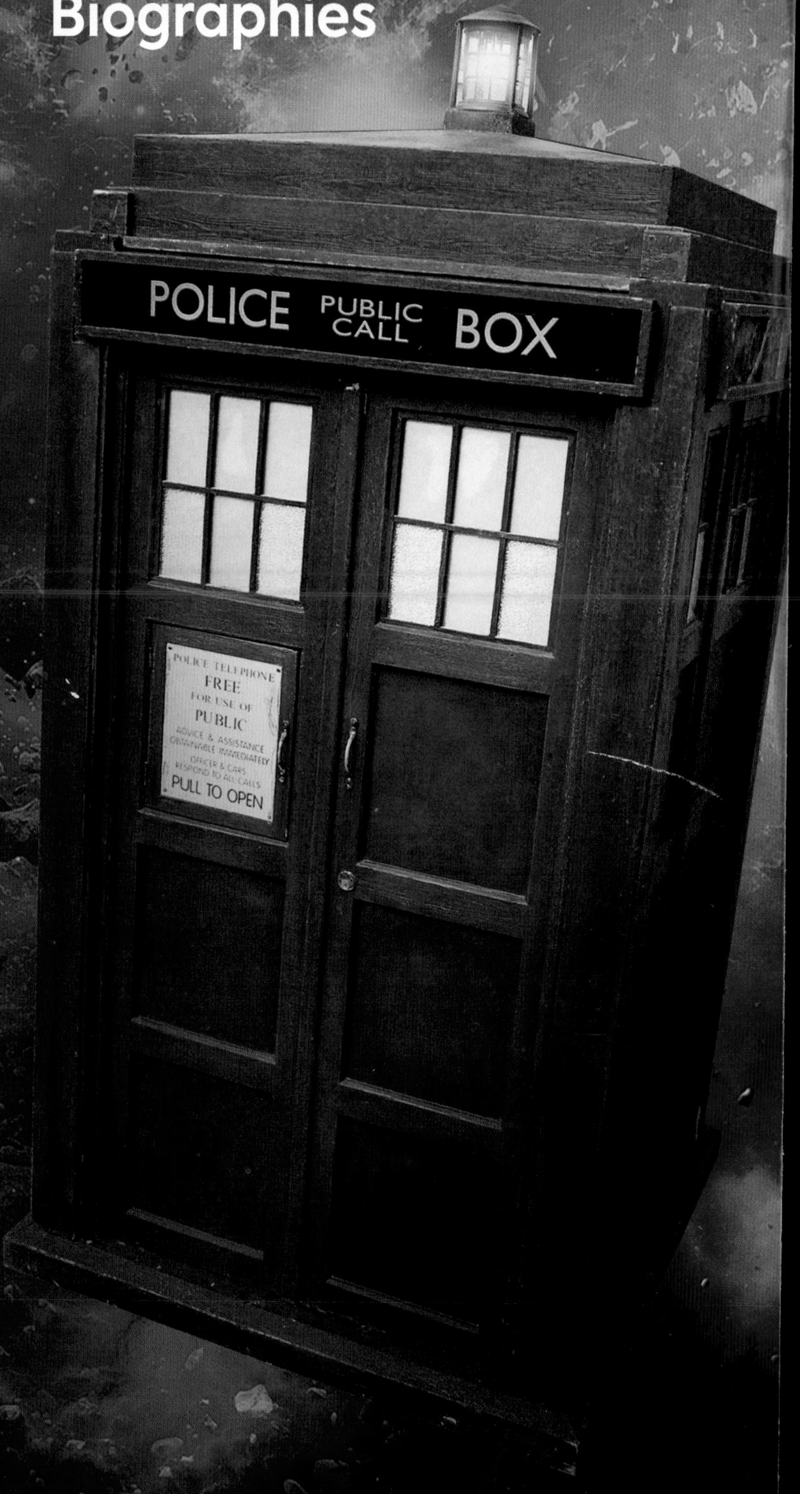
POLICE PUBLIC CALL BOX
POLICE TELEPHONE
FREE
FOR USE OF
PUBLIC
ADVICE & ASSISTANCE
OBTAINABLE IMMEDIATELY
OFFICER & CARS
RESPOND TO ALL CALLS
PULL TO OPEN

### Jody Houser

is a prolific writer of comics, perhaps best known for her work on *Faith* and *Mother Panic*. She has also written *Star Wars: Rogue One*, *Star Wars: Age of Republic*, *Amazing Spider-Man: Renew Your Vows*, and *Spider-Girls*, *The X-Files: Origins* and *Orphan Black*, and *Stranger Things*, *StarCraft*, and *Halo*.

### Roberta Ingranata

is an Italian comic artist. She worked for various Italian publishers before making the leap to US comics. Titles she has leant her considerable talents to include the highly acclaimed *Witchblade* series, *Robyn Hood*, and *Van Helsing*.

### Enrica Eren Angiolini

is a colorist and illustrator from Italy. Enrica's rich colors go from strength to strength, as demonstrated by her work on *Warhammer 40,000*, *Shades of Magic: The Steel Prince*, and *Doctor Who: Thirteenth Doctor* for Titan Comics, and cover work for various other publishers.